Brother Dave

2 CORINTHIANS

Something to read - sometime!
with love in the Lord

John

JANUARY 2020

2 CORINTHIANS

by
John M Riddle

RITCHIE
John Ritchie Publishing

40 Beansburn, Kilmarnock, Scotland

ISBN-13: 978 1 912522 64 4

Copyright © 2019 by John Ritchie Ltd.
40 Beansburn, Kilmarnock, Scotland

www.ritchiechristianmedia.co.uk

Typeset by John Ritchie Ltd., Kilmarnock
Printed by Bell & Bain Ltd., Glasgow

Contents

2 Corinthians

Preface

Unlike previous publications in this series, this book is not the product of Bible Class discussions at Mill Lane Chapel. Strictly speaking, therefore, it does not belong under the umbrella emblazoned 'Mill Lane Bible Studies', even though, through the good offices of Mr. Eric Browning, the underlying notes were distributed some years ago to everybody on the 'mailing list'. This means that although the notes now published reflect Bible Reading discussions in various places, plus addresses in various assemblies, they have not passed through the ultimate 'refining process' – the Friday Night Bible Class! The sessions there lead to a 'balanced view' and 'correct' the misconceptions and misunderstandings of 'the man at the front' (or, better, 'the man in the middle'!). He is most grateful for all the valued help given over many years.

Long before the original notes were distributed, they were kindly checked, in 2006/2007, by Miss Fiona Parker of Brookfield, Renfrewshire.

These notes are now published, at the suggestion of John Ritchie Ltd, to complement the recently-published Bible Class notes on 1 Corinthians. Once again, and not as mere courtesy, the Bible Class at Cheshunt remains genuinely indebted to John Ritchie Ltd for their willingness to publish its notes (even though '2 Corinthians' isn't quite in that category), something first mooted by Mr. John Grant, and to Mr. Fraser Munro and the John Ritchie 'team' for their invaluable help in formatting and editing the material submitted to them.

John Riddle
Cheshunt, Hertfordshire
November 2019.

2 Corinthians

2 CORINTHIANS

1) Introduction

This introduction to 2 Corinthians covers the following: *(1)* the historical background; *(2)* the relationship with 1 Corinthians; *(3)* Paul's circumstances at the time; *(4)* the structure of the epistle.

1) THE HISTORICAL BACKGROUND

The historical background to the two Epistles to the Corinthians begins with Paul's first visit to Corinth during the course of his *second missionary journey*. The details are given in Acts 18 verses 1-17. From Corinth Paul returned to Antioch via Ephesus. See Acts 18 verses 18-22.

From Antioch, Paul embarked on his *third missionary journey* which took him "over all the country of Galatia and Phrygia in order, strengthening all the disciples" (Acts 18: 1-17). Paul's next port of call was Ephesus (Acts 18: 18-22) where he "purposed in the spirit, when he had passed through *Macedonia* and *Achaia*, to go to Jerusalem, saying, After I have been there, I must also see Rome" (Acts 19: 21).

This brings us to the Corinthian epistles. Paul had evidently notified the believers at Corinth, before writing his first epistle to them, that he intended to travel *directly* from Ephesus to Corinth. See 2 Corinthians 1 verses 15-16, where he sets out his proposed itinerary: Ephesus – Corinth – Macedonia (to collect their gift for the needy saints in Judaea) – Corinth – Judaea.

But whilst at Ephesus news reached him of the disorders at Corinth, whereupon Paul wrote 1 Corinthians to correct these malpractices. It was written to correct certain behavioural, moral and doctrinal disorders, and to answer several questions.

1 Corinthians was therefore written from Ephesus. Hence we read, "But I will tarry at Ephesus until Pentecost" (1 Cor.16: 8); "The churches of Asia salute you" (16: 19). Stephanas, Fortunatas and Achaicus had evidently *come* from Corinth *to* Ephesus (16: 17). The letter was then conveyed to Corinth by Titus (2 Cor. 2: 13; 7: 6-7; 7: 14-15).

In his first letter Paul announced a *change of route*. "But I will come unto you, when I shall *have passed* through Macedonia; for I do pass through Macedonia" (1 Cor. 16: 5 RV). So instead of proceeding directly to Corinth as originally intended (2 Cor.1: 15-16), he in fact travelled north to Troas (instead of west to Corinth), where he expected to rendezvous with Titus bringing news of reaction at Corinth to 1 Corinthians.

Having despatched 1 Corinthians, Paul then left Ephesus to follow the amended route announced in 1 Corinthians 16 verse 5. Hence in Acts 19 verse 21 we read, as noted above, And "after these things were ended, Paul purposed in the spirit, when he had passed through *Macedonia* and *Achaia*, to go to Jerusalem, saying, After I have been there, I must also see Rome", and in Acts 20 verse 1,"And after the uproar was ceased, Paul called unto him the disciples, and embraced them, and departed for to go into Macedonia".

He travelled, as also noted above, via Troas, expecting to rendezvous with Titus returning from Corinth: 2 Corinthians 2 verse 13. But Titus was not there, and Paul then crossed the northern Aegean into Macedonia where he finally met him. (See 2 Cor.7: 5-6).

2 Corinthians was therefore written from Macedonia, possibly Philippi, in response to Titus' report of the Corinthian's reaction to the 1 Corinthians. It was evidently conveyed, again, by Titus: see Chapter 8 verses 16-24.

From Macedonia, Paul then journeyed south to Achaia, where Corinth was located (Acts 20: 2-3).

2) THE RELATIONSHIP WITH THE FIRST EPISTLE

In this connection, we should notice at least three things: *(a)* the change of plan; *(b)* the motives for writing; *(c)* unfinished business.

a) The change of plan

Paul altered his itinerary for good reasons. These are set out in 2 Corinthians 1 verse 23 to Chapter 2 verse 1: "Moreover I call God for a record upon my soul, that to spare you I came not as yet unto Corinth...But I determined this with myself, that I would not come again to you in heaviness". He had no wish to come "with a rod" (1 Cor. 4: 21).

From this we notice a most important lesson: ministry must be given *time to take effect.*

But the change of route fuelled the animosity of his adversaries at Corinth, who said that he never intended to come at all. We hear their voices in 1 Corinthians 4 verse 18, "Now some are puffed up as though I would not come unto you..." As we have seen, Acts 20 verses 1-2 records that from Macedonia, Paul did visit Corinth, remaining there for three months, before returning by the same route to avoid an assassination plot: Acts 20 verse 3.

The change of plan gave rise to the charge of fickleness. See 2 Corinthians 1 verse 17. Paul thus emphasises why it was necessary: had he implemented his original intention, a stern ministry would have been necessary. See 2 Corinthians 1 verse 23.

We should notice that there was a second change of plan about this time. In the first place, as already noted, the change was necessitated by conditions in the assembly at Corinth. In the second place, this further alteration of route was necessitated by known hazards. See Acts 20 verse 3. He had intended to sail from Corinth to Syria, but because "the Jews laid in wait from him", he returned to Macedonia, thence to Caesarea via Philippi, Troas, Miletus, Patara, and Tyre. Thence to Jerusalem.

b) The motives for writing

Whilst references to Paul's love for the Corinthians are not lacking in the First Epistle (see, 1 Corinthians 4: 14), the Second Epistle reveals his motives. He wrote:

i)   To avoid the sorrow which would have resulted from a personal visit to correct the disorders. "And *I wrote* this same unto you, lest when I came, I should have sorrow from them of whom I ought to rejoice" (2: 3).

Discipline is not an enjoyable thing. Judgment is God's "strange work" (Isa. 28: 21).

ii)   To express his love for them. "For out of much affliction and anguish of heart *I wrote* unto you with many tears, not that ye should be grieved, but that ye might know the love which I have more abundantly unto you" (2: 4).

iii)   To be assured of their obedience to divine truth. "For to this end also *did I write*, that I might know the proof of you, whether ye be obedient in all things" (2: 9). Compare Philemon verse 21.

iv)   To express his care for them. "Wherefore though *I wrote* unto you, I did it not for his cause that had done the wrong (he did not write vindictively), nor for his cause that suffered wrong (he did not write out of sentiment), but that our care for you in the sight of God might appear unto you" (7: 12).

Four good reasons for writing a letter!

c) Unfinished matters

There were at least three matters in this category: *(i)* the excommunicated brother; *(ii)* the collection for the saints; *(iii)* the antagonism against Paul.

i)   **The excommunicated brother.** The Corinthian believers had been slow to **put him away** from assembly fellowship: "and ye are puffed up, and have not rather mourned that he that hath done this deed might be taken away from among you" (1 Cor. 5: 2).

Now they were slow in **bringing him back** into fellowship. See 2 Corinthians 2 verses 6-8, "Sufficient to such a man is this punishment, which was inflicted of many. So that contrariwise ye ought rather to forgive him, and comfort him, lest perhaps such a one should be swallowed up with overmuch sorrow. Wherefore I beseech you that ye would confirm your love toward him". See also Chapter 7 verse 7, "he (Titus) told us your earnest desire, your **mourning**, your fervent mind toward me".

It was most important to deal with the matter: "Lest Satan should get an advantage of us: for we are not ignorant of his devices" (2 Cor 2: 11).

ii) **The collection for the saints.** Paul had said, "Now concerning the collection for the saints, as I have given order to the churches of Galatia, even so do ye. Upon the first day of the week let every one of you lay by him in store, as God hath prospered him, that there be no collections when I come. And when I come, whosoever ye shall approve by your letters, them will I send to bring your liberality unto Jerusalem" (1 Cor. 16: 1-3).

The church at Corinth had been tardy in this respect, and Paul was obliged to deal with the matter in 2 Corinthians 8-9.

iii) **The antagonism against Paul.** In this connection, we should note the following in 1 Corinthians: "Now some are puffed up as though I would not come unto you" (1 Cor. 4: 18-21); "Am I not an apostle? Am I not free? have I not seen Jesus Christ our Lord? are ye not my work in the Lord?... Mine answer to them that do examine me is this. Have we not power to eat and to drink?..." (1 Cor. 9: 1-6).

Hence, in the second epistle we read: "Do we begin again to commend ourselves? Or need we, as some others, epistles of commendation to you, or letters of commendation from you?" (2 Cor. 3: 1). But see, particularly, 2 Corinthians 10-13. For example, "For his letters say they are weighty and powerful, but his bodily presence is weak, and his speech contemptible" (10: 10); "For such are false apostles, deceitful workers..." (11: 13).

Paul is therefore obliged to speak about himself and to vindicate his actions. Not out of self-assertion, but because he knew that if the "false apostles" could successfully undermine his character and authority, they would then be in a pole position to overthrow the faith of the Corinthian believers. The false teachers, who attempted to corrupt the purity of their faith, had first to discredit Paul before achieving the object. Discredit Paul, and his ministry could then be discredited. (This emphasises the need for personal integrity as well as doctrinal purity: see 1 Timothy 4 verse 16, "Take heed unto *thyself*, and unto the doctrine".)

Hence, he vindicates his revised itinerary which had brought the charge of insincerity against him (1: 17); he draws attention to his accreditation as an apostle in view of the accusations of his detractors (3: 1); he states his personal credentials (chs.10-12).

3) THE CIRCUMSTANCES OF THE WRITER

These can be summed up in two verses: "For when we were come into Macedonia, our flesh had no rest, but we were troubled on every side; *without were fightings, within were fears"* (7: 5); "Besides those *things that are without*, that which cometh upon me daily, *the care of all the churches*" (11: 28).

a) "Without were fightings"

This refers to external pressure. See 1 verses 8-10; 4 verse 8 to 5 verse 1 and 11 verses 23-27. He was subject to gale force adversity in the form of persecution.

b) "Within were fears"

This refers to internal pressure. Paul was deeply concerned about the welfare of the believers at Corinth. It is summed up in Chapter 11 verses 2-3; "For I am jealous over you with godly jealousy: for I have espoused you to one husband, that I may present you as a chaste virgin to Christ. But I fear, lest by any means, as the serpent beguiled Eve though his subtilty, so your minds should be corrupted from the simplicity that is in Christ".

Paul was a man of deep concern and with a tender heart. He desired the best for them. There was nothing arrogant or self assertive about him, although he was authoritative in dealing with the matter.

But God was to Paul "the God of all comfort" (1: 3). He was "God that comforteth those that are cast down" (7: 6). He was "the God of all comfort" in delivering him from death (see, for example 1:9-10), and that "God that comforteth those that are cast down" in delivering him from despondency (see, for example, 7: 6 above).

The recurrent theme is therefore *strength in weakness*. P.E.Hughes sets this out clearly in his *'The Second Epistle to the Corinthians'* (Erdmans 1962), pp. xxxi/xxxii. See, for example, again Chapter 1 verses 8-9; 4

verses 7-11 and 12 verse 9: "And he said unto me, My grace is sufficient for thee: for my strength is made perfect in weakness".

So far as *"fightings"* are concerned, Paul mentions them, but not for self-gratification or self-esteem. So far as *"fears"* are concerned, Paul is constantly obliged to justify his service and conduct: he was under scrutiny and attack for the most unworthy motives. The false teachers wanted nothing less than dominion over the Corinthian believers: "For ye suffer, if a man bring you into bondage, if a man devour you, if a man take of you, if a man exalt himself, if a man smite you on the face" (11: 20).

It was therefore necessary that Paul should (i) justify his conduct; (ii) expose his critics.

Both were motivated by his love for the Corinthians: "As the truth of Christ is in me, no man shall stop me of this boasting in the regions of Achaia (that is, that he accepted no financial support at Corinth). Wherefore? Because I love you not? God knoweth" (11: 10-11); "And I will very gladly spend and be spent for you; though the more abundantly I love you, the less I be loved" (12: 15); "Again, think ye that we excuse ourselves unto you? we speak before God in Christ: but we do all things, dearly beloved, for your edifying" (12: 19).

4) THE STRUCTURE OF THE EPISTLE

2 Corinthians has been described as Paul's most emotionally charged epistle. In Chapters 1-7 we have his **explanation**, in Chapter 8-9 his **exhortation**, and in Chapters 10-13 his **exasperation.** Hence the different tone in Chapters 10-13!

The structure of the epistle follows the order of its historical background. Paul had come from **Asia**, he was writing from **Macedonia,** and he was going to Corinth in **Achaia.**

The epistle may therefore be divided as follows *(a)* what had happened in Asia (chs.1-7): that was past; *(b)* what was happening in Macedonia (chs.8-9): that was present; *(c)* what would happen in Corinth (chs.10-13): that was future or prospective.

All three sections emphasise that Paul is coming to Corinth. Each section could, possibly, be described in one word; *(a)* Chapters 1-7: suffering, perhaps 'triumphing'; *(b)* Chapter 8-9: giving; *(c)* Chapters 10-13: glorying.

a) The Asian section, Chapters 1-7

The historical framework is clearly set out in Chapter 1 verse 8, "For we would not, brethren, have you ignorant of our trouble which came to us in **Asia**".

In Chapters 1-2, Paul reveals his **motives** towards them:

- In travelling (1: 12 - 2: 1)
- In writing (2: 2 -13);
- In preaching (2: 14 - 17)

In Chapter 3, Paul describes his **service** to them. He describes himself and his colleagues as "ministers of the new testament (covenant)" (3: 6), and does so in view of the nationality of the "false apostles": "Are they Hebrews? So am I; are they Israelites? So am I; are they the seed of Abraham? So am I...." (11: 22). Hence he describes the new covenant: "written not with ink, but with the Spirit of the living God; not in tables of stone, but in fleshy tables of the heart...not of the letter, but of the spirit..." (3: 3, 6). The new covenant is not "the ministration of death" or the "ministration of condemnation", but the "ministration of the spirit" and "the ministration of righteousness" (3: 7-9)

In Chapters 4-5, Paul expresses his **assurance** to them, whether in life (Ch. 4) or in death (Ch. 5).

- As to **life**: "we have this treasure in earthen vessels, that the excellency of the power may be of God and not of us" (4: 7).

- As to **death**: "For we know that if our earthly house of this tabernacle were dissolved, we have a building of God, an house not made with hands, eternal in the heavens" (5: 1).

The result is expressed in Chapter 5 verse 9, "Wherefore we labour (we are ambitious), that, whether present or absent, we may be accepted (well-pleasing) of him". Whether or not we have been well-pleasing to him will be revealed at the judgment seat of Christ (5: 10).

In Chapters 6-7, Paul makes his appeals to them. In this connection, we should note the following:

- *"Receive not the grace of God in vain"* (6: 1). The ground of the appeal is the wonderful display of divine grace in Chapter 5 verse 21. By heeding false teaching they would have 'received the grace of God in vain'.

- *"Be ye also enlarged"* (6: 13). The ground of this appeal is "our heart is enlarged" (6: 11).

- *"Be ye not unequally yoked together with unbelievers"* (6: 14). The ground of the appeal is "my people" (6: 16).

- *"Receive us"* (7: 2). The ground of the appeal is "ye are in our hearts to die and live with you" (7: 3).

b) The Macedonian section, Chapters 8-9

This section *begins* with the example of the Macedonian believers, and *ends* with the example of God Himself: "Thanks be unto God for his unspeakable gift" (9: 15). The Corinthians are told to prove "the sincerity of your love" (8: 8) as the Lord Jesus did: "For ye know the grace of our Lord Jesus Christ, that, though he was rich, yet for your sakes he became poor, that ye through his poverty might be rich" (8: 9).

c) The Corinthian section, Chapters 10-13

Here we should notice the emphasis on 'boasting' or 'glorying'. Some twenty of the thirty-six occurrences of the word occur in this section of the epistle.

We should notice that when Paul thinks of *glorying* (Chs.10-13), he thinks of Christ: "But he that glorieth, let him glory in the Lord" (10: 17). When he thinks of *giving* (Chs.8-9), he thinks of Christ: "For ye know the grace of our Lord Jesus Christ..." (8: 9) When he thinks of *suffering* (Chs.1-7), he thinks of Christ: "For as the sufferings of Christ abound in us..." (1: 5).

2 Corinthians

2 CORINTHIANS

"The God of all comfort"

Read Chapter 1:1-11

As we have noticed in our Introduction to the book, Paul refers particularly in this Epistle to his adversity. He emphasises this more than anywhere else in his New Testament correspondence. It can be summed up in the words, "we were troubled on every side; without were fightings, within were fears" (7: 5).

After the introduction (vv.1-2) the chapter may be divided by reference to this statement as follows: *(i)* "without were fightings" (vv.3-11); *(ii)* "within were fears" (vv.12-24). The words "without were fightings" are illustrated in vv.8-9, and the words "within were fears" are illustrated in vv.23-24.

The chapter demands at least two studies, and we will deal with the passage as suggested above: *(1)* Paul's introduction to the letter (vv.1-2); *(2)* Paul's sufferings for the Gospel (vv.3-11); *(3)* Paul's concern for the assembly (vv.12-24).

1) PAUL'S INTRODUCTION, vv.1-2

This may be divided as follows: *(a)* the writer (v.1); *(b)* the recipients (v.1); *(c)* the greeting (v.2).

a) The writer, v.1

i)   "Paul, an apostle of Jesus Christ by the will of God, and Timothy our brother…" JND has "apostle of Jesus Christ": the RV has "an apostle of Christ Jesus".

Note: all three translations have "Jesus Christ" in Romans 1 verse 1; 1

Corinthians 1 verse 1; Galatians 1 verse 1; Philippians 1 verse 1 ("the servants of Jesus Christ"); Titus 1 verse 1. In Ephesians 1 verse 1 the AV/ JND has "Jesus Christ" whilst the RV has "Christ Jesus". In Colossians 1 verse 1 and Philemon verse 1 ("a prisoner of…"), the AV has "Jesus Christ", whilst RV/JND has "Christ Jesus". In 1 Timothy 1 verse 1 and 2 Timothy 1 verse 1, the AV has "Jesus Christ": the RV has "Christ Jesus": JND has "Jesus Christ" with the footnote 'or Christ Jesus'.

It is often said that whilst Peter describes himself as "an apostle of Jesus Christ" (1 Pet. 1: 1; 2 Pet. 1: 1), Paul describes himself as 'an apostle of Christ Jesus', and that this reflects the way in which the two apostles first knew Him. Peter knew Him on earth ("*Jesus* Christ") whereas Paul knew Him after His ascension ("*Christ* Jesus"). Whilst the concluding statement is correct, the references above suggest that the supporting argument is 'not proven'.

The important thing to notice is that Paul describes himself as "an apostle of Jesus Christ *by the will of God*". This is evidently emphasised in view of his detractors who were "false apostles, deceitful workers, transforming themselves into the apostles of Christ" (11: 13).

ii)   Paul associates Timothy with him: "and Timothy, our brother". The italics indicate that Paul simply calls him "brother". JND/RV have "*the* brother", suggesting that Timothy was an example of all that should be expected in a brother. We are told that "a brother is born for adversity" (Prov. 17: 17) and that "there is a friend that sticketh closer than a brother" (Prov. 18: 24). Paul wrote about Timothy as follows: "I have no man likeminded who will naturally care for your state ('who will care with genuine feeling how ye get on', JND). For all seek their own, not the things which are Jesus Christ's. But ye know the proof of him, that, as a son with the father, he hath served with me in the gospel" (Phil. 2: 19-22). It is noteworthy that we have the older and more experienced man linked with the young and less experienced man. Paul was not jealous of the young man (a lesson here), but neither does he push the young man forward.

b) The recipients, v.1

"Unto the church of God which is at Corinth, with all the saints which are in all Achaia." We should notice the dignity of the description of the assembly ("the church of God which is at Corinth") and of God's people ("all the saints"). We should note the following:

i) The epistle is addressed to "the church of **God**...at **Corinth**". Corinth was famed for its licentiousness and depravity. Job said, "Who can bring a clean thing out of an unclean? Not one" (Job 14: 4). He was wrong! See 1 Corinthians 6 verses 9-11; "Be not deceived: neither fornicators, nor idolators, nor adulterers, nor effeminate, nor abusers of themselves with mankind, nor thieves, nor covetous, nor drunkards, nor revilers, nor extortioners, shall inherit the kingdom of God. *And such were some of you: but ye are washed, but ye are sanctified, but ye are justified in the name of the Lord Jesus, and by the Spirit of our God".*

ii) The scope of the epistle is extended: "with all the saints which are in all **Achaia**". Compare 1 Corinthians 1 verse 1, "Unto the church of God which is at Corinth": no mention is made there of Achaia. This might indicate that the trouble at Corinth had spread. Bad news travels very quickly. It was therefore important that everybody in the locality should know that the difficulties and troubles had been addressed. Notice in passing that Paul makes clear that his ministry in 1 Corinthians was not limited to that one place. See, for example, 1 Corinthians 1 verse 2; 11 verse 16 and 14 verse 33.

c) The greeting, v.2

"Grace be to you and peace, from God our Father, and from the Lord Jesus Christ." We should notice:

i) The order. It is "grace...peace". Grace is what He brought (Titus 2: 11), and peace is what He left (John 14: 27). It is usually said that "grace" and "peace" represent the characteristic Greek and Hebrew greetings respectively.

ii) The joint source: "from God our Father, and (omit 'from', RV) the Lord Jesus Christ". The equality of the Lord Jesus with the Father, and therefore His absolute deity, is taught here.

2) PAUL'S SUFFERINGS, vv.3-11

This section of the chapter may be divided as follows: *(a)* the resources in suffering (v.3); *(b)* the results of suffering (vv.4-7); *(c)* the reality of suffering (vv.8-9); *(d)* the respite from suffering (vv.10-11). It should be said that in this passage Paul is evidently referring to his sufferings in his service for God.

a) The resources in suffering, v.3

"Blessed be God, even (omitted by RV/JND) the Father of our Lord Jesus Christ, the Father of mercies, and the God of all comfort": hence 'Blessed be the God and Father of our Lord Jesus Christ' (RV/JND). In the teeth of gale-force adversity, Paul can write **"Blessed be God!"** Compare Ephesians 1 verse 3 and 1 Peter 1 verse 3. In each case, the word "blessed" translates *eulogia* (not *makarios*). It has been pointed out that reference is made to the past in 2 Corinthians 1 verse 3, to the present in Ephesians 1 verse 3, and to the future in 1 Peter 1 verse 3.

We should notice that He is called "the Father of mercies" (here); the "Father of glory" (Eph. 1: 17); the "Father of spirits" (Heb. 12: 9); the "Father of lights" (James 1: 17).

If the greeting, "from God our Father and the Lord Jesus Christ", conveys **equality**, then the ascription of praise, 'Blessed be the God and Father of our Lord Jesus Christ', conveys **relationship.**

We should observe:

i) His relation to the **Lord Jesus** as God and Father. He is the "**God**... of our Lord Jesus Christ": the God whom He served. He is "**the Father**...of our Lord Jesus Christ". He is the Father whom He loved.

It is worth mentioning that the expression "God...of our Lord Jesus Christ" has particular reference to the Lord as man, which leads us to say that the words "God...of our Lord Jesus Christ" convey the **humanity** of the Lord Jesus whereas "Father...of our Lord Jesus Christ" convey His **deity.**

ii) His relation to **us** as Father and God. He is "the Father of mercies, and the God of all comfort".

The words, "the **Father** of mercies", convey divine **love**: the exercise of pity and compassion towards the suffering. The word "mercies *(oiktirmos)* means "pity, compassion for the ills of others" (W.E.Vine). JND has 'compassions'. See Psalm 103 verse 13, "Like as a father pitieth his children, so the Lord pitieth them that fear him"; Lamentations 3 verses 22-23: "It is of the Lord's mercies that we are not consumed, because his compassions fail not. They are new every morning: great is thy faithfulness".

The words, "the *God* of all comfort", emphasise His *power* to encourage us in suffering. The word *paraklesis* is rendered either "comfort" (vv.3-5) or "consolation" (vv.6-7) and means 'to encourage' or 'exhort'.

b) The results of suffering, vv.4-7

While these verses refer particularly to the benefits that other believers received through Paul's sufferings, we should notice that verses 4-11 outline four results: others in similar circumstances are helped (v.4); character is refined by suffering (v.9); God's faithfulness is proven in suffering (v.10); God is glorified by the deliverance He gives from suffering (v.11). In these verses, Paul makes a number of statements in connection with his present sufferings. He traces the hand and purpose of God in them. He looks beyond his immediate circumstances. We should notice the following:

i) *The sharing of comfort, v.4.* "Who comforteth us in all our tribulation, that we may be able to comfort them which are in any trouble, by the comfort wherewith we ourselves are comforted of God." We should notice:

- *"Tribulation"* *(thlipsis).* It is rendered "afflicted" *(thlibo)* in v.6 and "trouble" *(thlipsis)* in vv.4, 8. It means 'pressing' or 'pressure'. See also Chapter 4 verse 8, "we are troubled ('pressed', JND) on every side".

- *"Comfort"* *(paraklesis).* In verses 3-7 there are ten occurrences of the word rendered 'comfort' or 'consolation', or its associated words. The word occurs twenty-nine times in the epistle.

The words "*any* trouble" perhaps suggest that Paul is not necessarily referring to one particular aspect of suffering.

This emphasises the blessing of sharing with others what we have received from God. It stresses the benefit accruing to others through our own experience. Paul can speak out of experience: we cannot lift anyone higher than ourselves or our own experience.

> *Have you had a kindness shown?*
> *Pass it on!*
> *'Twas not given for thee alone:*
> *Pass it on!*
> *Let it travel down the years,*

> *Let it wipe another's tears,*
> *Till in heaven the deed appears –*
> *Pass it on!*

Our experience of God's help is therefore twofold in purpose: It has in view our blessing ("who comforteth us") and the blessing of others ("that we might be able to comfort").

But the emphasis is *not* on his suffering, but on God's grace to him: "Blessed be God…*who* comforteth us in all our tribulation". Thus, in his sufferings: *God* is glorified, Paul himself is encouraged, and *others* are helped.

ii) The sufficiency of comfort, v.5. "For as the sufferings of Christ abound in us, so our consolation also aboundeth by Christ." We should notice that the "consolation" (encouragement) matches the sufferings. Both "abound". In both cases the word "abound" translates is *perisseuo,* meaning 'an exceeding measure' (W.E.Vine).

The word ***"sufferings"*** (vv.5, 6, 7) translates *pathema*. (However, the word "suffer" in v.6, "which we also suffer", translates *pascho*). The word *pathema* is used of the Lord's sufferings. See 1 Peter 1 verse 11; Chapter 4 verse 13; Chapter 5 verse 1; Philippians 3 verse 10; Hebrews 2 verses 9-10; Acts 26 verse 23.

Paul's sufferings are described as the "sufferings of ***Christ***". This is illustrated in Acts 9 verses 3-5: "And he (Saul of Tarsus) fell to the earth, and heard a voice saying unto him, Saul, Saul, why persecutest thou me? And he said, Who art thou, Lord? And the Lord said, I am Jesus whom thou persecutest". Paul calls this "the fellowship of his sufferings" (Phil. 3: 10).

Since they are His sufferings, He compensates: "so our consolation also aboundeth by Christ". We have an example at Corinth: "Then spake ***the Lord*** to Paul in the night by a vision, Be not afraid, but speak, and hold not thy peace: for I am with thee, and no man shall set on thee to hurt thee: for I have much people in this city" (Acts 18: 9-10). See also 2 Timothy 4 verses 16-17, "At my first answer no man stood with me … Notwithstanding ***the Lord*** stood with me, and strengthened me…"

Samuel Rutherford said: "When I am in the cellars of affliction, I look for the king's wine".

iii) ***The salvation through comfort, v.6.*** "And whether we be afflicted (*thlibo*), it is for your consolation and salvation, which is effectual (wrought) in the enduring of the same sufferings (*pathema*) which we also suffer (*pascho*): or whether we be comforted, it is for your consolation and salvation".

That is, salvation from ***despair*** in suffering. Compare Philippians 1 verses 18-19, "What then? Notwithstanding, every way, whether in pretence or in truth, Christ is preached; and I therein do rejoice, yea, and will rejoice. For I know that this shall turn to my salvation through your prayer, and the supply of the Spirit of Jesus Christ".

Paul's afflictions (tribulation) were beneficial to them in the sense that when they passed through the same experiences, they could remember that he had passed through, or was passing through, the same experiences. They could be encouraged in the knowledge that he fully understood their circumstances. See Philippians 1 verse 30, "Having the same conflict which ye saw in me, and now hear to be in me".

Similarly, they could be encouraged in his encouragement. He had received divine encouragement in his circumstances, and this assured them that they would receive encouragement as well. So

- Paul speaks of his affliction (*thlibo*) and states this to be for Corinthians' benefit: "your consolation and salvation".

- Paul speaks of his comfort (encouragement) and states that this was to be for the Corinthians' benefit: "your consolation (omit 'and salvation')".

That is, 'whether we be afflicted, it is for your good' and 'whether we be comforted, it is for your good'. How was this "effectual" (wrought out)? Paul's own experiences were an example to them in their afflictions. As the Corinthians observed Paul's sufferings and consolation, they were enabled to endure their own affliction patiently. His suffering and consolation became helpful to them in their own circumstances.

iv) ***The certainty of comfort, v.7.*** "And our hope of you is stedfast, knowing (*oida,* the idea of perceiving) that as ye are partakers of the sufferings (*pathema),* so shall ye be also of the consolation."

Paul can confidently assert that his experience would be their experience as well. He now refers to his sufferings.

c) *The reality of suffering, vv.8-9*

"For we would not, brethren, have you ignorant of our trouble which came to us in Asia, that we were pressed out of measure, above strength, insomuch that we despaired even of life: but we had the sentence of death in ourselves, that we should not trust in ourselves, but in God which raiseth the dead."

As Albert McShane observes, "There has been much speculation as to the precise nature of this trial. Some suggest that it must have been a physical malady, so severe as to threaten his life. Others imagine that he was faced with some attack by hostile mobs or from a tumult in Ephesus. (Ephesus was in the province of Asia.) The weakness of the former view is that the word 'tribulation' used here hardly fits the idea of sickness, and the weakness of the latter opinion is that it scarcely suits 'pressed beyond strength', which seems to imply a weakening process". Some commentators suggest that Paul is referring here to his experience described in 1 Corinthians 15 verse 32, "I have fought with beasts at Ephesus" or to events described in Acts 19 verses 23-41.

The fact remains that Paul gives no further details. The absence of further information is probably quite deliberate. If we knew Paul's particular circumstances here we might be disposed to think that his ministry is hardly relevant to ourselves since we are not in the same precise position. The withholding of details therefore makes his teaching of general application. Compare the unidentified "thorn in the flesh" (12: 7).

As noted above (in connection with v.4), the word "trouble" *(thlipsis)* means 'a pressing' or 'pressure'. The words "pressed *(bareo)* out of measure" mean 'weighed down' or 'burdened'. The RV has "we were weighed down exceedingly". "Out of measure" *(huperbole)* means, literally, 'a throwing beyond' (W.E.Vine). "Above strength" means, "beyond our power" (RV). "We despaired even of life" recalls Psalm. 23 verse 4: "Yea, though I walk through the valley of the shadow of death".

According to W.E.Vine, the word "sentence" denotes a 'judicial sentence'. The RV has 'answer'. A. McShane suggests that Paul could only discern one answer to his circumstances, and that was *death!* Compare 1 Corinthians

15 verses 30-31, "Why stand we in jeopardy every hour?…I die daily": 'death is our constant companion'.

The result of suffering for Paul and his companions was **greater faith in God:** "that we should not trust in ourselves, but in God which raiseth the dead". The intense sufferings and dangers through which Paul passed accomplished this desirable result. God makes no mistakes in His dealings with us. Compare Chapter 12 verses 9-10.

d) The respite from suffering, vv.10-11

"Who delivered us from so great a death, and doth deliver: in whom we trust that he will yet deliver us; ye also helping together by prayer for us, that for the gift bestowed upon us by the means of many persons, thanks may be given by many on our behalf." Paul's deliverance had three results:

i) **Paul was encouraged.** His confidence was strengthened. Note the three tenses: "who delivered us…and doth deliver…will yet deliver us" (v10). The RV has: 'will deliver and still will deliver'. We are reminded that:

His love in times past forbids me to think,
He'll leave me at last in ruin to sink…

ii) **Their prayers were answered.** "Ye also helping together by prayer for us." The Corinthians were party to Paul's deliverance. The expression "helping together" refers to an underworker or helper (*sunupourgeo*). The word "prayer" is 'supplication' (*deesis*), meaning prayer particularly out of a sense of special need. Compare Philippians 1 verse 19, "For I know that this shall turn to my salvation through **your prayer** *(deesis)*…."

P.E.Hughes comments here: 'Though the apostle's hope is firmly fixed on God, yet he also relies on the prayers of fellow-believers on his behalf, especially of those whom, like the Corinthians, his ministry of the Gospel had closely linked him. Their supplications play an important role in his expectation of deliverance. Prayer is indeed a mystery, but it is stressed over and over again in the New Testament as a vital prerequisite for the release and experience of God's power. It is true that it is *God* who delivers, and that God stands in no need of human prayers before He can act on behalf of His afflicted servants. Yet there is the manward as well as the Godward aspect of such a deliverance, and the manward side is summed up in the duty of Christians to intercede in prayer for their fellow-believers who are enduring affliction…Thus the duty of prayer is not a modification of God's power, but a glorification of it'.

iii) **God was glorified.** "That for the gift (*charis* - grace, that is, of deliverance) bestowed upon us by the means of many persons, **thanks may be given** by many on our behalf." Compare Chapter 4 verse 15, "For all things are for your sakes, that the abundant grace might, through the thanksgiving of many, redound to the glory of God".

Very clearly, Paul is not thinking so much of his own benefit in this way, but rather of God's glory.

3) PAUL'S CONCERN, vv.12-24

In this connection we will notice in our next study *(a)* his attitude to them (v.12); *(b)* his letter to them (vv.13-14); *(c)* his visit to them (vv.15-24).

2 CORINTHIANS

"All the promises of God in him are yea, and in him Amen"

Read Chapter 1:12-22

As we noted in our previous study, Paul refers particularly in this Epistle to his adversity. He emphasises this more than anywhere else in his New Testament correspondence. It can be summed up in the words, "we were troubled on every side; without were fightings, within were fears" (7: 5).

We also noted that after the introduction (vv.1-2) the chapter may be divided by reference to this statement as follows: *(i)* "without were fightings" (vv.3-11); *(ii)* "within were fears" (vv.12-24), and that the passage therefore falls into three sections: *(1)* Paul's introduction to the letter (vv.1-2); *(2)* Paul's sufferings for the Gospel (vv.3-11); *(3)* Paul's concern for the assembly (vv.12-24).

1) PAUL'S INTRODUCTION, vv.1-2

In these introductory verses we noted *(a)* the writer (v.1); *(b)* the recipients (v.1); *(c)* the greeting (v.2).

2) PAUL'S SUFFERINGS, vv.3-11

We also noted that this section of the chapter may be divided as follows: *(a)* the resources in suffering (v.3); *(b)* the results of suffering (vv.4-7); *(c)* the reality of suffering (vv.8-9); *(d)* the respite from suffering (vv.10-11). While Paul is evidently referring to his sufferings in his service for God, there are lessons for general application.

This brings us to the third section of the chapter in which Paul refers to his concerns for the assembly at Corinth. These, as we have seen, can be summed up in the words, "within were fears". So:

3) PAUL'S CONCERN, vv.12-22

In these verses, Paul deals with his relationship with the assembly at Corinth, and, in particular, his attitude of heart to the saints. There were evidently people at Corinth who used the alteration in Paul's plans to visit them as an opportunity to accuse him of caprice and unreliability: "When I was therefore thus minded (that is, to travel directly to them from Ephesus), did I use lightness? Or the things that I purpose, do I purpose according to the flesh, that with me there should be yea yea, and nay nay?" (v.17). He therefore makes two things clear in a passage that extends to Chapter 2 verse 13:

- That his original plans were made in good faith (1:12-22).

- That his original plans were altered for good reasons (1: 23 - 2: 13).

We should notice three things in connection with Paul's relationship with the assembly: *(A)* his attitude to them (1: 12); *(B)* his letter to them (1: 13-14); *(C)* his visit to them (1: 15 - 2: 13). Note the expressions "to you-ward" (v.12); "unto you" (v.13); "unto you" (v.15).

A) HIS ATTITUDE TO THEM, 1: 12

"For our rejoicing is this, the testimony of our conscience, that in simplicity and godly sincerity, not with fleshly wisdom, but by the grace of God, we have had our conversation in this world, and more abundantly to you-ward." We must notice the link with their prayers. Paul assures them that they had been praying for people who had their best interests at heart. "Ye also helping by prayer for us... *For* our rejoicing is this... that in simplicity and godly sincerity... we have had our conversation... more abundantly to you-ward" (vv.11-12). It follows that we can hardly be confident of the prayers of the saints unless we are marked by integrity towards them!

a) It was with a clear conscience

"For our rejoicing (*kauchesis*: 'glorying', RV) is this, the testimony of our conscience..." The word *kauchesis* occurs in Chapter 7 verses 4 and 14; Chapter 8 verse 24; Chapter 9 verse 4 and Chapter 11 verses 10 and 17.

Paul's reference to "our conscience" reminds us that he said before the Jewish council, "Men and brethren, I have lived in all **good conscience** before God unto this day" (Acts 23:1) and, before Felix, "And herein do I exercise myself to have always a **conscience void of offence** toward God, and toward men" (Acts 24:16). Compare 1 Corinthians 4 verse 4, "I know nothing by (i.e. 'against') myself...."

When Paul thought about his relationship with the assembly at Corinth, he rejoiced with a clear conscience. What about **us?** Can **we** rejoice with a clear conscience when we think of our assembly membership? Have **we** got the right attitude to our fellow-believers? Are **we** giving our very best to the work of the assembly?

b) It was genuine

"In simplicity." As it stands, "simplicity" translates *'haplotes'* meaning simplicity as opposed to duplicity. This accords well with the context. The word occurs again in Chapter 8 verse 2; Chapter 9 verses 11 and 13; Chapter 11 verse 3. We are told, however, that the best manuscripts have *hagiotes,* the abstract quality of holiness. This does not constitute a major problem since moral purity is in view.

"And godly sincerity" is literally 'and sincerity of God' or "sincerity before God" (JND) with a marginal note, "'simplicity and sincerity of God': the force I take to be, such as God would have, and God would produce". It was not Paul's innate goodness.

"Sincerity" *(eilikrinia),* meaning 'unalloyed, pure... it was used of unmixed substances' (W.E.Vine). It is often said that in view of the fact that the word is probably a compound of two words meaning 'the heat of the sun' and 'to judge', it means, literally, 'tested by sunlight'. So, 'buyer beware'. A vase for sale in a market should be held up to the light to make sure that the stallholder is not a fraudster who has filled the cracks in the vase with wax!

We should conduct our relationships with one another in the assembly with genuine hearts and genuine motives.

c) It was spiritual

"Not with fleshly wisdom, but by the grace of God." Paul did not manipulate people or circumstances to achieve his own ends. He did not attempt to manoeuvre in order to outwit people. He did not resort to human ingenuity, *but* relied upon divine guidance.

The words, "we have had our conversation (behaviour or conduct) in the world, and more abundantly to you-ward", emphasise that fact that the Corinthians had more opportunity to witness it than most people.

B) HIS LETTER TO THEM, 1: 13-14

"For we write none other things unto you than what ye read or acknowledge; and I trust ye shall acknowledge even to the end; as also ye have acknowledged us in part, that we are your rejoicing, even as ye also are ours in the day of the Lord Jesus."

We should notice that Paul's letter flowed from his attitude to them in verse 12: "not with fleshly wisdom, but by the grace of God, we have had our conversation in the world, and more abundantly to you-ward. *For* we write none other things unto you than what ye read or acknowledge" (vv.12-13).

There was no hidden or mysterious meaning in his epistle. He meant what he said, and said what he meant: nothing more, nothing less.

It is important to remember here that when Paul says, "we write none other things unto you than what ye read or acknowledge", he is not referring to teaching, but to his *relationship with them.* There are some important lessons here:

a) He wanted them to take his letters at face value

"For we write none other things unto you than what ye read or acknowledge (RV, 'even acknowledge')." Paul did not resort to ambiguity or conceal hidden meanings in his epistles. When he spoke of "simplicity and godly sincerity", that is exactly what he meant! We too must avoid bring deliberately ambiguous and misleading. What passes for 'diplomacy' can be downright 'deception'. This does not mean, of course, that we should dispense with courtesy and care in the interests of truth! It is all very well to be 'Joe Blunt', but "be courteous" (1 Pet. 3: 8) *is* a divine injunction!

We can make a general application here. Paul's words, "For we write none other things unto you than what ye read or acknowledge", remind us the

Bible does not require us to perform incredible feats of mental gymnastics! So often we look for 'deep meanings' and completely miss the clear lesson staring us in the face!

b) He wanted their unbroken fellowship

"For we write none other things unto you than what ye read or acknowledge; **and I trust ye shall acknowledge even to the end**", or "I hope ye will acknowledge unto the end" (RV).

The expression "the end" must be understood with reference to the coming of the Lord Jesus and attendant events. See 1 Corinthians 1 verse 8, "who shall also confirm you unto **the end**, that ye may be blameless in the day of our Lord Jesus Christ". It must therefore be linked with "the day of the Lord Jesus" (v.14).

It would be helpful in this connection to treat the words "as also ye have acknowledged us in part" (v.14) as a parenthesis. So, "we write none other things unto you than what ye read or acknowledge; and I trust ye shall acknowledge even to the end... that we are your rejoicing, even as ye also are ours in the day of the Lord Jesus". Why such mutual rejoicing? See 1 Corinthians 4 verse 15: "For in Christ Jesus, I have begotten you through the gospel." It was Paul who had evangelised them initially. Hence the desire for mutual joy. Compare 1 Thessalonians 2 verses 19-20, "For what is our hope, or joy, or crown of rejoicing? Are not even ye in the presence of our Lord Jesus Christ at his coming? For ye are our glory and joy". Paul desired that their mutual fellowship on earth be consummated with mutual rejoicing in heaven!

The following should be noted in connection with "day of the Lord Jesus", which should be carefully distinguished from "the day of the Lord":

- "Blameless in the **day** of our Lord Jesus Christ" (1 Cor. 1: 8).

- "Every man's work shall be made manifest for the **day** shall declare it" (1 Cor. 3: 13).

- "That the spirit may be saved in the **day** of the Lord Jesus" (1 Cor. 5: 5).

- "Will perform it until the **day** of Jesus Christ" (Phil. 1: 6).

- "That ye may be sincere and without offence till the *day* of Christ" (Phil. 1: 10).

- "That I may rejoice in the *day* of Christ" (Phil. 2: 16).

- "That *day*" (2 Tim. 4: 8).

c) He wanted their complete fellowship

Returning now to the parenthesis: "As also ye have acknowledged us in part". The meaning is not that the entire assembly had only partly acknowledged him, but that only part of the assembly had done so. Not all the members acknowledged him. P.E.Hughes puts it clearly: "But already the shadow under which this epistle is written is becoming apparent: their acknowledgement of his integrity, founded on the assurance of personal fellowship, is but partial. They should *all* have complete confidence in him who is their divinely appointed apostle; but the calumnies and insinuations of the false apostles who had invaded his territory had caused some to waver and others even to transfer their allegiance". Paul was still subject to opposition by some at Corinth.

This is an appropriate opportunity to stress the necessity for assembly members to be in *complete* fellowship with each other. The existence of cliques and coteries spells disaster to assembly fellowship and must have a weakening effect on testimony.

C) HIS VISIT TO THEM, 1:15 - 2:13

In this section, Paul discusses *(a)* his original plan (1: 15-22); *(b)* his amended plan (1: 23 - 2: 13).

a) His original plan, 1: 15-22

We must notice *(i)* that he states his original intention (vv.15-16); *(ii)* that he confirms the integrity of his original intention (v.17); *(iii)* that he places his original intention on the highest possible level (vv.18-20); *(iv)* he attributes his ministry to God alone (vv.21-22).

i)   The details of his original intention, vv.15-16

"And in this confidence I was minded to come unto you before (previously) that ye might have a second benefit; and to pass by you into Macedonia, and to come again out of Macedonia unto you, and of you to be brought on my way toward Judaea."

The words "and in this confidence" refer to the clarity of his conscience and the integrity of his intentions (vv.12-13). The word "benefit" (*charis*) means 'grace'. It must be said that from one point of view "benefit" is a very good definition of grace! The word 'grace' is, of course, a most comprehensive word!

Referring now to verse 16, Paul's intended route, as outlined in the introduction, was Ephesus - Corinth - Macedonia - Corinth – Judaea. This was altered to (see 1 Cor. 16: 5), Ephesus - Macedonia – Corinth, and ultimately, back to Macedonia thence to Judaea.

ii)   The integrity of his original intention, v.17

"When I therefore was thus minded, did I use lightness? Or the things that I purpose, do I purpose according to the flesh, that with me there should be yea yea, and nay nay? But as God is true, our word toward you was not yea and nay." In passing, the Greek word rendered "yea" is *nai:* it almost looks like a contradiction!

"When I therefore was thus **minded**" or "Having therefore this purpose" (JND). The word *(bouluomai)* means 'counsel' or 'purpose'. The word is used twice more in the verse: "the things that I **purpose** (bouluomai), do I **purpose** (bouluomai)…" The word "lightness" ('fickleness', RV) means 'levity'. His plans were made not in fickleness, nor in a fleshly way, but with integrity.

The words "do I purpose according to the flesh" should be compared with verse 12: "not with fleshly wisdom". That is, what characterises nature: saying **"yea yea"** one moment (twice for emphasis) and **"nay nay"** the next (again, twice for emphasis). This reminds us that believers should be people of their word. They should mean what they say, and say what they mean.

iii)   The character of his original intention, vv.18-20

It was in accord with the character of God. "But as God is true, our word toward you was not yea and nay" (v.18). "But as God is true": that is, faithful. What God says He means. He is totally reliable.

It was in accord with the word of God. "For the Son of God, Jesus Christ, who was preached among you by us, even by me and Silvanus and Timotheus, was not yea and nay, but in him was yea" (v.19). It does seem that the words that follow ("for all the promises of God in him are yea, and in him Amen") are a parenthesis, and that the continuity of the passage is as follows: "For the Son of God, Jesus Christ, who was preached among you by us, even by me and Silvanus and Timotheus, was not yea and nay, but in him was yea...unto the glory of God by us".

We should notice four statements in connection with the preaching: (*kerusso*, meaning 'proclaim'):

- ***The subject of the preaching***. "The Son of God, Jesus Christ" (v.19). His deity and dignity.

- ***The fellowship in the preaching***. "By me, and Silvanus, and Timotheus" (v.19). See Acts 18 verse 5. They all preached the same thing!

- ***The certainty of the preaching***. "Not yea and nay, but in him was yea" (v.19).

- ***The result of the preaching***. "Unto the glory of God by us" (v.20).

It was in accord with the promises of God. "For all the promises of God in him are yea, and in him Amen, unto the glory of God" (v.20) or "For whatsoever promises of God there are, in him is ***the*** yea...' (JND); "For how many soever be the promises of God, in him is the yea. Amen" (RV).

"Yea": that is the promise; "Amen": that is the fulfilment. See Deuteronomy 7 verse 9, "Know therefore that the LORD thy God, he is God, the faithful (Strong 539) God", literally, 'the Amen God'. See also Isaiah 65 verse 16, "He who blesseth himself in the earth shall bless himself in the God of truth (Strong 543)", with the margin reading, 'God of Amen'. "Amen" when used of God means 'it is, and shall be so'.

We must remember that God's purposes for ourselves individually, for the church collectively, for Israel, for the world, for the planet, will all be completed by Christ.

So Paul determined in a godly manner ("as God is true") to travel as intended in verse 16. There was no discrepancy between the integrity of the messengers and the integrity of the message ("for the Son of God…who was preached among you"). Faithful preaching was undertaken by faithful men.

iv) He attributes his ministry to God alone, vv.21-22

Paul "does not lay claim to integrity as a personal achievement; all is attributed to the redeeming and recreative activity of the Holy Trinity" (P.E.Hughes). Hence: "Now he which stablisheth us with you in **Christ** (JND margin, literally 'unto Christ', meaning 'attaches firmly to…connects firmly with'), and hath anointed us, is **God**; who also hath sealed us, and given the earnest of the **Spirit** in our hearts". Notice that Paul does not regard himself as a special case: hence "stablisheth us with **you**…" "Stablisheth" means 'to make firm, to establish, to secure'. Paul reminds them that this is something concrete in their own experience, and therefore "to suspect his reliability was, in fact, to cast a shadow over their own stability, for it is a case of 'us with you in Christ', not 'us different from you', but all dynamically united in the unchanging Son of God" (P.E.Hughes). This has been accomplished by the Holy Spirit, whose ministry is described in three ways:

- **"Anointed us"**. In the Old Testament, prophets, priests and kings were anointed, signifying that God had set them apart for their particular service and empowered them to undertake their work. This is true of every believer. See 1 John 2 verse 20, "But ye have an unction (anointing) from the Holy One, and ye know all things"; 1 John 2 verse 27, "But the anointing which ye have received of him abideth in you".

- **"Sealed us"**. This indicates ownership and security. Compare Ephesians 1 verse 13, "Sealed with that Holy Spirit of promise"; Revelation 7 verse 2, where sealed with "the seal of the living God" indicates ownership and security; Jeremiah 32 verse 10 in connection with the property of "Hanameel my uncle's son", Jeremiah 32:8.

- **"Given the earnest of the Spirit in our hearts"**. 'The term "earnest" (*arrabon*) means "a deposit which is in itself a guarantee that the full amount will be paid later"' (P.E.Hughes). According to W.E.Vine the word refers originally to "earnest-money deposited by the purchaser and forfeited if the purchase was not completed". W.E.Vine notes that it "was probably a Phoenician word, introduced into Greece. In general usage it came to denote a pledge or earnest of any sort". Compare Ephesians 1 verse 14, "Which is the earnest of our inheritance until the redemption of the purchased possession"; 2 Corinthians 5 verse 5, "Now he that hath wrought us for the self-same thing is God, who also hath given unto us the earnest of the Spirit". 'In modern Greek, *arrabona* is an engagement ring' (W.E.Vine). Now that is most interesting!

b) His amended plan, 1: 23 - 2: 13

See next study.

2 CORINTHIANS

"The love which I have more abundantly unto you"

Read Chapter 1:23 - 2:13

As we have noted in previous studies, Paul refers particularly in this Epistle to his adversity. He emphasises this more than anywhere else in his New Testament correspondence. It can be summed up in the words, "we were troubled on every side; without were fightings, within were fears" (7: 5). We have also noticed that these words are an appropriate summary of Chapters 1 & 2.

i) *"Without were fightings"*

This describes Chapter 1 verses 3-11. Notice particularly verse 8: "For we would not, brethren, have you ignorant of our trouble which came to us in Asia, that we were pressed out of measure, above strength, insomuch that we despaired even of life".

ii) *"Within were fears"*

This describes Chapter 1 verse 12 to Chapter 2 verse 13, in which Paul expresses his deep concern for the assembly. See, for example, Chapter 2 verse 4: "For out of much affliction and anguish of heart I wrote unto you with many tears…that ye might know the love which I have more abundantly unto you"; Chapter 2 verses 12-13, "Furthermore, when I came to Troas to preach Christ's gospel…I had no rest in my spirit, because I found not Titus my brother: but taking my leave of them, I went from thence into Macedonia".

As we have seen, this section may be divided as follows: *(A)* his attitude to them (1: 12); *(B)* his letter to them (1: 13-14); *(C)* his visit to them (1:15 – 2:13).

A) His attitude to them, 1: 12

When Paul thought about the assembly at Corinth, he was able to rejoice with a clear conscience. He had acted at all times towards them with "simplicity and godly sincerity".

B) His letter to them, 1: 13-14

He did not say one thing and mean something quite different. His letters reflected his "simplicity and godly sincerity": thus, "We write none other things unto you, than what ye read or acknowledge" (v.13).

C) His visit to them, 1: 15 – 2: 13

In this section, Paul discusses *(a)* his original plan (1: 15-22); *(b)* his amended plan (1: 23 - 2: 13).

a) His original plan, 1: 15-22

"And in this confidence I was minded to come unto you before (previously) that ye might have a second benefit; and to pass by you into Macedonia, and to come again out of Macedonia unto you, and of you to be brought on my way toward Judaea."

The words, "and in this confidence", refer to the clarity of his conscience and the integrity of his intentions (vv.12-15). Paul makes it clear that these plans were made in good faith. It was his firm intention to follow this route. It was his determined itinerary. There was nothing fickle in his intentions.

As stated in verse 16 above, Paul's intended route, notified to them before 1 Corinthians was written, was Ephesus - Corinth - Macedonia - Corinth - Judaea.

ii)   His amended plan, 1: 23 - 2: 13

While Paul does not set out his amended plan in the same way as his original plan, we know that he refers to this in 1 Corinthians 16 verse 5: "But I will come unto you, when I shall **have passed** through Macedonia; for I do pass through Macedonia" (RV). So instead of proceeding **directly** to Corinth as originally intended (2 Cor. 1: 15-16), Paul amended his journey so that he travelled **indirectly** to them via Macedonia. Instead of travelling west from Ephesus to Corinth, he travelled north to Troas (2: 12-13), thence into Macedonia (2: 12-13) where he met Titus bringing news of reaction at Corinth to his first letter to them (7: 5-8).

We know from Acts 20 verses 1-6 that he then visited Greece (Achaia, where Corinth was located), and then returned to Macedonia before setting sail from Philippi to Judaea.

It was this amendment that caused a furore (1: 17) on the part of his detractors at Corinth, and Paul now explains why he changed his route. He did so for very good reasons indeed, not the least in the interests of the Corinthians themselves.

This brings us to the present passage, and we should notice the following: **(1)** the reason for his alteration (1: 23 - 2: 3); **(2)** the reality of his concern (2: 4); **(3)** the response to his letter (2: 5-6); **(4)** the requirement of the assembly (2: 7-11); **(5)** the restlessness of his spirit (2: 12-13).

1) THE REASON FOR HIS ALTERATION, 1: 23 – 2: 3

Paul gives two reasons for altering his itinerary: **(a)** "To spare you, I came not as yet unto Corinth" (1: 23); **(b)** "I would not come again to you in heaviness (sorrow)" (2: 1). He explains that it was for the reasons above that he had written to them: "and I wrote this same unto you, lest, when I came, I should have sorrow for them of whom I ought to rejoice" (2: 3).

Had he come directly to Corinth as originally intended, and not have first **written** to give them the opportunity to deal with the flagrant case of immorality (1 Cor. 5), it would have been unpleasant **for them** (1: 23), and unpleasant **for him** (2: 1). There was everything to be gained by waiting, even though it meant considerable stress for him. See Chapter 2 verses 12-13.

This reminds us that whilst there are occasions when action must be taken expeditiously, particularly in cases of immorality and erroneous doctrine, there is a great deal to be gained by allowing time for teaching to be 'marked, learned and inwardly digested'. Paul gave the assembly at Corinth time to deal with the matters raised in his first epistle before visiting them.

We must also notice here that Paul is not dealing with a theoretical situation:

he is dealing with real people. But there is no 'naming and shaming'. He is tender, compassionate, and diplomatic. He is certainly not seeking publicity for himself.

a)   As to them, 1: 23-24

"Moreover I call God for a record upon my soul, that to spare you I came not as yet unto Corinth. Not for that we have dominion over your faith, but are helpers of your joy: for by faith ye stand." Attention is drawn to the following:

- *"I call God for a record upon my soul..."* The word "record" signifies 'testimony'. Compare 1 Thessalonians 2 verse 5, "For neither at any time used we flattering words, as ye know...God is **witness**". See also 1 Thessalonians 2 verse 10: "Ye are **witnesses**...and God also, how holily, and justly, and unblameably, we behaved ourselves among you that believe". Paul calls for the highest possible witness to vouch for his integrity in the matter. Can we speak of **our** motives with the same confidence?

- *"To spare you".* Paul did not delight in censure. Compare 1 Corinthians 4 verse 21, "What will ye? Shall I come unto you with a rod, **or** in love, and in the spirit of meekness?"; 2 Corinthians 13 verse 2, "If I come again, I will not spare"; 2 Corinthians 13 verse 10, "Lest being present. I should use sharpness" (literally, 'in a manner that cuts'). Paul exhibited a divine quality here for judgment is God's "strange (alien) work" (Isaiah 28: 21). It is His "strange work" because "he delighteth in mercy" (Micah 7:18). Do **we** delight in reprimanding people? Some preachers seem to think that they are being unfaithful to God's word if they are not 'hammering' the saints!

- *"Not that we have dominion over your faith".* "Dominion" means 'lordship'. The word is used in a strengthened form in 1 Peter 5 verse 3 ("Neither as being lords over God's heritage"). Paul had no desire to act dictatorially or autocratically. He was not their master.

- *"But as helpers of your joy..."* That is, the joy in doing what is right. "Helpers" means 'fellow-workers', as in 2 Corinthians 8 verse 23 ("Whether any do enquire of Titus, he is my partner and fellow-helper concerning you") and Romans 16 verses 3 & 9 ("Greet Priscilla and Aquila my helpers in Christ Jesus...Salute Urbane, our helper in Christ"). The need for us **all** to recognise this: it will save us from 'pride of place'. Note: "as helpers of your **joy**", not 'of your sorrow!'

- *"For by faith ye stand."* That is, by faith alone. Paul recognised their relationship with the Lord, and therefore he had no desire to dominate them, but simply to *help* them.

b)   As to himself, 2: 1-3

"But I determined this with myself (see 1: 15), that I would not come unto you again in heaviness" (v.1). The expression, "but I determined *(krino)* this with myself", indicates that Paul's changed plan was the result of careful consideration. His detractors had charged him with fickleness (1: 17), but Paul had not changed his mind on the spur of the moment, and he was not subject to whims and fancies, or making casual promises. The situation had altered since he first indicated his intention to revisit Corinth, and that demanded a change in his plans.

Paul used spiritual intelligence in deciding whether or not to proceed as originally intended. Had he done so, he would have "come again to you in heaviness (*lupe*, meaning 'grief' or 'sorrow')". This is something he wanted to avoid, and in order to achieve this he had written the First Epistle to them. He therefore continues: "For if I make you sorry, who is he then that maketh me glad, but the same which is made sorry by me. And I wrote this same unto you, lest when I came, I should have sorrow from them of whom I ought to rejoice…" (vv.2-3). Paul's joy was wrapped up with the joy of God's people, and so was his pain.

There is a play on words here. Paul resolved not to revisit them in grief (AV "in heaviness", *lupe*), and in order to avoid this he had caused them grief (AV "make you sorry", *lupeo*) by writing to them in order that the very people he had grieved (AV "made sorry", *lupeo*) by his letter should make him glad. In summary, to avoid personal grief, Paul caused them grief so that his own grief would be removed!

This emphasises that sin (in this case the tolerated sin of immorality at Corinth) interrupts fellowship and mutual joy. Paul's grief over the situation at Corinth could only be removed by the party which caused it, which in this case was the assembly itself which had failed to deal with the matter. See 1 Corinthians 5 verse 2, "And ye are puffed up, and have not rather mourned, that he that hath done this deed might be taken away from among you". This stresses the need to put things right promptly and properly.

While the situation at Corinth was grave in the extreme, the opportunity must be taken to say, sadly, that fellowship can be easily fractured, sometimes by very small things. With this in mind we must endeavour not to **give** offence, and not to **take** offence.

It was with this in mind, the avoidance of a grievous meeting, that Paul had written to them: "I wrote this same unto you, lest when I came, I should have sorrow *(lupe)* from them of whom I ought to rejoice". He had therefore given them instructions, accompanied by solid reasons, to "put away from among yourselves that wicked person" (1 Cor. 5: 13).

He had delayed his visit to them in order that the assembly at Corinth could deal with matter before his arrival, and had done so with confidence that they would do this: "Having confidence in you all, that my joy is the joy of you all". That is, the joy which comes when a matter is put right and dealt with properly. As in verse 2: a mutual joy in putting things right.

The assembly ought to be a place which brings **joy** through **obedience,** rather than **sorrow** through **disobedience.** The apostle John would certainly agree with that: "I have no greater joy than to hear that my children walk in truth" (3 John 4).

2) THE REALITY OF HIS CONCERN, 2: 4

"For out of much affliction (*thlipsis*, meaning 'pressure') and anguish ('distress', *sunoche*: it occurs only here and in Luke 21: 25: "distress of nations") of heart, I wrote unto you with many tears" (v.4). We must bear in mind that Paul founded the assembly at Corinth (1 Cor. 3: 10), though he acknowledged that it was "according to the grace of God...given unto me" that "as a wise master builder" he had "laid the foundation". Changing the metaphor, the assembly at Corinth was his own virgin daughter. See 2 Corinthians 11 verse 2: "I have espoused you to one husband, that I may present you as a chaste virgin to Christ". We can therefore understand his deep personal grief over the condition of the assembly. Paul had the spirit of the Lord Jesus, who wept over Jerusalem.

But Paul always had deep concern over the welfare of God's people. Compare Acts 20 verse 31, "I ceased not to warn every one (at Ephesus) night and day with tears". See also Philippians 3 verse 18; Acts 20 verse 19. Godly men exhibited such grief throughout Scripture. See, for example,

Nehemiah: "And it came to pass, when I heard these words, that I sat down and wept and mourned certain days, and fasted, and prayed before the God of heaven" (Neh. 1: 4). Jeremiah was known as 'the weeping prophet'. How concerned are **we** about each other, about the testimony of the assembly, and about the Lord's work in general. We grumble, criticise and sometimes shout, but we seldom weep before God.

His letter was the expression of his concern: he had written the first epistle "not that ye should be grieved (again, *lupeo*), but that ye might know the love which I have more abundantly unto you" (v.4). This does not contradict his earlier statement. His object in writing was not simply to cause sorrow full stop, but to show his *love*. It was a love that wanted the very best for them, even though it involved sorrow on their part. What prompts **us** in such circumstances? **Love for the saints** must underlie discipline and correction, since it is for their ultimate good. Notice that Paul does not say 'the love which I have for you', but "the love which I have more **abundantly** unto you".

3) THE RESPONSE TO HIS LETTER, 2: 5-6

In these verses Paul refers to the fact that as a result of his letter to them (1 Corinthians) the believers at Corinth had shared his grief over the tolerated immorality in the assembly. We say 'as a result of his letter to them' because it is evident that they had not shared his grief before. See 1 Corinthians 5 verses 1-2, "It is reported commonly (RV 'It is actually reported'), that there is fornication among you, and such fornication as is not so much as named amongst the Gentiles, that one should have his father's wife. And ye are puffed up, and have not rather mourned, that he that hath done this deed might be taken away from among you".

Hence, Paul now writes: "But if any have caused grief *(lupeo)*, he hath not grieved *(lupeo)* me, but in part: that I may not overcharge you all" (v.5), meaning 'But if any one have caused grief, he hath not grieved me (i.e. me alone), but in some measure, not to put it too severely (he has grieved) all of you'.

The words, "that I may not overcharge (overburden) you all" carry the meaning 'that I press not too heavily' (RV) or 'that I put it not too severely'. This may well refer to 1 Corinthians 5 verses 2, 6: "And ye are puffed up, and have not rather mourned...Your glorying is not good". But they now appreciated the serious nature of the situation: once they were "puffed up" but now they are 'grieved'. They had "sorrowed *(lupeo)* to repentance: for ye were made sorry *(lupeo)* after a godly manner" (7: 9).

Paul is stating that he does not wish to press his own concern excessively since the situation had grieved them as well. This is important. Situations can arise in assembly life and even though they have been addressed and resolved, some brethren never let the matter rest! Paul was not of that ilk. His attitude in this way was quite justified: he had not compromised: the assembly at Corinth **had** dealt with the matter: "Sufficient to such a man is this punishment which was inflicted by many".

The words, "this punishment (penalty, *epitimia*) which was inflicted by **many**", refer to the exclusion of the guilty brother from fellowship (the "punishment") by the entire assembly ("inflicted by many") in accordance with Paul's instructions in 1 Corinthians 5 verses 4-5, "In the name of our Lord Jesus Christ, when ye are gathered together…to deliver such an one to Satan for the destruction of the flesh…" Compare Matthew 18 verses 17-20. They had dealt with the matter with spiritual zeal: "For behold this selfsame thing that ye sorrowed after a godly sort, what carefulness it wrought in you, yea, what clearing of yourselves…In all things ye have approved yourselves to be clear in this matter" (2 Cor. 7: 11).

But was that the end of the matter? The guilty man had been dealt with and that was that. It must be remembered that assembly discipline has repentance and restoration in view. The man had evidently repented of his sin, hence the words "swallowed up with overmuch sorrow" (v7). This brings us to:

4) THE REQUIREMENT OF THE ASSEMBLY, 2: 7-11

We should notice three things here: *(a)* what they were to do (vv.7-8); *(b)* whose authority was involved (vv.9-10); *(c)* why they were to act in this way (v.11).

a) What they were to do, vv.7-8

Paul now tells them how they were to act in view of the man's repentance: "So that contrariwise, ye ought rather to forgive him, and comfort him, lest perhaps such an one should be swallowed up with overmuch sorrow. Wherefore I beseech you, that you would confirm your love towards him". Note: there had been *laxity* in dealing with the case in the first place: now there seems to have been **legality** obstructing restoration. They had been slow in putting the man away from fellowship: now they were slow in bringing him back into fellowship. We should notice:

i) **"Forgive him."** Literally, 'to show grace' (*charizomai*: 'to bestow a favour unconditionally', W.E.Vine). The word occurs again in verse 10. See also Ephesians 4 verse 32, "And be ye kind one to another, tenderhearted, forgiving one another, even as God for Christ's sake hath forgiven you".

ii) **"Comfort him."** Literally, 'encourage him'. Where there is true repentance, encouragement can be given. It is a mistake to sympathise and socialise with people who have not repented. That will not bring about their repentance. But as in this case there had been repentance, the assembly needed now to act lest the man should lose all hope of ever enjoying the fellowship of the Lord's people again: "lest perhaps such an one should be swallowed up with overmuch sorrow". His case was not hopeless, but it might look like that to him. The man must be assured of their love for him. It is most important to remember that assembly discipline should not be exercised at the expense of love. Discipline does not mean that the assembly have abandoned their love for the person concerned, since they have their best interests at heart. So:

iii) **"Confirm your love toward him."** The word "confirm" *(kuroo)* means 'ratify' or 'make valid'. It occurs again in Galatians 3 verse 17, "the covenant that was confirmed before of God". In 1 Corinthians 5, Paul commands the assembly, but here it is "I **beseech** you..." We cannot command people to love each other.

b) Whose authority was involved, vv.9-10

"For to this end did I write that I might know the proof of you, whether ye be obedient in all things. To whom ye forgive anything, I forgive also: for if I forgave anything, to whom I forgave it, for your sakes forgave I it, in the person of Christ." We learn of Paul's involvement:

i) At the time he wrote the **first** epistle (v.9). "For to this end also did I write that I might know the proof of you, whether ye be obedient in all things." Here he is recalling the time **when the situation needed correction.**

The word "proof" *(dokime)* means the process of proving. It occurs again in

Philippians 2 verse 22 ("ye know the proof of him") and Romans 5 verse 4 where it is rendered "experience" ("tribulation worketh patience; and patience experience; and experience, hope"). The proof of the Lord's people is their obedience: "whether ye be obedient in all things". Compare Romans 6 verse 17; 1 Peter 1 verse 14.

ii)   At the time he wrote the **second** epistle (v.10). **Now that the situation has been corrected**, Paul comments: "To whom ye forgive anything, I forgive also: for if I forgave anything, to whom I forgave it, for your sakes forgave I it, in the person of Christ".

We should notice that Paul acts in fellowship with the assembly: "To whom ye forgive anything, I forgive also". But he also acts in fellowship with Christ: "for your sakes forgave I it, in the person of Christ". We should notice that the forgiveness corresponds to the discipline:

1 Cor 5: 4	*2 Cor 2: 10*
"In the name of our **Lord Jesus**"	"In the person of **Christ**"
"When **ye** are gathered together"	"To whom **ye** forgive"
"And **my** spirit"	"**I** forgive also"

The Lord Jesus, the assembly at Corinth and the apostle Paul are involved in the exclusion from fellowship and the restoration to fellowship.

The words, "For your sakes have I forgiven it in the person (margin: 'or, presence') of Christ" (RV) recall Matthew 18 verse 18, which can be rendered: "Whatsoever ye shall bind on earth shall be (Amplified Version: 'shall have been') bound in heaven: and whatsoever ye shall loose on earth shall be (ditto) loosed in heaven". It is not that heaven will ratify the assembly acting in discipline, or in forgiveness, but that the assembly implements heaven's judgment in the matter. So the assembly is to be in touch with heaven about the matter. (For other references to "In...Christ", see Chapter 1 verse 21, Chapter 2 verses 14 & 17).

c) Why they were to act in this way, v.11

"Lest Satan should get an advantage over us, for we are not ignorant of his devices." In 1 Corinthians 5 verse 5, it is to "deliver such an one to Satan": now it is, "Lest Satan should get an advantage over us".

The word "advantage" *(pleonekteo)* means, literally, 'seek to get more' (W.E.Vine). 'The word "devices" *(noema)* means 'thoughts'. Failure to recognise the need to restore the repentant brother was a victory for Satan. He is set on the spiritual destruction of the saints, if not by one way, then by another. We are not to be "ignorant" of his intentions.

For further references to ignorance, see 1 Corinthians 10 verse 1 ("Moreover, brethren, I would not that ye should be *ignorant*, how that all our fathers..."); 1 Corinthians 12 verse 1 ("Now concerning spiritual gifts, brethren, I would not have you *ignorant*"); 1 Thessalonians 4 verse 13 ("But I would not have you to be *ignorant*...").

5) THE RESTLESSNESS OF HIS SPIRIT, 2: 12-13

These verses connect with verse 4 where Paul describes his "affliction and anguish of heart" *at the time of writing.* Now he points out that his deep inward concern did not cease with the despatch of the first epistle, but remained: "Furthermore, when I came to Troas to preach Christ's gospel, and a door was opened unto me of the Lord, I had no rest in my spirit, because I found not Titus my brother: but taking my leave of them, I went from thence into Macedonia". 2 Corinthians 7 verses 5-6 add to this: "For when we were come into Macedonia, our flesh had no rest, but we were troubled on every side; without were fightings, *within were fears*".

It is worth noting that Paul made three visits to Troas: during the outward leg of his second journey (Acts 16: 9-11); during the outward leg of his third journey (as related here: see Acts 20: 1; *en route* for Macedonia); during the homeward leg of his third journey (Acts 20:6-12). Eutychus would have remembered the last of these very well indeed!

Paul was deeply affected by the situation at Corinth. These verses do not imply that he immediately left Troas, but describe his spiritual concern for the saints at Corinth whilst he was at Troas. We should also notice:

i) **His description of the gospel:** "when I came to Troas to preach Christ's gospel" (v.12), or "for the gospel of Christ" (RV). Compare, for example, Romans 1 verse 16; 1 Thessalonians 2 verse 2. We must never forget that it is "the gospel of the glory of Christ" (2 Cor. 4: 4, RV).

ii) *His recognition of God's sovereignty:* "a door was opened unto me of the Lord (in the Lord', RV)" (v.12). Compare Revelation 3 verse 8. Paul recognised the sovereignty of God in his service and circumstances, reminding us that we are utterly dependent upon Him for blessing. Compare 1 Corinthians 16 verse 9.

But although deeply burdened over conditions at Corinth, Paul was enabled to continue faithfully in Gospel preaching: "*But* thanks be to God, who always leads us in triumph in the Christ, and makes manifest the odour of his knowledge through us in every place" (v.14, JND).

We will discuss this in our next study.

2 CORINTHIANS

"We are unto God a sweet savour of Christ"

Read Chapter 2: 14-17

We have noted several times that Paul refers particularly in this Epistle to his adversity. He emphasises this more than anywhere else in his New Testament correspondence. It can be summed up in the words, "we were troubled on every side; without were fightings, within were fears" (7: 5). We have also noticed that these words are an appropriate summary of Chapters 1 & 2.

i) "Without were fightings"

This describes Chapter 1 verses 3-11. Notice particularly verse 8: "For we would not, brethren, have you ignorant of our trouble which came unto us in Asia, that we were pressed out of measure, above strength, insomuch that we despaired even of life".

ii) "Within were fears"

This describes Chapter 1 verse 12 - Chapter 2 verse 13, in which Paul expresses his deep concern for the assembly. See, for example, Chapter 2 verse 4: "For out of much affliction and anguish of heart I wrote unto you with many tears…that ye might know the love which I have more abundantly unto you"; Chapter 2 verses 12-13, "Furthermore, when I came to Troas to preach Christ's gospel…I had no rest in my spirit, because I found not Titus my brother: but taking leave of them, I went from thence into Macedonia".

When Paul reached Troas (on the outward leg of his second journey), he had no doubt about his mission there ("to preach Christ's gospel") and was deeply conscious of the Lord's help ("a door was opened unto me of the Lord"), but he remained deeply burdened about conditions at Corinth (2:

12-13). Compare 1 Corinthians 16 verses 8-9 which refer to his gospel work at Ephesus prior to leaving for Troas. Current service, evidently blessed of God, did not make him oblivious of need elsewhere.

His deep concern was evident at the time he wrote 1 Corinthians (2 Cor. 2: 4), after its despatch (2 Cor. 2: 12-13), and in Macedonia (2 Cor. 7: 5-6) where he looked for the return of Titus from Corinth.

But in it all, Paul was deeply conscious of divine guidance and divine blessing. His deep concerns over Corinth did not damp down his zeal for the Gospel. God enabled him to press on victoriously. Circumstances at Corinth, so burdensome to him, did not impede the progress of the Gospel. If Paul had been so affected by the state of the assembly at Corinth that he had ceased to preach, Satan would have achieved a signal victory. The lesson for *us* is clear. Nothing must blunt our evangelical zeal.

The remaining verses of 2 Corinthians 2 may be divided as follows: *(1)* the progress of the messengers (v.14a); *(2)* the preaching of the messengers (vv.14b-16) *(3)* the purity of the messengers (v.17).

1) THE PROGRESS OF THE MESSENGERS, v.14a

"Now thanks be unto God, which always causeth us to triumph in Christ" or "*But* thanks be unto God, which always leadeth us in triumph in Christ" (RV, supported by JND). Although deeply burdened in spirit with regard to affairs at Corinth, the apostle was enabled to continue faithfully in Gospel testimony. The pressures were intense, but he was 'led in triumph in Christ'. The sense of 'triumph' is evidently 'triumph over', that is, over "fightings without...fears within". But it is far more than dogged determination. In the midst of the difficulties which faced him, he rejoiced and exclaimed, "But thanks be unto God..."

It is generally thought that Paul alludes here to the Roman 'triumph'. A victorious general would be accorded a 'triumph', that is, a triumphal entrance to the capital city. He would ride in a magnificent chariot drawn by two white horses, although there were variations. We are told that Pompey's chariot was drawn by elephants, Mark Anthony's by lions, and Aurelius' by deer! The general's sons and senior officers rode behind his chariot, and the procession would include captives and the acquired spoils of war.

But where was Paul and his colleagues in the procession? The answer is 'amongst the captives!' See 1 Corinthians 4 verses 9 and 13: "I think that God hath set forth us the apostles last, as it were appointed to death: for we are made a spectacle unto the world, and to angels, and to men…we are made as the filth of the world, and are the offscouring of all things unto this day". That's how the world saw them, but from the perspective of heaven they were the result of Christ's victory. Once the enemies of God (Rom. 5: 10), they had been overcome and taken captive by Him and were led by Him as trophies of divine grace. We must note the following:

i) **God was in control**. "But thanks be unto **God,** which always leadeth us in triumph in Christ" (RV). Paul and his colleagues were not victims of circumstances. Neither were they left to their own devices. They were led and directed by God Himself. Paul did not take credit for the triumph of divine grace in his life. He exclaims, 'Thanks be unto God'. Compare Chapter 4 verse 7, "But we have this treasure in earthen vessels, that the excellency of the power may be of **God**, and not of us".

But they were not led to defeat! Compare Romans 8 verses 35-39: "Who shall separate us from the love of Christ? Shall tribulation, or distress, or persecution, or famine, or nakedness, or peril, or sword? As it is written, For thy sake we are killed all the day long; we are accounted as sheep for the slaughter. Nay, in all these things we are more than conquerors through him that loved us". 'Led in triumph' indeed! It has often been said that 'the blood of the martyrs is the seed of the church'.

Moreover, God makes no mistakes: "But thanks be unto God, which **always** leadeth us in triumph in Christ". We can exclaim "As for God his way is perfect" (Psalm 18: 30). Paul himself bears testimony to God's unfailing grace: "who delivered us from so great a death, and doth deliver: in whom we trust that he will yet deliver us" (1: 10).

If He is consistent (*"always"* leadeth us in triumph in Christ") then we should be consistent too: "**Always** abounding in the work of the Lord" (1 Cor. 15: 58); "Therefore we are **always** confident" (2 Cor. 5: 6); "Giving thanks **always** for all things unto God and the Father in the name of our Lord Jesus Christ" (Eph. 5: 20); "**Always** in every prayer of mine for you all making request with joy" (Phil. 1: 4). After all, His resources are never diminished: "God is able to make all grace abound toward you: that ye **always** having all sufficiency in all things, may abound to every good work" (2 Cor. 9: 8).

ii) **Christ was their resource**. "But thanks be unto God, which always leadeth us in triumph in **Christ**." RV "In Christ" means in His strength and sufficiency. It was His strength and sufficiency that enabled Paul to triumph over circumstances and opposition. This is expressed elsewhere: "I can do all things through Christ that strengtheneth me" (Phil. 4: 13); "Notwithstanding the Lord stood with me and strengthened me…" (2 Tim. 4: 17).

iii) **They were recipients**. "But thanks be unto God, which always leadeth *us* in triumph in Christ." It is "God…us…Christ!" No wonder Paul interrupts the main thrust of his epistle to say "But thanks be unto God…" We must never lose sight of the immense privilege of being led by God, yes, almighty God, and fully resourced in Christ.

2) THE PREACHING OF THE MESSENGERS, vv.14b-16

"God…maketh manifest the savour of his knowledge by us in every place. For we are unto God a sweet savour of Christ, in them that are saved, and in them that perish. To the one we are the savour of death unto death; and to the other the savour of life unto life."

The words, "and maketh manifest the savour of his knowledge", could also allude to the Roman 'triumph'. The procession would be attended by the burning of incense on the altars lining the route of the triumphal procession. Alternatively, it has been suggested that the incense was scattered by members of the triumphant cavalcade. It has been said that "Paul sees his apostolic progress through the world as a continuous triumph, by which the knowledge of Christ is spread abroad like perfume". We must notice the following:

a) The power

"**God**…maketh manifest the savour of his knowledge *(gnosis)* by us in every place" (v.14b). It is His work. It is "the savour of *his* knowledge". He reveals Himself . Not now in creation (see Rom 1:19, "that which may be known *(gnostos)* of God is manifest in them; for God hath shewed in unto them"), but through the Gospel.

The word "savour" *(osme)* comes from a root meaning 'to smell' *(ozo)*. It also occurs in verse 16, "the savour of death unto death…the savour of life unto life". It means a smell, or an odour. (From which comes the English word 'ozone': "a condensed form of oxygen with pungent refreshing odour", the

Oxford Dictionary). The word is used in John 12 verse 3, "The house was fill with the **odour** of the ointment". (The word translated "savour" in v.15 is *euodia* meaning 'fragrance'.)

b) The people

"Us"! "God…maketh manifest the savour of his knowledge **by us** in every place" (v.14b). The words "by us" occur several times in the epistle, and make a profitable study: "For the Son of God, Jesus Christ, who was preached among you **by us**" (1: 19); "unto the glory of God **by us**" (1: 20); "maketh manifest the savour of his knowledge **by us**" (2: 14); "the epistle of Christ ministered **by us**" (3: 3); "Now then we are ambassadors for Christ, as though God did beseech you **by us**" (5: 20).

The words "by us" indicate the immense privilege of communicating the gospel message.

c) The place

Everywhere! "God…maketh manifest the savour of his knowledge by us in **every place**" (v.14b). Compare 1 Thessalonians 1: 8, "In **every place** your faith to God-ward is spread abroad; so that we need not to speak any thing".

The testimony in "every place" can be illustrated from Paul's life and journeys. It began at Damascus: "straightway he preached Christ in the synagogues, that he is the Son of God" (Acts 9: 20). At Pisidian Antioch: "of this man's seed (David's seed) hath God according to his promise raised unto Israel a Saviour, Jesus" (Acts 13: 23). At Thessalonica: "Opening and alleging, that Christ must needs have suffered, and risen again from the dead; and that this Jesus, whom I preach unto you, is Christ" (Acts 17: 3). At Corinth: "I determined not to know any thing among you, save Jesus Christ, and him crucified" (1 Cor. 2: 2). At Troas: "Furthermore, when I came to Troas to preach Christ's gospel" (2 Cor. 2: 12).

Can it be said of **us** that we are so much at God's disposal that through **us** He can make "manifest the savour of his knowledge…in every place"?

d) The perfume

"For we are unto God a sweet savour of Christ, in them that are saved and

55

in them that perish. To the one we are the savour of death unto death; and to the other the savour of life unto life" (vv.15-16). We must notice the effect of the preaching Godward and manward.

i) Godward

The effect of the gospel Godward: "We are unto God a sweet **savour** of Christ" (v.15) This is how God views the Gospel preacher. Notice that Paul does **not** say 'our preaching is unto God a sweet savour of Christ', but "**we** are unto God a sweet savour of Christ". If Paul is alluding to the incense accompanying the Roman 'triumph', then it may well be that he is thinking of the product of suffering. The flame has to be applied to incense before it releases its fragrance. Paul's adversity only served to reveal the character of Christ in Him. Irrespective of the response, "we are unto God a sweet savour of Christ". This must be set alongside the words, "maketh manifest the **savour** of his knowledge by us in every place" (v.14).

It is worth pointing out that in relation to men ("the savour of his knowledge by us in every place...to the one we are the savour of death unto death; and to the other the savour of life unto life") the word used is *osme*, but in relation to God the word used is *euodia*. Possibly this indicates that Christ in the full fragrance of His Person can only be fully appreciated by God Himself. In the meal offering, all the frankincense was for God. See Leviticus 2 verse 2.

However, both words are used together elsewhere in the New Testament: in Ephesians 5 verse 2, "And walk in love, as Christ also hath loved us, and hath given himself for us, an offering to God for a sweetsmelling *(euodia)* savour *(osme)*" or "for an **odour** *(osme)* of a **sweet smell** *(euodia)*" (RV): in Philippians 4 verse 18, "Having received of Epaphroditus the things which were sent from you, an **odour** *(osme)* of a **sweet smell** *(euodia),* a sacrifice acceptable, well-pleasing to God".

Putting the three passages together teaches us that we may exude Christ in all His sweetness in three ways:

- *In our mutual love.* "And walk in love, as Christ also hath loved us, and hath given himself for us, an offering and a sacrifice to God for a **sweetsmelling** *(euodia)* **savour** *(osme)*" (Eph. 5: 2).

- *In Gospel testimony.* "The **savour** *(osme)* of his knowledge by us in every place…we are unto God a sweet *savour* (*euodia*) of Christ" (2 Cor. 2: 14-16).

- *In our stewardship*. "Having received of Epaphroditus the things which were sent from you, an *odour* (*osme*) of a *sweet smell* (*euodia*), a sacrifice acceptable, well-pleasing to God" (Phil. 4: 18). Note that Paul emphasises the sacrificial nature of their giving: "a *sacrifice* acceptable, well-pleasing to God".

ii) Manward

"For we are unto God a sweet savour of Christ, *in them that are saved and in them that perish.* To the one we are the savour of death unto death; and to the other the savour of life unto life" (vv.15-16). Compare John 3 verses 18-21: "He that believeth on him is not condemned: but he that believeth not is condemned already, because he hath not believed in the name of the only begotten Son of God. And this is the condemnation, that light is come into the world, and men loved darkness rather than light, because their deeds were evil. For every one that doeth evil hateth the light, neither cometh to the light, lest his deeds should be reproved *('the savour of death unto death').* But he that doeth truth cometh to the light, that his deeds may be made manifest, that they are wrought in God *('the savour of life unto life')*".

We must remember that however men might view the Gospel preacher, he remains in both cases "unto God a sweet savour of Christ" -

- *"In them that are saved"*. Literally, 'being saved'. To them the Gospel is "the savour of life unto life". They regard it as a message of life, and in receiving it they have life: "whosoever believeth in him should not perish, but have everlasting life" (John 3: 16). It has been described as 'a vital fragrance that leads to life'. It is welcomed and received. The result is eternal life. "Of life": that is its quality; "unto life": that is its result.

- *"In them that perish"*. Literally, 'are perishing'. To them the Gospel is the very reverse of a message of life. It is "the savour of death unto death". It warns of condemnation and leads to the second death. It has been described as 'a fatal aroma which ends in death'. It condemns men now, with fearful results in the future. Those of whom Paul and Barnabas said, "ye put it from you, and judge yourselves unworthy of everlasting life" (Acts 13: 46), face eternal death. Similarly those who "mocked" at Athens (Acts 17: 32). Paul concludes, "And who is sufficient for these things?" (v.16). That is, 'how is this ministry maintained?' He gives the full answer in Chapter 3 verses 5-6, "Not that we are sufficient of ourselves to think anything as of ourselves; but our sufficiency is of God; who hath also made us able ministers of the new testament". However, we do not have to wait that long for an explanation: he points out that only men empowered by God and faithful to Him can undertake such ministry (v.17).

3) THE PURITY OF THE MESSENGERS, v.17

"For we are not as many, which corrupt the word of God: but as of sincerity, but as of God, in the sight of God speak we in Christ." We must notice Paul's reference to "many" and to themselves:

a) "Not as many"

The word "corrupt" (*kapeleuo*) means to retail or to peddle. W.E.Vine tells us that the word "corrupt" comes "from *kapelos*, an inn-keeper, a petty retailer, especially of wine, a huckster, a pedlar…hence to get base gain by dealing in anything, and so, more generally to do anything for sordid personal advantage". So here, it means to adulterate the word of God by an admixture of foreign elements (adding water to wine) such as Judaism or paganism.

We should compare Titus 1 verse 11, "teaching things they ought not for **filthy lucre's** sake"; 1 Timothy 3 verse 8, "not greedy of **filthy lucre**"; Titus 1 verse 7, "not given to **filthy lucre**"; 1 Peter 5 verse 2, "taking the oversight thereof…not for **filthy lucre**".

In the context of this epistle, this refers to false teachers whose motive was base gain. See Chapter 11 verse 20: "For ye suffer, if a man devour you, if a man take of you, if a man exalt himself, if a man smite you on the face". There was no "sweet savour of Christ" to God in these people. Paul resorted to none of these things: see Chapter 11 verses 7-10. What about **our** motives in serving the Lord?

b) "Speak we in Christ"

i)   "**But** as of sincerity". The word rendered "sincerity" (*eilikrines*) means unalloyed, pure. It is used of unmixed substances. There was no preaching the word of God from impure motives with Paul. We have already noted (1: 12) that *eilikrines* is probably a compound of two words meaning 'the heat of the sun' and 'to judge, with the suggested meaning, 'tested by sunlight'.

ii) "***But*** as of God". In this they resembled Jeremiah who spoke "from the mouth of the LORD" (2 Chron. 36: 12). It was a case of "Thus saith the LORD". The Old Testament prophets faithfully repeated what God had told them. They did ***not*** interpret what God had told them to say. See 2 Peter 1 verses 20-21, "no prophecy of the scripture is of any private interpretation. For the prophecy came not in old time by the will of man: but holy men of God spake as they were moved by the Holy Ghost". Paul and his colleagues followed in their train. Their preaching originated with God ("as of God"), and was delivered before God ("in the sight of God"). The words "in Christ" indicate that their preaching was undertaken in fellowship with Him and in His strength.

2 CORINTHIANS

"Able ministers of the new testament"

Read Chapter 3:1-6

In our last study we noticed Paul's thanksgiving to God for enabling him to triumph over adverse circumstances (2:14-17). The question with which Chapter 3 commences suggests that he now takes steps to ensure that his thanksgiving is not distorted by his detractors at Corinth. Hence, "Do we begin again to commend ourselves?" (v.1). The word "*again*" may well refer to such statements in the First Epistle as: "Am I not an apostle? am I not free? have I not seen Jesus Christ our Lord? are not ye my work in the Lord?" (9: 1). See also Chapter 4 verse 16 ("Wherefore I beseech you, be ye followers of me"); Chapter 11 verse 1 ("Be ye followers of me even as I am of Christ").

The very fact that in this chapter Paul contrasts the glory of the Old Covenant with the glory of the New Covenant clearly identifies his opponents. It must be said that the line of demarcation between Paul and the Judaisers is very clear. Paul refers to their **corruption** (2: 17), their **credentials** (3: 1), and their **craftiness** (4: 2). Having dealt with the charge of fickleness against him (1: 17), he now deals with a further attempt to discredit him.

We must notice how the epistle reflects Paul's mixed feelings over the Corinthians. On the one hand, he rejoices over their obedience to the First Epistle in dealing with immorality in the assembly. See Chapter 2 verses 6-11 and Chapter 7 verses 11-16. On the other, he has to censure the perverse suggestions about him by the false teachers at Corinth, who used every opportunity to discredit him.

Bearing this in mind, the chapter may be analysed as follows: *(1)* the commendation of his ministry (vv.1-3); *(2)* the competence of his ministry (vv.4-6); *(3)* the character of his ministry (vv.7-18).

1) THE COMMENDATION OF HIS MINISTRY, vv.1-3

In these verses, Paul raises and answers the question of his commendation. "Do we begin again to commend ourselves... Ye are our epistle written in our hearts, known and read of all men."

a) The question raised, v.1

"Do we begin again to commend (*sunistano*: used in 5: 12; 10: 12) ourselves? or need we, as some others, epistles of commendation (*sustatikos*) to you, or letters of commendation (*sustatikos*) from you?" Paul had no need

- *To commend himself*: "Do we begin again to commend ourselves?"

- *To be commended to them*: "or need we, as some others, epistles of commendation to you...?"

- *To be commended by them*: "or letters of commendation from you...?"

Note the expression, "*as some others*". Compare Chapter 2 verse 17, "for we are not as *many* which corrupt the word of God". Doubtless, these references are to the same persons. Quite obviously, these people were saying, 'We have a letter, but Paul hasn't'. Their letters of commendation had enabled them to gain entry at Corinth, where they had evidently made a good living out of their ministry, and a similar letter from Corinth would enable them to continue their lucrative practices elsewhere. Paul needed no such letters, for the simple reason that the quality of his work spoke for itself. The very salvation of the believers at Corinth, the planting of the assembly there, and the character of the ministry given, was in itself Paul's commendation. *They knew what manner of man Paul was:* others were acting questionably, and sought appropriate cover by commendatory letters.

This is not to say that letters of commendation were unnecessary in New Testament times, or unnecessary today. Paul is simply saying that *he did not need one!* The false teachers were without accreditation: Paul's very commendation was the existence of the assembly at Corinth, as we shall see.

In connection with letters of commendation, see Acts 18 verse 27, "And when he (Apollos) was disposed to pass into Achaia, the brethren (at Ephesus) wrote, exhorting the disciples to receive him"; Romans 16 verse

1, "I commend unto you Phebe our sister, which is a servant of the church which is at Cenchrea: that ye receive her in the Lord, as becometh saints"; Colossians 4 verse 10, "Marcus, sister's son to Barnabas (touching whom ye received commandments: if he come unto you receive him)".

b) The question answered, vv.2-3

"Ye are our epistle, written in our hearts, known and read of all men: forasmuch as ye are manifestly declared to be the epistle of Christ ministered by us, written not with ink, but with the Spirit of the living God; not in tables of stone, but in fleshy tables of the heart."

Paul had no need to commend himself because – "Ye are our epistle written in our hearts, known and read of all men". **Paul did have a letter** of commendation. It was not written with ink on paper however: it was a human letter! The Corinthians themselves were his letter of commendation. See Acts 18 verses 8, 11: "Many of the Corinthians hearing believed, and were baptized…And he continued there a year and six months, teaching the word of God among them"; 1 Corinthians 9 verses 1-2: "Am I not an apostle? am I not free? have I not seen Jesus Christ our Lord? are not ye my work in the Lord? If I be not an apostle unto others, yet doubtless I am to you: for the seal of mine apostleship are ye in the Lord". The letter was:

i) **"Written in our hearts".** This was **inward testimony.** In the place of love and affection. Compare 1 Corinthians 4 verse 15, "For though ye have ten thousand instructors in Christ, yet have ye not many fathers: for in Christ Jesus I have begotten you through the gospel". Hence he says, "I write not these things to shame you, but as my beloved sons (children) I warn you". The expression "written in our hearts" means that Paul loved them: he did not use them for financial gain as others: his love for them was not superficial. **Paul's love for them was his letter of commendation.** This recalls the stones on Aaron's breastplate: "And Aaron shall bear the judgment of the children of Israel upon his heart, when he goeth in unto the holy place" (Ex. 28: 29-30).

ii) **"Known and read of all men".** According to J.N.Darby (see his marginal note), "The word translated 'read' means also 'well known'; a thing read of all, not private". We may therefore say, 'well read of all men'. This was **outward testimony.** Compare 1 Corinthans 9 verse 2, "The seal of mine apostleship are ye in the Lord".

Having said this, Paul did not claim to be the author of his letter of commendation. He attributes their salvation to Christ. He was the Author. Paul was the scribe. So, "forasmuch as ye are manifestly declared to be *the epistle of Christ ministered by us*". That is, Paul and his companions served the interests of Christ, just as an amanuensis serves the interests of an author. We must notice the features of Paul's letter of commendation by asking and answering five questions:

- *Who was the author of the letter?* Answer – "Christ". They were "the epistle of Christ". They were saved by His grace, on the basis of His death and resurrection. We must notice the humility of the apostle here: "Do we begin again to commend *ourselves?*" No, they did not! The Corinthians owed everything to Christ.

- *Who wrote the letter?* Answer – "us". "Ministered by us". Do notice the expression "by us" in Chapter 1 verses 19 & 20, Chapter 2 verse 14, Chapter 3 verse 3 and Chapter 5 verse 20.

- *How was it written?* Answer – "*Not* with ink (by man who can only write with ink), *but* by the Spirit of the living God". That is, not human, but divine. Do notice the words "Spirit of the *living* God". (This must be borne in mind in interpreting the remainder of the chapter). It was written with divine power. See 1 Corinthians 6 verse 11, "But ye are washed, ye are sanctified, but ye are justified in the name of the Lord Jesus, and by the *Spirit of our God*".

- *Where was it written?* Answer – "*Not* in tables of stone" (that is, outwardly, demanding something of them), "*but* in fleshy tables of the heart" (that is, inwardly, imparting something to them). This refers to the New Covenant. See Jeremiah 31 verse 33, "I will put my law in their inward parts, and write it in their hearts". We will deal with this in more detail later. The word "heart" denotes the seat of the intellect (Gen. 6: 5), the seat of the emotions (Gen. 6: 6), and the seat of the will, volition (Gen. 8: 21). The words, "not in tables of stone, but in fleshy tables of the heart", would forcibly remind the assembly at Corinth that they had not been saved by law-works, but by divine power. The following verses will amplify and develop this.

We should notice that it was most appropriate that the law should have been written "in tables of stone". Nothing was so lifeless. The law made demands on men and women but did not impart the ability to fulfil its demands. It seems unlikely, as some suggest, that the words "not with ink" refer to the commendation of the Judaisers, and the words "not in tables of stone" to their ministry.

- **Who read it?** Answer – "Known and read of all men".

2) THE COMPETENCE OF HIS MINISTRY, vv.4-6a

"And such trust ('confidence', RV) have we through Christ to God-ward: not that we are sufficient (*hikanos*) of ourselves to think anything, as of ourselves; but our sufficiency (*hikanotes*) is of God: who also hath made us able (*hikanoo*) ministers (*diakonos*) of the new testament" or "And such confidence have we through the Christ towards God: not that we are competent of ourselves to think anything as of ourselves, but our competency is of God; who has also made us competent, as ministers of the new covenant" (JND). We should remember that the words "testament" and "covenant" translate the same word (*diatheke*).

Paul is confident that his work at Corinth was a standing testimony to his divinely-given commission. The words, **"through Christ to God-ward"**, emphasise that this was not self confidence, but confidence through Christ. That is, it was Christ's work, not Paul's. Compare Romans 12 verse 3 and 1 Corinthians 4 verse 7.

The words, **"to God-ward"**, emphasise that it was a confidence that would stand divine inspection. That is, a confidence undisturbed in the presence of God. The reason follows: "Not that we are sufficient of ourselves to think anything of ourselves". That is, 'we have no grounds for claiming personal credit', because "our sufficiency is of God, who also hath made us able ('sufficient', RV) ministers of the new testament". We should note the words "made us". The aorist tense here signifies a definite occasion when this took place. (See, for example, Acts 9: 3). Compare 1 Timothy 1 verse 12, "I thank him that enabled me, even Christ Jesus our Lord, for that he counted me faithful, appointing me to his service" (RV); 1 Corinthans 15 verse 10, "I laboured more abundantly than they all; yet not I, but the grace of God which was with me".

3) THE CHARACTER OF HIS MINISTRY, vv.V6b-18

"Our sufficiency is of God; who also hath made us able ('sufficient as', RV) ministers (*diakonos*) of the **new testament** ('covenant', RV/JND)." Reference has already been made to this in verse 3: "not in tables of stone, but in fleshy tables of the heart", referring to Jeremiah 31 verses 33-34.

It is important to notice that Paul does **not** say, 'God…who also hath made us able ministers of the **gospel**' but "able ministers of the **new testament**". This is to emphasise that the blessings currently enjoyed by believers are no less than those that will be enjoyed by Israel in the future. The reference to the Jewish teachers at Corinth is clear. Leaving aside for the moment their duplicity and covetousness, Paul is simply pointing out that they were outmoded and outdated. They were 'behind the times'. How could they possibly advocate compliance with the old covenant (the law) when believers were already enjoying the blessings of the new covenant? To put it in everyday language, Christians were 'streets ahead' of Judaism!' They enjoyed the greatest of all covenants! They did so through the Gospel which clearly enshrines the principles of the new covenant.

The Epistle to the Hebrews deals with the superiority of the new covenant at length. See the addendum. Here are its terms of the new covenant: "*I will* put my laws into their mind, and write them in their hearts: and *I will* be to them a God, and they shall be to me a people…*I will* be merciful to their unrighteousness, and their sins and their iniquities *will I* remember no more" (Heb. 8: 10-12). In other words, God himself alone will enact the covenant. It is a divine work. This should be compared with the terms of the Gospel: "For by grace are ye saved through faith; and that not of yourselves: it is the **gift of God**: not of works, lest any man should boast" (Eph. 2: 8-9). In other words, salvation is a divine work. Men and women, in both cases, are regenerated by God alone. The new covenant and the gospel are one in nature.

Paul now emphasises the superlative qualities of the new covenant. It is "not of the **letter,** but of the **spirit:** for the **letter** killeth, but the **spirit** giveth life". This summarises the essential difference between the two covenants. In the following verses, Paul contrasts the respective glories of the two covenants, and does so with reference to Exodus 34 verses 29-35, "Behold the skin of his face shone; and they were afraid to come nigh him (v.30)… Moses put a veil over his face" (v.35).

But before considering the contrasts, we should give attention to the expressions, "the letter" and "the spirit".

i) **Both expressions refer to the law.** See Romans 2 verses 28-29, "For he is not a Jew, which is one outwardly; neither is that circumcision, which is outward in the flesh: but he is a Jew, which is one inwardly; and the circumcision is of the heart, in the spirit, and not in the letter; whose praise is not of men, but of God". The Lord Jesus is "a life-giving spirit ('quickening spirit', AV)" (1 Cor. 15: 45, RV).

ii) **The "letter" refers to the law externally.** Hence, "written and engraven in stones" (v.7). That is, the written commandments of God. See verse 3, "written...in tables of stone". Stone is **lifeless material.** As such, the "letter killeth". It stated divine requirements without providing the power to meet them. It said, "Thou shalt...thou shalt not..." In itself, it was "holy, and just and good" (Rom 7: 12). It was "unto life" (Rom. 7: 10, RV). But it said, "The soul that sinneth, it shall die" (Ezek. 18: 4, 20). It imposed a curse on all who transgressed: "Cursed is every one that continueth not in all things which are written in the book of the law to do them" (Gal. 3: 10).

iii) **The "spirit" refers to the law internally.** Thus Paul affirms that the ministry committed to him concerns a fundamental change within men. Not now a case of God requiring men to meet His just demands, but God actually intervening, in regeneration, to give both the desire and ability to display the righteousness of the law. While it could be argued that the expression "of the spirit" does not refer directly to the Holy Spirit, but to the living reality of the things expressed in the "letter" (as in Romans 2: 28-29 above), the words "but the spirit giveth life" must refer to the Holy Spirit. J.N.Darby is clear about this: "For the letter kills, but the Spirit quickens". In this connection, it should be noted that Paul has already said that the believers at Corinth were "manifestly declared to be the epistle of Christ...written not with ink, but with **the Spirit of the living God**" (v.3). This is confirmed by the fact that the new covenant with Israel will be enacted in the power of the Holy Spirit: "A new heart also will I give you, and a new spirit will I put within you; and I will take away the stony heart out of your flesh, and I will give you an heart of flesh. And I will put **my Spirit within you,** and cause you to walk in my statutes" (Ezek. 36: 26-27).

To summarise. *(i) "The letter"* refers to the external command: it **commands** good things: it makes men hearers of the word; it depends on human nature. *(ii) "The spirit"* refers to internal nature: it **confers** good things; it makes men doers of the word; it is accomplished by the indwelling Holy Spirit.

The following verses (vv.7-16) are a parenthesis. This is clear by reading verses 5-6 in immediate conjunction with verses 17-18: "our sufficiency is of God: who also hath made us able ministers of the new testament; not of the letter, but of the spirit: for the letter killeth, but the spirit ('Spirit', JND) giveth life…Now the Lord is that Spirit: and where the Spirit of the Lord is, there is liberty. But we all, with open face beholding as in a glass the glory of the Lord, are changed into the same image from glory to glory, even as by the Spirit of the Lord".

ADDENDUM

The Old and New Covenants

The Epistle to the Hebrews presents the new covenant in a variety of ways, and these can be summarised in the following way:

1) Its titles

i) It is called "*new*" as opposed to "old". See Hebrews 8 verse 13, "In that he saith, A new covenant, he hath made the first old".

ii) It is called "*second*" as opposed to "first". See Hebrews 8 verse 7, "For if that first covenant had been faultless, then should have no place been sought for the second".

iii) It is called "*better*" as opposed to one with "fault". See Hebrews 8 verses 6-8, "He is the mediator of a better covenant…for if that first covenant had been faultless…for find fault with them…"

iv) It is called "*everlasting*" as opposed to temporary. See Hebrews 13 verses 20, "through the blood of the everlasting covenant"; Hebrews 8 verse 13, "that which decayeth and waxeth old is ready to vanish away".

2) Its benefits

i) **What is its essential difference?** Answer: under the new covenant God will do for men and women what they cannot do for themselves.

- The old covenant (see Hebrews 8: 13) rested on **men**: "Thou shalt…Thou shalt not". Hence, it was "weak through **the flesh**" (Rom. 8: 3); "For finding fault **with them**…" (Heb. 8: 8). Men were required to act.

67

- The new covenant rests on **God**: "*I* will make...*I* will put...*I* will be...will *I* write...will *I* remember no more". See Jeremiah 31 verses 33-34, cited in Hebrews 8 verses 10-12; Hebrews 10 verses 16-17. God acts.

ii) **But how can God do this in view of man's sinfulness?** Answer: He will remit sins and iniquities. "For I will be merciful (propitious) to their unrighteousness, and their sins and iniquities will I remember no more" (Heb. 8: 12).

iii) **But how can God do this righteously?** Answer: by the provision of a final sacrifice. Man's sin is put away in a Man. The **old covenant** required "sacrifices which they offered year by year continually" (Heb. 10: 1); "Every priest standeth daily ministering and offering oftentimes the same sacrifices which can never take away sins" (Heb. 10: 11). It is categorically stated that "it is not possible that the blood of bulls and of goats should take away sins" (Heb. 10: 4). The **new covenant** provides "one sacrifice for sins for ever" (Heb. 10: 12); "Christ was once offered" (Heb. 9: 28).

- Of the **old covenant**, it is said: "offer up **sacrifices**" (Heb. 7: 27); "offer **gifts** and **sacrifices**" (Heb.8: 3), and "offering **oftentimes**" (Heb. 10: 11).

- Of the **new covenant,** it is said "offered up **himself**" (Heb. 7: 27); "offered **one** sacrifice for sins for ever" (Heb. 10: 12); "For by **one** offering" (Heb. 10: 14). With this in view, the Saviour said, "A body hast thou prepared me" (Heb. 10: 5-9).

iv) **What will be the result of this?** The benefits of the new covenant cannot be doubted. The new covenant bestows what the old covenant could never impart.

- The **old covenant** gave no peace to conscience. "Gifts and sacrifices that could not make him that did the service ('the worshipper', RV) perfect, as pertaining to the conscience" (Heb. 9: 9); "For then would they (that is, 'those sacrifices which they offered year by year continually') not have ceased to be offered? Because that the worshippers once purged should have had no more conscience of sins" (Heb. 10: 1-2). There was no peace for the conscience under the old covenant because it gave no final settlement to the sin question: "But in those sacrifices there is a **remembrance again made** of sins every year" (Heb. 10: 3). In fact, "It is not possible that the blood of bulls and of goats should take away sins" (Heb. 10: 4).

- The **new covenant** gives peace to the conscience. "How much more shall the blood of Christ...purge your conscience from dead works..." (Heb.9: 14). Our "hearts are sprinkled from an evil conscience" (Heb. 10: 22). There is peace for the conscience under the new covenant because, on the grounds of the work of Christ, God can say, "Their sins and iniquities will *I remember no more*" (Heb. 8: 12; 10: 17). The sin question has been settled.

3) Its Mediator

The mediator of the Old Covenant was **Moses.** See Galatians 3 verse 19, "Wherefore then serveth the law? It was added because of transgressions, till the seed should come to whom the promise was made; and it was ordained by angels in the hand of a mediator".

The mediator of the New Covenant is **Christ.** See Hebrews 12 verse 24, "But ye are come to...Jesus the mediator of the new covenant, and to the blood of sprinkling that speaketh better things than that of Abel".

4) Its inauguration

The old covenant was inaugurated with "the blood of goats and calves" (Heb. 9: 13, 19).

The new covenant was inaugurated with the "blood of Christ" (Heb. 9: 14).

5) Its permanence

The **old covenant** required "sacrifices which they offered year by year continually" (Heb. 10: 1); "Every priest standeth daily ministering and offering oftentimes the same sacrifices which can never take away sins" (Heb. 10: 11). It is categorically stated, as already noted, that "it is not possible that the blood of bulls and of goats should take away sin" (Heb.10: 4).

The **new covenant** provides "one sacrifice for sins for ever" (Heb.10: 12); "Christ was once offered" (Heb.9: 28).

The blessings of the new covenant are brought before us in the Lord's supper. The Lord Jesus said, "This cup is the new testament in my blood, which is shed for you" (Luke 22: 20; 1 Cor .11: 25).

2 CORINTHIANS

"Changed into the same image from glory to glory"

Read Chapter 3:7-18

As we have noticed, this chapter may be divided as follows: *(1)* the commendation of his ministry (vv.1-3); *(2)* the competence of his ministry (vv.4-6); *(3)* the character of his ministry (vv.7-18).

1) THE COMMENDATION OF HIS MINISTRY, vv.1-3

The Corinthians themselves were Paul's letter of commendation: "Ye are our epistle written in our hearts, known and read of all men". But he gladly acknowledges that the Lord Jesus was the author of the letter. Paul and his colleagues were the scribes! Paul does two things here:

i) He refers to the servants: "Do we begin again to commend ourselves? Or need we, as some others, epistles of commendation…"

ii) He refers to the service: "Ye are our epistle… manifestly declared to be the epistle of Christ ministered by us, written not with ink, but with the Spirit of the living God; not in tables of stone, but in fleshy tables of the heart". Two things must be noted here: the *power* of his ministry ("not with ink, but with the *Spirit of the living God*") and the *effectiveness* of his ministry ("not in tables of stone, but in fleshy tables of the heart").

The words "Spirit of the living God" must be borne in mind when interpreting the remaining part of the chapter. The words "not in tables of stone, but in fleshy tables of the heart" clearly indicate the old and new covenants respectively. "Tables of stone" needs no further explanation. "Fleshy tables of the heart" refers to Ezekiel 36 verse 26, and to the future regeneration of Israel.

2) THE COMPETENCE OF HIS MINISTRY, vv.4-6

Not self-confidence! "Not that we are sufficient of ourselves to think any thing as of ourselves; but our sufficiency is of God; who also hath made us able ministers of the **new testament** (covenant)…"

Leaving aside now the actual competence given to Paul and his colleagues (we have already dealt with this), we must notice his description of the ministry itself. This brings us to:

3) THE CHARACTER OF HIS MINISTRY, vv.7-18

This is introduced with the words, "Our sufficiency is of God; who also hath made us able ministers of the **new testament** (covenant); not of **the letter,** but of **the spirit:** for the letter killeth, but the spirit giveth life" (v.6). The expression "new covenant" summarises the statement, "written not with ink, but with the Spirit of the living God; **not in tables of stone, but in fleshy tables of the heart**" (v.3). As we noted in our previous study:

- The words "**new covenant**" refer to Jeremiah 31 verses 31-33: "Behold, the days come, saith the LORD, that I will make a new covenant with the house of Israel, and the house of Judah; not according to the covenant that I made with their fathers…which covenant they break…but this shall be the covenant that I will make with the house of Israel…I will put my law in their inward parts, and write it in their hearts". We should notice the way in which this passage contrasts the old and new covenants.

- The words "**fleshy tables of the heart**" refer, as noted above, to Ezekiel 36 verses 26-27 which describes the same covenant: "A new heart also will I give you, and a new spirit will I put within you; and I will take away the stony heart out of your flesh, and I will give you an heart of flesh. And I will put **my Spirit** within you, and cause you to walk in my statutes".

The statement, "not of the **letter,** but of the **spirit:** for the **letter** killeth, but the **spirit** giveth life", summarises the essential difference between the two covenants. Both refer to the law, but with a vast difference:

- The expression "**the letter**" refers to the requirements the law **demanded,** and describes the law written **outwardly** on "tables of stone". "**The letter** *killeth*" because none can fulfil its demands. "All have sinned", and "the wages of sin is death".

- The expression "*the spirit*" refers to the requirements of the law *imparted,* and describes the law written *inwardly* on "the fleshy tables of the heart" of believers. Compare Romans 2 verses 28-29. "*The spirit giveth life*" because those in whose heart the law has been written are regenerate people. This involves a fundamental change in the very nature of men and women, and the words, "the spirit giveth life" ('the Spirit quickens', JND), tell us how this inward change is achieved. It is effected by the *Holy Spirit.* Hence "written not with ink, but with the *Spirit of the living God*" (v.3).

Divine life is communicated by the Holy Spirit, and it is to this that Paul refers in saying, "Therefore, seeing we have *this ministry*, as we have received mercy, we faint not" (4: 1). His ministry did not concern outward compliance (the old covenant) but inward transformation (the new covenant).

The following verses (vv7-16) are a parenthesis. This is clear by reading verses 5-6 in immediate conjunction with verses 17-18: "our sufficiency is of God: who also hath made us able ministers of the new testament; not of the letter, but of the spirit: for the letter killeth, but the spirit ('Spirit', JND) giveth life...Now the Lord is that Spirit: and where the Spirit of the Lord is, there is liberty. But we all, with open face beholding as in a glass the glory of the Lord, are changed into the same image from glory to glory, even as by the Spirit of the Lord". Although the various occurrences of the word "Spirit" here (together with v.8) present difficulties to the expositor, it seems clear that Paul is referring to the Holy Spirit in each case.

Having pointed out the essential difference between the two covenants, Paul now contrasts their respective glories. He does so with reference to Exodus 34 verses 29-35, "Behold the skin of his face shone; and they were afraid to come nigh him...and till Moses had done speaking with them, he put a vail on his face...and the children of Israel saw the face of Moses, that the skin of Moses' face shone: and Moses put the vail upon his face again, until he went in to speak with him". The argument is clear: since the new covenant is superior to the old, it must have a greater glory than the old.

The section may be divided as follows: *(A)* The glory seen in the face of Moses (vv.7-12). Having considered three ways in which the new covenant is invested with a greater glory, Paul observes, "Seeing then that we have such hope, we use great plainness ('boldness', RV) of speech". *(B)* The glory veiled on the face of Moses (vv.13-18). Having considered the transfer of that veil from the face of Moses to the hearts of Israel, Paul observes, "but *we* all with open ('unveiled', RV) face..."

A) THE GLORY SEEN IN THE FACE OF MOSES, vv.7-12

We should note its effect on Israel: "so that the children of Israel *could not stedfastly behold* (compare v.13: "could not stedfastly look") the face of Moses for the glory of his countenance; which glory was to be *done away*" (*katargeo,* rendered 'abolished' in v.13). This is a *literal* statement. If glory of this magnitude attended the law, how much more the magnitude of the glory associated with the new covenant?

The glory of the old covenant was seen in the face of Moses in connection with a covenant that had *(a)* no power to give life (vv.7-8), *(b)* no ability to acquit from guilt (v.9), and *(c)* no continuing existence (v.11).

Put positively, the new covenant is greater in glory than the old covenant: *(a)* because of the power it imparts (vv.7-8): it imparts life, not death; *(b)* because of the position it gives (v.9-10): it gives righteousness, not condemnation; *(c)* because of its permanence (v.11).

a) The old covenant had no power to give life, vv.7-8

"But if the ministration of *death,* written and engraven in stones, was glorious (RV 'came with glory: JND 'began with glory'), so that the children of Israel could not stedfastly behold the face of Moses for the glory of his countenance; which glory was to be done away: how shall not the ministration of the *spirit* be *rather glorious?*"

The law was "*the ministration* (*diakonia:* service or ministry) *of death*". None could meet its demands. The gospel is the "*ministration of the spirit*". Paul and his colleagues were "able ministers of the new covenant"! (v.6). All are empowered to fulfil its demands. We should note the following:

- *"The ministration of death".* This describes the law. It did not *cause* death. It *punished* by death. There was no justification by the law. It was "glorious": it 'came with (or 'in') glory' (RV). This must be so: it came from *God.* The effect on Israel as they saw its glory in the face of Moses is described as follows: they "could not stedfastly behold the face of Moses for the glory of his countenance". Exodus 34 verse 30 indicates that this was because of fear: "and they were afraid to come nigh him". The law kept men at a distance. The words, "which glory was to be done away", are elsewhere rendered, "which glory was passing away' (RV) or "which is annulled (*katargeo*)" (JND).

- ***"The ministration of the spirit".*** This describes the new covenant as conveyed by the Gospel. The expression "ministration of the spirit" ('ministry of the Spirit', JND) refers to the work of the Holy Spirit. The words "be rather glorious" are elsewhere rendered "be with glory" (RV). In verse 7, we have two time markers: a ***beginning*** ("came with glory") and an ***end*** ("to be done way" or "passing away", RV), but in verse 8 there is no reference to time: "***be with glory***" (RV).

If the covenant which commanded men to "do, and thou shalt live" was invested with glory: much more the covenant which said, "*I* will write...". As J.M.Davies observes, "This ministry of the 'letter' that killeth is illustrated in the 3,000 killed at Sinai (Exodus 32: 28), at the inauguration of the Old Covenant, while the ministry of the Spirit, the life-giving ministry, is illustrated in the 3,000 saved on the day of Pentecost (Acts 2: 41)".

b) The old covenant had no ability to acquit from guilt, vv.9-10

If there was glory attaching to a covenant that had no ability to acquit from guilt, how much more in connection with a covenant through which righteousness is imparted. "For if the ministration of **condemnation** be glory, much more doth the ministration of **righteousness** exceed in glory". "**Condemnation**" is the consequence of **breaking the law,** for under law, "every transgression and disobedience received a just recompence of reward" (Heb. 2: 2). "**Righteousness**" is imputed because the Lord Jesus has met the demands of the law. "By **him** all that believe are justified from all things, from which ye could not be justified by the law of Moses" (Acts 13: 39).

Paul draws a conclusion: "For even that which was made glorious had no glory (it had no intrinsic glory) in this respect, by reason of the glory that excelleth" or "For verily that which hath been made glorious hath not been made glorious in this respect, by reason of the glory that surpasseth" (RV). The greater glory of the "the ministration of the Spirit" (v.8) and "the ministration of righteousness" (v.9) must utterly surpass the glory associated with "the ministration of death" (v.7) and "the ministration of condemnation", to the extent that it "may be said to be no longer glorious" (P.E.Hughes). That is, as the glory of the sun transcends the glory of the moon, and as the day causes the brilliance of the lamp to pass away. (Car headlamps at night are no longer necessary in daytime - unless you drive a Volvo!).

c) The old covenant had no continuing existence, v.11

If there was glory attaching to an impermanent covenant, how much more to a permanent covenant: "For if that which is done away (RV, 'which passeth away') was glorious ('with glory', RV), much more that which remaineth *is* glorious" ('in glory', RV). That is, established in the sphere of glory. We should notice the contrasting expressions, '*with glory*' and '*in glory*'.

This completes a progression: *(i)* "with glory" (v.8, RV); *(ii)* "exceed in glory" (v.9); *(iii)* "the glory that surpasseth" (v.10, RV); *(iv)* "in glory" (v.11,RV).

In view of this, Paul spoke boldly: "Seeing then that we have *such hope,* we use great plainness ('boldness', RV) of speech" (v.12). The "hope" to which he refers here is the permanence and superlative glory of the new covenant. He preached a message which brought permanent blessing - eternal blessing - quite unlike the law.

There can be no doubt that he stresses this in view of the Jewish teachers who had invaded Corinth. "Are they Hebrews? So am I. Are they the seed of Abraham? So am I" (11: 22).   This introduces the second section of the passage, viz:

B) THE GLORY VEILED ON THE FACE OF MOSES, vv.13-18

In v erse 12, Paul has stated that he used *no* concealment or reserve in relation to men: "we use great plainness (boldness) of speech", in view of "that which remaineth" (v.11). But there *was* concealment and reserve so far as Moses was concerned: thus, "and not as Moses, which put a vail over his face, that the children of Israel could not steadfastly look to the end of that which is abolished" (v.13). Moses did not "speak boldly".

As a result, "the children of Israel could not stedfastly look (see also verse 7) to the end of that which is abolished". This refers to Exodus 34 verse 33,

"And *till* Moses had done speaking with them, he put a vail on his face". The RV renders this as follows: "*When* Moses had done speaking with them, he put a veil over his face". That is, *not* during, but *after* his speech. Hence Exodus 34 verse 35, "And the children of Israel saw the face of Moses, that the skin of Moses' face shone: and Moses put the vail upon his face again, until he went in to speak with him". This was evidently the customary practice of Moses: "Moses *used to place* a vail (AV 'put a vail') over his face" (Exodus 34: 33). The verb is in the imperfect tense.

This section can be divided into two paragraphs: *(a)* t*he diminishing glory* in the face of Moses (vv.13-16), and *(b) the developing glory* in the lives of believers (vv.17-18).

a) The diminishing glory in the face of Moses, vv.13-16

We can call this, *(i)* the veil and Israel in the past (v.13); *(ii)* the veil and Israel in the present (vv.14-15); *(iii)* the veil and Israel in the future (v.16).

i)   *In the past: the veil in place on Moses' face, v.13.* Two questions arise. *Firstly:* Why, when he was speaking to the people, did Moses *not* veil his face? Answer: this indicated his authority. The people feared. The very face of Moses radiated the glory and the authority of God Himself. *Secondly:* Why, when he had spoken unto them, did Moses *then* veil his face? The answer, in the context of Exodus 34, must be that had he not done so, Israel would have been kept at a distance from him because they were incapable of beholding such glory. It reminds us that the law kept men at a distance. Alternatively, it could mean that Israel was not worthy to behold it. In which case the veiling of his face condemned the people.

But Paul looks at it *another way:* he says that the veil prevented Israel from seeing how soon the brightness faded from Moses' face. So, "And not as Moses, which put a vail over his face that the children of Israel could not stedfastly look to *the end* of that which is abolished". The word "abolish" means, literally, reduced to inactivity (W.E.Vine). It is rendered "was passing away" by the RV. This statement must be taken *literally throughout.* It would be inconsistent to make the first part literal, and the second part figurative or allegorical. We must therefore understand the words, "that which is abolished", to refer to *the visible brightness on the face of Moses,* and "the end" to refer to *the termination of that brightness.* (Note: v.13 does not specifically state that the veil hid the fading or diminishing glory in the face of Moses). The expression, "to the end of that which is abolished", means to "look right on to the end of that which was transient".

So by putting on the veil, which was *not* a deliberate attempt to mislead Israel, Moses *also* hid the fading glory in his face. That veil hid the transience of the glory of the law from them. Paul now uses this as a picture of their spiritual position. They *still* could not see the diminishing glory of the law. Hence verses 14-15:

ii) *In the present: the veil in place on Israel's mind, vv.14-15.* "But their minds were blinded: for until this day remaineth the same veil untaken away in the reading of the old testament; which vail is done away in Christ. But even unto this day, when Moses is read, the vail is upon their heart". Note the words, "minds" and "heart". Compare Jeremiah 31 verse 33, "I will put my law in their inward parts, and write it in their hearts"; Hebrews 8 verse 10, "I will put my laws into their minds, and write them in their hearts".

So, "their minds were blinded". That is, they were blinded to the message of the veil: that men are unworthy to behold the glory of God, and that the law was not able to make them worthy. The law itself taught this. The veil still exists, not now on the face of Moses, but on the heart of the nation. See Romans 10 verses 2-4, "For I bear them record that they have a zeal of God, but not according to knowledge. For they being ignorant of God's righteousness, and going about to establish their own righteousness, have not submitted themselves unto the righteousness of God. For Christ is the end of the law for righteousness to every one that believeth". The nation still fails to see that the law taught that men are unworthy to behold the glory of God. The nation glories in the law, but fails to realise its significance as exhibited on the face of Moses.

In the case of the face of Moses, they failed to understand what they *saw.* In the case of the writings of Moses, they fail to understand what they *read.* That is, that *approach to God cannot be on the basis of law.* On what basis can there be approach to God? The answer lies in verse 14: "Which (veil) is done away in Christ". That is, the veil remains until they join Paul in saying, "I count all things but loss for the excellency of the knowledge of Christ Jesus my Lord…and be found in him not having mine own righteousness, which is of the law, but that which is through the faith of Christ" (Phil. 3: 8-9). See also Romans 10 verse 4, "For Christ is the end of the law for righteousness to every one that believeth". At present their eyes and heart are veiled to the transience of the law. Our eyes and hearts have been opened to see the permanence of the new covenant, and this has **transformed** us.

(iii) In the future: the veil removed from Israel's heart, v.16. "Nevertheless, when it (i.e. the heart, or, perhaps, the nation) shall turn (the word "converted", as in Acts 3: 19) to the Lord (like Paul himself in Acts 9), the vail shall be taken away." (There is no reference here to Isaiah 25: 7-8. See addendum). This evidently refers to Exodus 34 verse 34, "But when Moses went in before the LORD to speak with him, he took the vail off, until he came out". Israel must turn to the same Lord to whom Moses turned in the tabernacle. That is, to Christ. Moses of course met Him again - on the mount of transfiguration. "On that mountain, Moses and Elijah appeared with Christ, but it was **Christ alone** who was transfigured with heavenly radiance before the eyes of Peter, James and John. It was **His** face that shone as the sun, and **His** garments that became white and dazzling. It was of **Him alone** that the voice from the cloud said, 'This is my beloved Son, in whom I am well pleased; hear ye him'. And thereafter the disciples saw no one, **save Jesus only.** It is He who abides" (P.E.Hughes).

b) The developing glory in the lives of believers, vv.17-18.

Whilst verses 7-16 are a parenthesis, and the main development can be discerned by reading verses 5-6 in conjunction with verses 17-18, there is certainly a connection between the parenthesis and verses 17-18. In the words of John Heading, "Yet how can such a transformation of opinion, outlook and faith take place (as in v.16) in a soul?...The only method of changing from one to the other is **by the Spirit of God**". There are two important things to notice here: *(i)* liberty (v.17) and *(ii)* transformation (v.18): RV

i)   Liberty, v.17 "Now the Lord is that Spirit: and where the Spirit of the Lord is, there is liberty." The words, "Now the Lord is **that Spirit**", mean 'the Spirit that quickens' (v.6, JND), that is, the Spirit whose ministry it is to implement the new covenant through the Gospel ('the ministry of the Spirit', v.8, JND). Altering the emphasis, the words, "Now **the Lord** is that Spirit" stress the deity of the Holy Spirit. "Now the 'Lord' here means the Spirit" (F.F.Bruce). The very Lord whose glory shone in the face of Moses, transforms us by His Holy Spirit. But Paul has something specifically in mind here, and so he adds, "and where the Spirit of the Lord is, there is liberty". We might ask, 'Liberty to **do** what?', to which the answer might be 'liberty to behold the glory of the Lord' or 'liberty to approach God'. But perhaps the question ought to be rephrased, 'Liberty *from* what?', in which case the answer must be 'from the letter which killeth' and the "ministration of death" (vv.6-7).

ii) *Transformation, v.18.* "But we all, with open face beholding as in a glass the glory of the Lord, are changed into the same image from glory to glory, even as by the Spirit of the Lord." When Moses returned from the summit of Mount Sinai, "he knew not that the skin of his face shone through his talking with him" (Ex. 34: 29, JND). As we have seen, Moses had to wear a veil when he spoke to the people, but whenever he entered the presence of God "he took the vail off, until he came out" (Ex. 34: 34). Paul now tells us that what was true of Moses is true of us! When Moses saw the Lord (Ex. 33: 11; Num. 12: 8) his face was transformed. The glory of the Lord shone in his face. In the Old Testament, this was confined to one man, but not now: "we *all*, with open face ('unveiled face': just like Moses) beholding as in a glass the glory of the Lord, are changed into the same image from glory to glory…"

We 'behold' the "glory of the Lord" in the word of God. We do not see Him at present *directly* (we *will* see Him face to face in heaven), but *indirectly*. It is in the Scriptures that we have "the light of the knowledge of the glory of God in the face of Jesus Christ" (2 Cor. 4: 6). This is indicated by the words, "But we all with open face, beholding as in *a glass* the glory of the Lord". (J.N.Darby has, simply, 'looking on the glory of the Lord'). The RV rendering, "reflecting as in a mirror", does not quite accord with the overall statement. We are transformed into the image of the Lord by *beholding* the glory of the Lord, not by reflecting it.

"But we all, with open face beholding as in a glass the glory of the Lord, are *changed into the same image*…" The word "changed" translates the Greek *metamorphoo*. It is used of the Lord's transfiguration (Mark 9: 2; Matt. 17: 2) and means to change into another form. It signifies the transfiguration of the actual person, as opposed to mere outward appearance. Thus, by beholding (a continuing process) the Lord Jesus in the word of God, we become progressively like Him in all His moral glory and beauty. (Compare Romans 12: 2, "be ye *transformed* by the renewing of your mind"). The progression in this wonderful process is indicated by the words, "changed into the same image *from glory to glory*", that is, from one degree of glory to another degree of glory.

This is accomplished by the Holy Spirit: we "are changed into the same image from glory to glory, *even as by the Spirit of the Lord*" or "even as by [the] Lord [the] Spirit" (JND). The RV margin has "the Spirit which is the Lord". Once again (see v.17), this emphasises the deity of the Holy Spirit. He is 'the Lord the Spirit'. We have a clear example of a man being "changed into the same image from glory to glory" in Stephen who, "being full of the *Holy Ghost*, looked up stedfastly into heaven, and *saw* the glory of God, and Jesus standing on the right hand of God, and said, Behold, I *see*…the Son of man standing on the right hand of God". With the result that he became *like the Lord Jesus* in saying, "Lord, lay not this sin to their charge" (Acts 7: 55-56, 60). Compare Luke 23 verse 34.

In the next chapter, Paul applies his teaching here to his evangelism: "Therefore seeing we have this ministry (the ministry described in vv.7-9) as we have received mercy, we *faint not* ('lack courage…lose heart…be fainthearted')".

Addendum

"And he will destroy ('swallow up') in this mountain the face of the covering cast over all people, and the vail that is spread over all nations. He will swallow up death in victory; and the Lord GOD will wipe away tears from off all faces; and the rebuke of his people shall he take away from off all the earth: for the LORD hath spoken it" (Isaiah 25: 7-8). Whilst there might, at first glance, appear to be a reference in the current passage to Isaiah 25, the evident meaning of verses 7-8 is that the universal joy of verse 6 will not be invaded by sorrow. To cover the face was a sign of mourning for the dead. An example occurs in 2 Samuel 19 verse 4, "But the king (David) covered his face, and the king cried with a loud voice, O my son Absalom, O Absalom, my son, my son!" As E.H.Plumptre observes, "to cover the face was, in the East, a sign of mourning for the dead…and to destroy that covering is to overcome death, of which it is thus the symbol". In the millennial age, there will be no cause for sorrow, for its chief cause will be annulled: "He will swallow up death in victory" (v.8).

2 CORINTHIANS

"We preach not ourselves, but Christ Jesus the Lord"

Read Chapter 4:1-6

As we have noted in previous studies, Paul refers particularly in this Epistle to his adversity. He emphasises this more than anywhere else in his New Testament correspondence. It can be summed up in the words, "we were troubled on every side; without were fightings, within were fears" (7: 5).

i) *"Without were fightings"*

This becomes evident on the very threshold of the Epistle. See Chapter 1 verses 8-9, "For we would not, brethren, have you ignorant of our trouble which came to us in Asia, that we were pressed out of measure, above strength, insomuch that we despaired even of life: but we had the sentence of death in ourselves, that we should not trust in ourselves, but in God which raiseth the dead". Paul refers again to external pressure in Chapter 4 verses 8-18, where he calls it "light affliction", in Chapter 6 verses 4-10, and in Chapter 11 verses 24-33.

ii) *"Within were fears"*

This describes Paul's deep concern for the assembly at Corinth. See, for example, Chapter 2 verse 4: "For out of much affliction and anguish of heart I wrote unto you with many tears…that ye might know the love which I have more abundantly unto you"; Chapter 2 verses 12-13, "Furthermore, when I came to Troas to preach Christ's gospel…I had no rest in my spirit, because I found not Titus my brother: but taking my leave of them, I went from thence into Macedonia". See also Chapter 7 verses 1-16, Chapter 11 verses 1-23. At the beginning of the Epistle, Paul discloses his heart to the assembly, particularly to rebut those who accused him of fickleness in regard to his promised visit. He explains that his love for them had made him change his plans, otherwise his arrival would have been sorrowful for them (1: 23) and sorrowful for him (2: 1).

But in it all, whether outward "fightings" or inward "fears", Paul describes himself as being led "in triumph in Christ" (2: 14, RV): It is generally thought that Paul alludes here to the Roman 'triumph'. A victorious general would be accorded a 'triumph', that is, a triumphal entrance to the capital city. He would generally ride in a magnificent chariot drawn by two white horses, although there were variations. The general's sons and senior officers rode behind his chariot, and the procession would include captives and the acquired spoils of war.

But where were Paul and his colleagues in the procession? The answer is 'amongst the captives!' See 1 Corinthians 4 verses 9 & 13: "I think that God hath set forth us the apostles last, as it were appointed to death: for we are made a spectacle unto the world, and to angels, and to men…we are made as the filth of the world, and are the offscouring of all things unto this day". That's how the world saw them, but from the perspective of heaven they were the result of **Christ's victory**. Once the enemies of God (Rom.5: 10), *they had been overcome and taken captive by Him and were led by Him as trophies of divine grace.*

Having then emphasised his love for the assembly at Corinth, and the purity of **motive** which underlay his attitude towards them, Paul continues by emphasising the purity of motive underlying his preaching: "For we are not as many which corrupt ('make a trade of') the word of God, but as of sincerity, but as of God, in the sight of God speak we in Christ" (2: 17).

He then describes his ministry with its superiority over the law (3: 1-18) and proceeds in Chapter 4 verse 1 to Chapter 5 verse 21) to describe the impact of that ministry upon him: "Therefore seeing we have this ministry, as we have received mercy, we faint not" (4: 1).

This brings us to Chapter 4, and the passage may be divided as follows: *(1)* persevering in service (v.1); *(2)* purity of motive (v.2); *(3)* preaching the gospel (vv.3-6); *(4)* power from God (v.7); *(5)* persecution from men (vv.8-12); *(6)* prospect for the future (vv.13-18). It has been said that in verses 1-6, we have renunciation, manifestation and illumination.

1) PERSEVERING IN SERVICE, v.1

"Therefore seeing we have this ministry, ('even', RV) as we have received mercy, we faint not." Three expressions call for comment:

a) "We have this ministry"

The "ministry" (*diakonia,* meaning 'service') to which Paul refers is described in the previous chapter. Hence the connecting word "Therefore" (v.1). It is described as:

i) "The ministration (*diakonia*) of the spirit" as opposed to "the ministration of death" (Ch 3 vv.7, 8). Very clearly, the expression "ministration of death" refers to the law. It is appropriately called "the ministration of death" in view of its penalty for non-compliance: "Cursed is every one that continueth not in all things which are written in the book of the law to do them" (Gal. 3: 10). The "curse" is death: eternal death. To this end it is deeply significant that the law was "written and engraven in stones". Nothing is so devoid of life as stone, and any attempt to "bend" stone will cause breakage!

But Paul was not engaged in "the ministration of death", but in "the ministration of the Spirit", reminding us that we "have begun in the Spirit" and that "we live in the Spirit" (Gal. 3: 3; 5: 25). It is a ministry of *life*, as opposed to a ministry of *death*. In fact "the law of the Spirit of life in Christ Jesus" has made us "free from the law of sin and death" (Rom. 8: 2).

ii) "The ministration of righteousness" as opposed to "the ministration of condemnation" (v.9). The "ministration of righteousness" is, of course, the doctrine of justification by faith. "But to him that worketh not, but believeth on him that justifieth the ungodly, his faith is counted for righteousness... Therefore being justified by faith, we have peace with God through our Lord Jesus Christ" (Rom. 4: 5; 5: 1).

Of this, Paul describes himself and his fellow-workers as "able ministers". "Our sufficiency is of God; who also hath made us sufficient as ministers (*diakonous*) of the new covenant" (3: 5-6, RV). The saints at Corinth are described as "the epistle of Christ ministered *(diakontheisa)* by us" (3: 3).

b) "As we have received mercy"

Compare 1 Timothy 1 verses 12-13, "I thank Christ Jesus our Lord, who hath enabled me: for that he counted me faithful, putting me into the ministry, who was before a blasphemer, and a persecutor, and injurious. But I obtained **mercy**, because I did it ignorantly in unbelief." Now, he was a "vessel unto honour". The word "mercy" indicates the succour available to those in need, and could well refer to the phrase following, "we faint not". That is, divine succour enabled him to continue.

There is, surely, a sense of wonder in Paul's heart here: to think that such a message could be committed to mortal men, especially to such a man as Paul, the onetime arch-persecutor of the church! See Galatians 1 verse 13.

c)   "We faint not"

"Faint not" (*enkakeo*) means 'to lack courage, lose heart, be faint-hearted' (W.E.Vine). It occurs again in verse 16, "For which cause we **faint not**". Compare Ephesans 3 verse 13, "Wherefore I desire that ye **faint not** at my tribulations for you, which is your glory"; Luke 18 verse 1, "Men ought always to pray, and not to **faint**"; 2 Thessalonians 3 verse 13, "But ye brethren, be not weary **(faint not)** in well doing…"

The superlative character of the ministry, together with inestimable privilege of engaging in that ministry, enabled Paul and his colleagues to persevere. It is said, "If thou faint in the day of adversity, thy strength is small" (Prov. 24: 10).

2) PURITY OF MOTIVE, v2

"But have renounced the hidden things of dishonesty, not walking in craftiness, nor handling the word of God deceitfully; but by manifestation of the truth commending ourselves to every man's conscience in the sight of God."

This verse can be divided with reference to the furtive, shadowy activities of the false teachers, with their hidden agenda, and the open declaration of truth by Paul and his colleagues:

a) The covert methods of the false teachers

i)   "But have renounced the hidden things of dishonesty". The word "dishonesty" means 'shame' (see margin). The word "renounced" is used in the sense of 'disowned'. This implies that there were those who had not done so.

What were 'the **hidden** things of shame?' 1 Corinthians 4 verse 5 refers to the coming of the Lord "who both will bring to light the **hidden** things of darkness, and make manifest the counsels of the hearts". The reference here (v.2) could therefore be to the hidden or concealed shameful motives of others as, for example, in Chapter 2 verse 17: "many which corrupt ('make a trade of') the word of God". The word "corrupt" (*kapeleuo*) means to retail or to peddle. According to W.E.Vine, it comes, as already noted, "from *kapelos*, an inn-keeper, a petty retailer, especially of wine, a huckster, a pedlar…hence to get base gain by dealing in anything, and so, more generally to do anything for sordid personal advantage". So, here, to adulterate the word of God by an admixture of foreign elements (adding water to wine) such as Judaism or paganism.

This, evidently, was their hidden and shameful motive. They would be ashamed to avow openly what their ends really were. Their machinations and manoeuvres were secret, as opposed to the openness, honesty and frankness of Paul in Chapter 3 verse 12 ("seeing then that we have such hope, we use great plainness of speech"). Paul renounced and disowned such motives.

ii) *"Not walking in craftiness"*. Compare Luke 20 verse 23, "He perceived their craftiness", that is, in endeavouring to trap Him with the device, "is it lawful for us to give tribute unto Caesar, or no?" Compare 2 Corinthians 11 verse 3, "as the serpent beguiled Eve in his craftiness (AV, subtilty)" (RV). See also Chapter 12 verse 16. The word "craftiness" means, literally, 'all working' or 'doing everything'. That is, ready to adopt any device or trickery. Cunning or sly. The word means someone who can do everything and is willing to do anything to accomplish his ends.

iii) *"Not handling the word of God deceitfully"*. The word "deceitfully" comesfrom from *dolos* meaning a 'bait or snare'.

But how can the scriptures ever become a bait or lure? Certainly not in themselves! Compare 1 Peter 2 verse 2, "desire the sincere *(adolos)* milk of the word", meaning 'guileless'. The Lord Jesus is "without guile". There was "no guile *(dolos)* found in his mouth" (1 Pet. 2: 22).

The scriptures cannot be a bait or lure in themselves, but they can be falsified. So, "not falsifying the word of God" (JND). How were the scriptures falsified in the context of this epistle? P.E.Hughes is helpful here: "But it seems preferable to understand 'the word of God' here to mean the message of Jesus Christ, in which case the deceitful handling of it would refer to the falsification of the gospel, probably by robbing it of its unique glory and essential content in a way as to suggest that the old covenant was still in force". This explanation is certainly supported by Chapter 3 verses 1-18. Paul calls the people responsible "false apostles, *deceitful (dolios)* workers, transforming themselves into the apostles of Christ" (2 Cor.11:13). 2 Corinthians 11 verse 3 sums up the purpose of such activity: "so your minds should be corrupted (be in an inferior or worse condition) from the simplicity that is in Christ".

We must remember, however, that "handling the word of God deceitfully" is not limited to New Testament times. It has been said that 'a text taken out of its context becomes a pretext', to which we add, 'for every idea imaginable'.

b) The clarity of Paul's ministry

The balance of the verse presents a vivid contrast with the above: "but by manifestation of the truth commending ourselves to every man's conscience in the sight of God". We should notice the following:

i) *"By manifestation of the truth".* If shameful motives require concealment, then truth can be displayed for all to see. Paul did not trade in the "hidden things of dishonesty (shame)", but in "the truth." He did not handle "the word of God deceitfully", but 'manifested' the truth.

False teachers always act furtively: see, for example Galatians 2 verse 4, "false brethren unawares brought in, who came in privily to spy out our liberty which we have in Christ Jesus"; 2 Peter 2 verse 1, "false teachers among you, who privily shall bring in damnable heresies"; Jude 4, "there are certain men crept in unawares". The contrast with "the manifestation of the truth" could not be greater. The Lord Jesus said, "I spake openly to the world; I ever taught in the synagogue, and in the temple, whither the Jews always resort; and in secret have I said nothing" (John 18: 20). Paul said, "the things that thou hast heard of me among many witnesses, the same commit thou to faithful men" (2 Tim. 2: 2).

ii) *"To every man's conscience".* Paul made no attempt to deceive the *mind:* he appealed to the *conscience* of his hearers and readers. A specious argument can deceive the mind: but there was a self-evidencing power about Paul's preaching.

The words, "commending ourselves" recall Chapter 3 verse 1, "Do we begin again to commend ourselves". Literally, "are we beginning again to commend ourselves" (RV), that is, in view of Chapter 2 verses 14-17. There was no need for Paul and his fellow-labourers to do this before the assembly at Corinth: its very existence was their commendation.

The commendation here (4: 2) is to the consciences of the hearers of his preaching. It had the 'ring of truth' about it, even though many would reject it. As the Jewish leadership listened to Stephen, "they were cut to the heart" (Acts 7: 54). An activated conscience can lead to repentance, but it can also lead to rage.

We should carefully note that Paul and his colleagues did not commend themselves by talking about themselves, but by manifesting of the truth. Compare 3 John verse 12, "Demetrius hath a good report of all men, and of the truth itself". The truth commended him. People who commended themselves attracted apostolic censure: "we dare not make ourselves of the number, or compare ourselves with some that commend themselves" (2 Cor. 10: 12).

iii) ***"In the sight of God".*** Unlike the false teachers, Paul and his colleagues acted in the consciousness that "Thou God seest me" (Gen. 16: 13). Compare 1 Thessalonians 2 verse 5, "For neither at any time used we flattering words, as ye know, nor a cloak of covetousness, God is witness"; 1 Thessalonians 2 verse 10, "Ye are witnesses, and God also, how holily, and justly, and unblameably we behaved ourselves among you that believe". Everything is open before God: "all things are naked and opened unto the eyes of him with whom we have to do" (Heb. 4: 13). It is impossible to disguise motives. God saw all that the false teachers did, and the underlying motives for their actions.

So, in summary (vv.1-2): The ministry of the new covenant ***(i)*** sustained him because of its superlative character and ***(ii)*** was accompanied by transparency of character. There was faithfulness in both ***motive*** and ***ministry.***

3) PREACHING THE GOSPEL, vv.3-6

"But if our gospel be hid, it is hid to them that are lost" (v.3) or "But and if our gospel is ***veiled***, it is ***veiled*** in them that are perishing" (RV).

We have noticed that Paul's business in life was to '*manifest* the truth'. He now discusses the barrier to its reception. The barrier lay, not in his preaching, but in the hearts of men. No charge could be laid against Paul if the gospel was non-effective. If the truth of the gospel was 'veiled in them that are perishing' (v.3) the responsibility for this could *not* be laid at the apostle's door. *He* had 'manifested the truth' (v.2).

But are *we* clear in the matter? Have we discharged, or are we discharging, our responsibility in preaching the Gospel? "How then shall they call on him in whom they have not believed? And how shall they believe in him of whom they have not heard? And how shall they hear without a preacher?" (Rom. 10: 14). We must notice the following expressions here:

i) *"Our gospel."* Compare 2 Thessalonians 2 verse 14 where, speaking of salvation, Paul says, "wherewith he called you by *our gospel*"; Romans 2: 16, "the day when God shall judge the secrets of men by Jesus Christ according to *my gospel*"; 2 Timothy 2 verse 8, "Remember that Jesus Christ of the seed of David, was raised from the dead, according to *my gospel*".

In what sense are the expressions "our gospel" and "my gospel" used? Certainly not in the sense of origin. See Galatians 1 verses 11-12, "But I certify you, brethren, that the gospel which was preached of me is not after man. For I neither received it of man, neither was I taught it, but by the revelation of Jesus Christ"; 1 Corinthians 15 verses 1-3: "For I delivered unto you first of all that which I also received..." Although it is the 'gospel of the glory of Christ' (v.4, RV), Paul describes it as "our gospel" and "my gospel" in the sense of its commitment to him. That is, it was the gospel which he preached: "for we preach not ourselves, but Christ Jesus the Lord ('as Lord', RV)". Compare 1 Thessalonians 2 verse 4, "But as we were allowed of God to be put in trust with the gospel, even so we speak..."

All else was spurious. See Galatians 1 verses 6-9: "I marvel that ye are so soon removed from him that called you into the grace of Christ unto another gospel..." Compare 2 Corinthians 11 verse 4.

ii) "But if our gospel be hid, it is hid to them that are lost" or 'If our gospel is *veiled*, it is *veiled* in them that are perishing' (RV). The connection with Chapter 3 is evident: there Paul uses the noun (*kalumma*, a covering); here he uses the corresponding verb (*kalupto,* to conceal or cover).

In Chapter 3, Paul refers to the veil on the face of Moses. A people under law were not fit to behold the glory of God. P.E.Hughes puts it succinctly: "Moses used to veil his face when he had done speaking with them, not so much for the convenience of the people as to show them, by a kind of enacted parable, that it was their iniquities which rendered them unable, and unworthy, to behold such a glory". The veil still exists, but on the heart of the nation. Israel still cannot see that a people under law are unfit to behold the glory of God. "But their minds were blinded…the veil is upon their heart".

Paul preached a message that could take away the veil, but if that message was non-effective it was not because the gospel was faulty but because men failed to discern its glory: "it is veiled *in* them that are perishing". The failure to appreciate the truth of the gospel lies *within* men. In the words of Calvin, "The blindness of unbelievers in no way detracts from the clearness of his gospel, for the sun is no less resplendent because the blind do not perceive its light".

This is now developed and we must notice *(a)* the work of Satan (v.4); *(b)* the work of the preacher (v.5); *(c)* the work of God (v.6).

a) The work of Satan, v.4

"In whom the god of this world hath blinded the minds of them which believe not lest the light of the glorious gospel of Christ, who is the image of God, should shine unto them…" See, again, Chapter 3 verse 14: "but their minds were blinded".

So the inability of men to appreciate the gospel derives from the activity of Satan. We must notice:

i) He is called "the god of *this* world", literally, 'the god of this age'. There is an age to come: see Ephesians 1 verse 21, "Far above all principality and power…named, not only in *this* world ('age') but also in that which *is to come*". See also Hebrews 6 verse 5, "And have tasted the good word of God, and the powers of the world ('age') *to come*…" (See also Luke 20: 35; 18: 30.) See further, for example, Galatians 1 verse 4 ("present evil world") and 2 Timothy 4 verse 10 ("present world") etc. Thus Satan has only temporary power: he is 'the god of *this* age', *not* 'the god of the age to come'.

ii) He is the *god* of this world." In what sense is he "god?" See 1

Corinthans 8 verses 4-6, "There is none other God but one...there is but one God...." Even though "there be that are called gods..." only God Himself is the true God: He alone is the "King eternal", literally, 'of the ages' (1 Tim. 1: 17).

Satan is but a creature: his demon hosts are called 'no-gods'. See 1 Corinthians 10 verse 20; Galatians 4 verse 8 (which refers to Deuteronomy 32: 17). He is called 'the god of this age' because:

- That is what he seeks to be. He will be worshipped as such. See Revelation 13 verse 4.

- That is what men make him by subjecting themselves to his power. Chrysostom puts it like this: "Scripture frequently uses the term 'god', not in regard to the dignity that is so designated, but of the weakness of those in subjection to it".

iii) He has "blinded the eyes of them which believe not". When does he do this? If the answer is 'on rejecting the gospel', then what of man's natural fallen state of blindness? The answer must be that those who believe not (RV 'the unbelieving') are **already blind**. How does this arise? Not initially from God, but as the result of Satan's activity in Eden. See Ephesians 4 verse 18, "Having the understanding darkened, being alienated from the life of God through the ignorance that is in them, because of the blindness of their heart". Compare Romans 11 verses 7-10: "God hath given them the spirit of slumber, eyes that they should not see..." Though Satan is the initiator of spiritual blindness, it is none the less judicial. With this result:

iv) "Lest the light (*photismos,* an illumination: see also v.6) of the glorious gospel of Christ, who is the image of God, should shine (*augazo,* to dawn) unto them" or "That the light of the gospel of the glory of Christ, who is the image of God, should not dawn upon them" (RV). (Note: the words "shine" and "shined" in v.6 translate *lampo*, 'to shine as a torch'). In Chapter 3, Israel could not see the glory in Moses' face: in Chapter 4 men generally cannot see the gospel of the glory of Christ.

So we learn from verse 4 that although through "the god of this world", men's minds are blinded, through Christ, "who is the image of God", illumination is available. The first is opposed to the second: how the second is effective will be seen in verse 6. Satan blinds men: the gospel enlightens men.

v)   The Gospel is described as "the gospel of the glory of Christ" (RV) It is "the gospel of the glory of Christ" because He is glorified in every way. For example:

- In pre-incarnation. "The glory which I had with thee before the world was" (John 17: 5).

- In incarnation. "We beheld his glory" (John 1: 14).

- In death. "Now is the Son of man glorified" (John 13: 31-32).

- In resurrection and ascension. "Received up in glory" (1 Tim.3: 16, JND); He has 'entered into his glory' (Luke 24: 26).

vi)   "Who is the image (the same word is used in 3: 18) of God." In 1 Corinthians 11 verse 7, the man is said to be "the *image* and glory of God"; in Revelaton 13 verse 15 the phrase occurs, "the *image* of the beast"; and in Matthew 22 verse 20, the coin showed "the *image* and superscription of Caesar". In each case the image is different from the original that it represents.

But the Lord Jesus exactly represents and manifests all that God is. The man is not God, only His image; the image is not the beast, only his image; the coin does not convey Caesar personally, only his image. *But Christ is God.* "He that hath seen me, hath seen the Father" (John 14: 9). See also Colossians 1 verse 15, "Who is the image of the invisible God"; John 1 verse 18; "No man hath seen God at any time; the only begotten Son, which is in the bosom of the Father, he hath declared him".

b) The work of the preacher, v.5

"For we preach not ourselves (the words "our gospel" do not contradict this: see note at v.3) but Christ Jesus the Lord; and ourselves your servants for Jesus sake."

The order, "Christ Jesus", gives emphasis to 'the gospel of the glory of Christ. He is the exalted Saviour who was once here on earth: He is "Christ Jesus". The emphasis is always placed on the first name. His title, "the Lord", stresses His authority. Compare Romans 10 verse 9; Acts 2 verse 36; Acts 10 verse 36.

Notice: "preach not *ourselves*…*ourselves*…servants". But why "servants for **Jesus'** sake?" He is the perfect Servant! Paul and his colleagues were the servants of the perfect Servant! "I am among you as one that serveth" (Luke 22: 27).

> *Jesus! It speaks a life of love*
> *And sorrows meekly borne:*
> *It tells of sympathy above*
> *Whatever griefs we mourn.*

We must carefully note that whilst the preacher cannot enlighten men and women, it is through his preaching that **God** gives enlightenment. Preachers are simply channels: the work itself is totally divine. But this does not minimise the work of the preacher. "How shall they hear without a preacher?" (Rom. 10: 14).

c) The work of God, v.6

"For God, who commanded the light to shine out of darkness, hath shined in our hearts, to give the light of the knowledge of the glory of God in the face of Jesus Christ." Not 'in the face of Moses'!

Not only is the message divine: the illumination is divine as well: "For God, who commanded the light to shine out of darkness". He shined creatively in Genesis 1 verse 3, when "darkness was upon the face of the deep": "And God said, Let there be light: and there was light". He has shined creatively again: "For God, who commanded the light to shine out of darkness, hath shined **in our hearts**". Unbelievers are hopelessly blinded by 'the god of this age', so that they cannot see the light of the gospel. Only God can give spiritual enlightenment. It was so in Paul's experience. See Acts 26 verse 13, "A light **from heaven** above the brightness of the sun".

If in verse 4, Satan has blinded the minds of men and women, then in verse 6, God enlightens the minds and hearts of men and women. He does so through Gospel preaching, and the preacher can rightly say:

> *Come to the Light, 'tis shining for thee;*
> *Sweetly the Light has dawned upon me;*
> *Once I was blind, but now I can see:*
> *The Light of the world is Jesus.*

2 CORINTHIANS

"We have this treasure in earthen vessels"

Read Chapter 4:7-18

If we were to attempt an 'overview' of 2 Corinthians Chapters 1-5, it might look like this:

Chapters 1 & 2 emphasise Paul's *motives.* *(i)* He explains why he changed his route from Ephesus to Corinth: "to spare you I came not as yet unto Corinth…I determined…that I would not come again to in heaviness" (1: 23; 2: 1). *(ii)* He explains why he wrote the First Epistle: "I wrote this same unto you, lest, when I came, I should have sorrow from them of whom I ought to rejoice…I wrote unto you with many tears…For to this end also did I write, that I might know the proof of you, whether ye be obedient in all things" (2: 3, 4, 9) *(iii)* He explains why he rejoiced in adversity: "now thanks be unto God, which always causeth us to triumph in Christ ('always leadeth us in triumph in Christ')" (2: 14).

Chapter 3 emphasises Paul's *service*: the character of his preaching. "Our sufficiency is of God; who also hath made us able ministers of the new testament; not of the letter, but of the spirit" (3: 6).

Chapters 4 & 5 emphasise Paul's *resources.* *(i)* In life, Chapter 4: "we have this treasure in earthen vessels…though our outward man perish, yet the inward man is renewed day by day" (4: 7, 16). *(ii)* In death, Chapter 5: "For we know that if our earthly house of this tabernacle were dissolved, we have a building of God, an house not made with hands, eternal in the heavens" (5: 1).

We have noted that 2 Corinthians 4 may be divided as follows: *(1)* persevering in service (v.1); *(2)* purity of motive (v.2); *(3)* preaching the gospel (vv.3-6);

(4) power from God (v.7); *(5)* persecution from men (vv.8-12); *(6)* prospect for the future (vv.13-18).

Alternatively, verses 8-18 could be summarised as follows: *(1)* the pressure of his sufferings (vv.8-12); *(2)* the purpose of his sufferings (vv.13-15): "all things are for your sakes" (v.15); *(3)* the prospect after suffering (vv.16-18): "a far more exceeding and eternal weight of glory…the things which are not seen are eternal" (vv17-18). This leads on to Chapter 5 verse 1: "we know…we have a building of God, an house not made with hands, eternal in the heavens".

1) PERSEVERING IN SERVICE, v.1

"Therefore seeing with have this ministry, as we have received mercy, we faint not." We have noted that by "this ministry", Paul refers to the new covenant. The new covenant, which he calls the ministration of life…righteousness" is infinitely superior to "the ministration of death… condemnation" (3: 7, 9).

2) PURITY OF MOTIVE, v.2

"But have renounced the hidden things of dishonesty ('shame'), not walking in craftiness, nor handling the word of God deceitfully; but by manifestation of the truth commending ourselves to every man's conscience in the sight of God."

3) PREACHING THE GOSPEL, vv.3-6

"But if our gospel be hid, it is hid to them that are lost" (v.3) or "But and if our gospel is *veiled*, it is *veiled* in them that are perishing" (RV). As we have noticed, Paul's business was to '*manifest* the truth'. He discusses the barrier to its reception. The barrier lay, not in his preaching, but in the hearts of men. The failure to appreciate the truth of the gospel lies *within* men. In this connection, we noticed *(i)* the work of Satan (v.4); *(ii)* the work of the preacher (v.5); *(iii)* the work of God (v.6). This brings us to:

4) THE POWER OF GOD, v.7

Having spoken of "the light of the knowledge of the glory of God in the face of Jesus Christ" (v.6), Paul continues: "But we have this treasure in earthen

vessels, that the excellency of the **power** may be of God, and not of us".
The expression "earthen vessels" refers not just to the physical body, but to
the whole weak frail man. Later he describes it as "our earthly house of this
tabernacle" and goes on to speak of "a building of God, an house not made
with hands, eternal in the heavens" (5: 1). In both cases, he is referring to
our bodies and their faculties. God has marvellous designs on our "earthen
vessels!" We should notice three things here:

a) The greatness of the treasure

The treasure is "the light of the knowledge of the glory of God in the face of
Jesus Christ" (v.6). God is revealed in Christ .When Paul was "apprehended
of Christ Jesus" (Phil. 3: 12) on the road to Damascus, he saw "a light from
heaven, above the brightness of the sun, shining round about me" (Acts
26: 13). John testified, "and we beheld his glory, the glory as of the only
begotten of the Father" (John 1: 14).

As P.E.Hughes observes, "there could be no contrast more striking than that
between the greatness of the divine glory and the frailty and unworthiness
of the vessels in which it dwells and through which it is manifested to the
world". So:

b) The frailty of the vessels

They are described as "earthen (*ostrakinos)* vessels *(skuos)*". This recalls
that Adam was formed by God "of the dust of the ground" (Gen. 2: 7) and that
the "the first man is of the earth, earthy" (1 Cor. 15: 47). God has bestowed
a great honour on His earthen vessels by making them the depositaries of
"the light of the knowledge of the glory of God in the face of Jesus Christ". It
has been suggested (P.E.Hughes) that "Paul's fondness for graphic similes
taken from the spectacle of a Roman triumph (see 2: 14 and 1 Cor. 4: 9)"
might be evident here as well. Just as a victorious Roman general would
commit the carriage of captured treasure to his men, so "it was very possibly
his intention here to suggest a picture of the victorious Christ entrusting His
riches to the poor earthen vessels of His human followers".

c) The clarity of the conclusion

"That the excellency *(huperbolee)* of the power *(dunamis)* may be of God,
and not of us" or "the exceeding greatness of the power may be of God, and

not of ourselves" (RV). "The purpose behind this almost incredible contrast between the brilliance of the treasure and the meanness of the vessel is that the surplus or excess of power may be, that is, may be apparent as being, of God (entirely God's) and not from himself (as something for which he could claim any credit)" (P.E.Hughes). Paul is emphasising here the perception of others, rather than the possibility of self-congratulation on the part of the preachers (see 1 Cor.1: 29, 31, citing Jer. 9: 23-24).

5) PERSECUTION FROM MEN, vv.8-12

These verses may be divided into two sections. In the first place, Paul describes the effect of persecution in a variety of ways (vv.8-9) and in the second he uses one figure "dying...death" (vv.10-12). In the first case, we have the details, and the second we have the summary.

a) The details of his sufferings, vv.8-9

These are expressed in four couplets *(i)* "troubled...not distressed"; *(ii)* "perplexed...not in despair"; *(iii)* "persecuted...not forsaken"; *(iv)* "cast down...not destroyed". In each case, the first words ("troubled... perplexed...persecuted...cast down") refer to what men did to the 'vessel', and the second words ("not distressed...not in despair...not forsaken... not destroyed") refer to the sustaining power of God: "the excellency of the power of God".

i)   "Troubled on every side, yet not distressed"

"Troubled" (see also 7: 5, "we were troubled on every side") means 'afflicted' with the idea of pressure (*thlipsis*). The word occurs in Chapter 1 verse 4 ("our tribulation"); Chapter 1 verse 6 ("afflicted"); Chapter 1 verse 8 ("affliction"). "Yet...

"Not distressed", meaning 'straitened'. That is, there is a way out. This can be illustrated by Chapter 7 verses 5-6, "we were troubled (*thlibo*) on every side...Nevertheless God, that comforteth those that are cast down, comforted us by the coming of Titus". Compare 1 Corinthians 10 verse 13, "God is faithful, who will not suffer you to be tempted above that ye are able; but will with the temptation also make a way to escape, that ye may be able to bear it". This is illustrated in 1 Samuel 23 verses 26-28

ii) *"Perplexed, but not in despair"*

The linguists tell us that there is a play on words here: "perplexed" is *aporeo:* "despair" is *exaporeo*

"Perplexed". The word "perplexed" means, literally, 'without a way'. So, 'in doubt' or 'at a loss'. See Luke 24 verse 4, "as they were much perplexed *(diaporeo)*". See also Acts 25 verse 20, (Festus to Agrippa) "And because I doubted *(aporeo)* of such manner of questions" or "And I, being perplexed how to enquire concerning these things" (RV). "Yet…

"Not in despair." Meaning, 'not utterly without a way' or 'not without any resource'. It seems, however, that Paul hadn't always seen it like that: see Chapter 1 verse 8: "we despaired even of life". But he proved that there were resources: "God…delivered us from so great a death" (1: 9-10).

iii) *"Persecuted, but not forsaken"*

"Persecuted". The word *(dioko)* means 'to put to flight, drive away…to pursue, whence the meaning to persecute' (W.E.Vine). It perhaps carries the idea of being hunted. Compare John 15 verse 20: "The servant is not greater than his lord. If they have persecuted me, they will also persecute you". "Yet…

"Not forsaken". So: "I will never leave thee…" (Heb. 13: 5); "When thou passest through the waters, I will be with thee" (Isa. 43: 2); "At my first answer…all men forsook me…Notwithstanding the Lord stood with me…" (2 Tim. 4: 16-17). Paul never had to cry, "My God, my God why hast thou forsaken me?"

iv) *"Cast down, but not destroyed"*

"Cast down", means 'smitten down'. Perhaps the "most remarkable instance known to us of his being, in a literal sense, hunted and struck down by the enemies of the gospel was the occasion when hostile Jews from Antioch and Iconium pursued him to Lystra, stoned him, and after dragging his apparently lifeless body out of the city, left him for dead; but he was miraculously raised up and restored to vigour (Acts 14: 19)" (P.E.Hughes). "Yet…

"Not destroyed". The word "destroyed" *(apollumi)* does not mean extinction, but ruin. Not loss of being, but loss of well-being.

The verses above have been expressed as follows:

> *We are hard pressed, but not suffocated;*
> *Puzzled, but not completely baffled;*
> *We are pursued, but not caught or over run by the hunters;*
> *Struck down, but not out of the fight.*

To summarise: 'At wits' end but never at hope's end'.

b) The summary of his sufferings, vv.10-12

"Always bearing about in the body the dying of the Lord Jesus ('Jesus, RV/ JND, that the life also of Jesus might be made manifest in our body. For we which live are always delivered unto death for Jesus' sake, that the life also of Jesus might be made manifest in our mortal flesh. So then death worketh in us, but life in you." These verses *(i)* make a statement about his sufferings (v.10); *(ii)* give an explanation of his sufferings (v.11); *(iii)* give a reason for his sufferings (v.12).

i)   A statement about his sufferings, v.10

The connection with the preceding verses is clear: "Persecuted, but not forsaken; cast down but not destroyed; always bearing about in the body the dying of the Lord Jesus ('Jesus', as above), that the life also of Jesus might be manifest in our body". Once again, the first statement ("always bearing about in the body the dying of Jesus", JND) refers to what men did to the 'vessel', and the second statement ("that the life also of Jesus might be manifest in our body") refers to the sustaining power of God: "the excellency of the power of God".

- "*Always bearing about in the body the dying of Jesus*" or "always bearing about in the body the putting to death of Jesus" (RV margin). Paul does not refer here to our identification with Him in death in relation to sin (Rom. 6: 3, 11), but to our identification with Him in His sufferings at the hands of men. This is why he says, 'the putting to death of Jesus', thus emphasising His manhood. The Lord Jesus was constantly exposed to death (see, for example, Luke 4: 29; John 8: 59), and Paul with his colleagues were therefore experiencing the "fellowship of his sufferings" (Phil. 3: 10). They too were exposed to constant death.

The Lord Jesus had warned His disciples that this would happen: "The servant is not greater than his lord. If they have persecuted me, they will also persecute you" (John 15: 20). Hence Romans 8 verse 36, "for thy sake we are killed all the day long; we are accounted as sheep for the slaughter"; 1 Corinthians 4 verse 9, "I think that God hath set forth us the apostles last, as it were appointed to death"; 1 Corinthians 15 verses 30-31, "And why stand we in jeopardy every hour? I protest by your rejoicing which I have in Christ Jesus our Lord, I die daily"; 2 Corinthians 1 verse 9, "But we had the sentence of death in ourselves…"

It is with this in mind that Paul writes, 'Always bearing about in the body the dying of Jesus' or 'Always bearing about in the body the putting to death of Jesus'.

- "*That the life also of Jesus might be made manifest in our body*". The same frail 'earthen vessel' manifested not only 'the putting to death of Jesus', but "the life also of Jesus". It is most important to notice that it is "the putting to death of *Jesus*", and "the life also of *Jesus*". We must not divorce the 'dying of Jesus' from 'the life of Jesus'. He could not be overcome by death. Similarly, Paul and his colleagues were sustained in all their sufferings and persecution by what Paul elsewhere calls "the power of his resurrection" (Phil. 3: 10). It was the power of Christ that enabled him to continue.

The words, "that the life also of Jesus might be made *manifest* in our body" emphasise that it was obvious that Paul did not undertake his service for God in his natural power, but in the power of Christ.

ii)   An explanation of his sufferings, v.11

Paul now enlarges on his statement. By saying, "Always bearing about in the body the dying (putting to death) of Jesus", he meant, "For we which live are always delivered unto death for Jesus' sake", and by saying "that the life also of Jesus might be made manifest in our body", he meant here and now (not referring to the future): "that the life also of Jesus might be made manifest in our mortal flesh".

- "*For we which live are always delivered unto death for Jesus' sake*". The continuity of his sufferings are emphasised: "*always* delivered unto death". See 2 Timothy 3 verses 10-11, "But thou hast fully known my… persecutions, afflictions, which came unto me at Antioch, Iconium, at Lystra:

what persecutions I endured: but out of them all the Lord delivered me". Here, again, is the frail earthen vessel.

'In speaking of himself as being constantly delivered, while living ("we which live"), unto death, Paul conjures up the picture of a man being thrown alive to the wild beasts in the arena – a fate experienced by many Christians in the apostolic age" (P.E.Hughes). See, again, 2 Corinthians 1 verse 9, "But we had the sentence of death in ourselves..." Compare "in deaths oft" (2 Corinthians 11 verse 23).

We must also notice that his sufferings in this way were "for **Jesus'** sake". Compare 1 Peter 4 verses 13-16, "But rejoice, partakers of Christ's sufferings... If ye be reproached for the name of Christ, happy are ye... But let none of you suffer as a murderer, or as a thief, or as an evildoer, or as a busybody in other men's matters. Yet if any man suffer as a Christian, let him not be ashamed; but let him glorify God on this behalf".

- "*That the life also of Jesus might be made manifest in our mortal flesh*". Paul changes his wording from "manifest in our body" (v.10) to "manifest in our mortal flesh" (v.11). This is evidently to stress the frailty of the 'earthen vessel'. The words "mortal flesh" refer to the body as liable to death. The "life of Jesus" is manifested in what is naturally the seat of decay and death. Compare, "our body of humiliation" (Phil. 3: 21, JND). Paul does not refer here to the resurrection body, for at the resurrection "this mortal shall... put on immortality" (1 Cor.15: 53-54).

iii)   The reason for his sufferings, v.12

"So then death worketh in us, but life in you..." The words, so then **death worketh in us"** summarise verses 8-11: "Troubled on every side... perplexed... persecuted... cast down... bearing about in the body the putting to death of Jesus... delivered unto death for Jesus' sake". It is summed up in the words, "so then death worketh in us".

But what of the words, "*but life in you?*" It has been suggested that Paul is being ironical as in 1 Corinthians 4 verses 8-10. But it seems better to say that he is rejoicing in the fact that his sufferings are not fruitless. See verse 15: "For all things are for your sakes, that the abundant grace might, through the thanksgiving of many, redound to the glory of God". As P.E.Hughes observes, "Through his endurance the gospel had been brought to them, and by believing its word they had passed from death to life".

6) PROSPECT FOR THE FUTURE, vv.13-18

When Paul thinks of death (v.12) he thinks of resurrection, and this brings us to the third section of the chapter. We should notice that Paul now turns to consider death itself. Two things call for attention here: *(a)* the assurance of resurrection (vv.13-14); *b)* the present effect of resurrection (vv.15-18).

a) The assurance of resurrection, vv.13-14

"We having the same spirit of faith, according as it is written, I believed, and therefore have I spoken; we also believe, and therefore speak" (v.13). Paul refers here to Psalm 116 verse 10 which is a psalm of thanksgiving for deliverance from death. "The sorrows of death compassed me, and the pains of hell gat hold upon me: I found trouble and sorrow (v.3)...I was brought low, and he helped me (v.6)...thou hast delivered my soul from death, mine eyes from tears, and my feet from falling (v.8)...I believed, therefore have I spoken" (v.10).

Paul confesses to the same spirit of faith as exhibited by the Psalmist, who could speak of life ("I will walk before the LORD in the land of the living", v.9) in the place of death. How did Paul appropriate the blessings of verses 8-12 in the midst of his sufferings? By faith! "We also believe...and speak." Referring to the reality of faith in the heart.

But that faith not only enabled Paul to continue under pressure and persecution: it also enabled him to look forward to the ultimate triumph. Thus:

"Knowing (note the assurance) that he which raised up the Lord Jesus, shall raise us up also by Jesus ('with Jesus', RV), and shall present us with you" (v.14). That is, His resurrection is the guarantee of our resurrection. He is the "firstfruits of them that slept." Why "Jesus?" See 1 Corinthians 15 verse 21, "For since by man came death, by man came also the resurrection of the dead". The essential unity of the believer with Him is taught here.

"And shall present (*paristemi*) us with you." That is, Paul anticipated the happy day in heaven when he would stand with the believers from Corinth, the fruit of his suffering and service, in the presence of God. Compare 1 Thessalonians 2 verses 19-20, "For what is our hope, or joy, or crown of rejoicing? Are not even ye in the presence of our Lord Jesus Christ at his coming? For ye are our glory and joy".

See also 2 Corinthans 11 verse 2, "that I might present (*paristemi*) you as a chaste virgin to Christ". The idea of presentation is found in Ephesians 5 verse 27, "that he might present (*paristemi*) it to himself a glorious church". See also Colossians 1 verse 22; "to present (*paristemi*) you holy and unblameable and unreprovable in his sight"; Jude verse 24, "present (*histemi*) you faultless".

The prospect of being presented with the Corinthian believers had a salutary effect on Paul, which brings us to:

b) The present effect of resurrection, vv.15-18

It enabled him to persevere through affliction and suffering. In view of the fact that in heaven, Paul will be presented with the saints at Corinth, he says: "all things are for your sakes (they are also 'for Jesus' sake', v.11), that the abundant grace might, through the thanksgiving of many, redound to the glory of God" (v.15). The RV is helpful here: "For all things are for your sakes (with this result) that the grace being multiplied through the many (saved) may cause the thanksgiving to abound unto the glory of God".

With this in mind, he continues: "For this cause we faint not; but though our outward man perish, yet the inward man is renewed day by day" (v.16). Why did Paul say, "we faint not"? Because although persecuted:

i)   He was enabled to triumph in Christ. *His* life enabled Paul to do so (vv.10-11).

ii)   Men were blessed as a result of Paul's ministry: "so then death worketh in us, but life in you" (v.12).

iii)   He anticipated a day of resurrection and presentation (v.14).

iv)   God was glorified through the thanksgiving of those saved: the "many" (v.15).

In view if this "wherefore we faint not" meaning, as in verse 1, 'we do not lose heart...lose courage'. This is not to say that he was not subject to the effects of the stresses and strains he experienced, but "though our outward man perish, yet the inward man is renewed day by day". To what does Paul refer here? *Not* to the outward man. This was subject to decay. *But* to the inward man. That was renewed day by day. He refers to inward strength, not outward strength.

But what is the "inward man?" **Not** our mental faculties. They decline too! It is the spiritual man: the life of the soul with its desires and aspirations that is "renewed day by day". Hence elderly saints, suffering saints, so often display a spiritual health and vitality far in excess of mind and body!

In the concluding verses of the chapter, Paul tells us how "the inward man is renewed day by day". "For our light affliction, which is but for a moment, worketh for us a far more exceeding and eternal weight of glory; while we look not at the things which are seen, but at the things which are not seen: for the things which are seen are temporal; but the things which are not seen are eternal" (vv.17-18). We should notice the contrasts:

i) As to his **experience:** here - "affliction": there - "glory".

ii) As to the **intensity** of his experience: here - "light": there - "weight".

iii) As to the **duration** of his experience: here - "moment": there - "eternal".

But what is meant by the verse?

i) Does it teach that glory will be commensurate with suffering? That is, that glory is dependant upon suffering? Paul is not speaking of a correspondence between the two, but of a contrast between them. The verse does **not** teach that suffering merits glory. On the contrary, the glory is said to utterly outweigh the suffering. The latter is called "light affliction", not because it was inconsiderable (see, for example, Chapters 1 & 11, as well as this same chapter, vv.8-11), but because of the "far more exceeding and eternal weight of glory". It is also "light affliction" because it is confined only to this life, "but for a moment", as opposed to eternity.

ii) It teaches us rather that God will ensure that the suffering of His servants will be compensated beyond their imagination. Hence Romans 8 verse 18, "For I reckon that the sufferings of this present time are not worthy to be compared with the glory which shall be revealed in us".

When Paul says, "While we look" *(skope),* he means 'to look at, to consider, implying mental consideration'. As in Hebrews 12 verse 15, "looking diligently" (RV 'looking carefully'). He continues: "we look **not** in things which are seen". That is, the vessel with all its suffering, humiliation and shame: things that men man can see, and only see. "**But** at the things which are not seen", that is, on the eternal glory.

2 CORINTHIANS

"Absent from the body...present with the Lord"

Read Chapter 5:1-8

As we have noted before, Paul refers particularly in this Epistle to his adversity. He emphasises this more than anywhere else in his New Testament correspondence. It can be summed up in the words, "we were troubled on every side; without were fightings, within were fears" (7: 5) or "Beside those things that are without, that which cometh upon me daily, the care of all the churches" (11: 28).

i)   *"Without were fightings"*

This becomes evident on the very threshold of the Epistle. See Chapter 1 verses 8-9, "For we would not, brethren, have you ignorant of our trouble which came unto us in Asia, that we were pressed out of measure, above strength, insomuch that we despaired even of life: but we had the sentence of death in ourselves, that we should not trust in ourselves, but in God which raiseth the dead". Paul refers again to external pressure in Chapter 4 verses 8-18, where he calls it "light affliction", in Chapter 6 verses 4-10, and in Chapter 11 verses 24-33.

ii)   *"Within were fears"*

This describes Paul's deep concern for the assembly at Corinth. See, for example, Chapter 2 verse 4: "For out of much affliction and anguish of heart I wrote unto you with many tears...that ye might know the love which I have more abundantly unto you"; Chapter 2 verses 12-13, "Furthermore, when I came to Troas to preach Christ's gospel...I had no rest in my spirit, because I found not Titus my brother: but taking my leave of them, I went from thence into Macedonia". His deep concern is also expressed in Chapters 7 and 11.

But the epistle does far more than highlight the pressure on Paul and his colleagues. It also reveals the resources on which Paul drew in order to withstand and triumph over those pressures. Whether in life or in death, Paul rested on divine sufficiency. The same assurance that marked him under suffering and affliction, marked him equally as he contemplated death. In Chapter 4 verses 7-18, Paul speaks of the sustaining grace of God in the midst of earthly sufferings, and in Chapter 5 verses 1-8, he speaks of the sustaining certainty of hope in the face of death itself. When speaking of his earthly sufferings, he describes his body and its faculties as an 'earthen vessel' (4: 7): when speaking of the possibility of death, he describes them as an 'earthly house of this tabernacle' or 'tent' (5: 1).

i) The 'earthen vessel' was actually a treasure chest!

The treasure was "the light of the knowledge of the glory of God in the face of Jesus Christ", and Paul says "we have this treasure in earthen vessels, that the excellency of the power may be of God, and not of us" (4: 6-7). He continues by describing the pressure on the 'earthen vessel', "troubled… perplexed…persecuted…cast down", together with the sustaining power of God: "not distressed…not in despair…not forsaken…not destroyed" (vv.8-9).

Having given us details of his sufferings and the power which sustained him in them, Paul summarises the position in the words, "Always bearing about in the body the dying (putting to death) of (the Lord) Jesus, that the life also of Jesus might be made manifest in our body. For we which live are alway delivered unto death for Jesus' sake (the 'earthen vessel'), that the life also of Jesus might be made manifest in our mortal flesh" (vv.10-11). The expressions "the body" and "mortal flesh" describe the 'earthen vessel', but those same 'earthen vessels' display the life of the risen Christ. He sustains them in all the pressure and adversity they encounter.

In view of assured resurrection (v.14), Paul looks again at the 'earthen vessel' and writes, "though our outward man perish, yet the inward man is renewed day by day", and then tells us why "the inward man is renewed day by day". Here is the reason: "For our light affliction, which is but for a moment, worketh for us a far more exceeding and eternal weight of glory; while we look not at the things which are seen, but at the things which are not seen: for the things which are seen are temporal; but the things which are not seen are eternal" (vv17-18). There are three contrasts here:

As to **experience:** here, it is "affliction": there, it is "glory".

As to the **intensity** of experience: here, it is "light": there, it is "weight".

As to the **duration** of experience: here, it is "moment": there, it is "eternal".

The verse does **not** teach that suffering merits glory. On the contrary, the glory is said to utterly outweigh the suffering. The latter is called "light affliction", not because it was inconsiderable (see, for example, Chapters 1 & 11, as well as this same chapter, vv.8-11), but because of the "far more exceeding and eternal weight of glory". It is also "light affliction" because it is confined only to this life, "but for a moment", as opposed to eternity.

ii) The tent on earth becomes a house in heaven.

This brings us to Chapter 5, which may be analysed as follows: *(1)* passing into the presence of Christ (vv.1-8); *(2)* appearing before the judgment seat of Christ (vv.9-10); *(3)* serving in view of the love of Christ (vv.11-15); *(4)* preaching reconciliation by Christ (vv.16-21). We must now consider the first of these:

1) PASSING INTO THE PRESENCE OF CHRIST, vv.1-8

Paul now enlarges on "the things which are not seen", that is, the "eternal" things (4: 18), and gives reasons for his complete confidence in the future. He deals with the assurance that garrisoned his heart in facing death itself. Why could Paul be so confident in saying, "we look not at the things which are seen, but at the things which are not seen"? The answer is given in this chapter. It is because the believer can look at death, not as "the king of terrors" (Job 18: 14) but as a wonderful transition from the present with all its limitations and difficulties to eternal blessedness.

Paul describes death for the believer in four ways: *(a)* it means a permanent dwelling (v.1); *(b)* it means passing from suffering (vv.2-4); *(c)* its means the promise fulfilled (v.5); *(d)* it means the presence of the Lord (vv.6-8).

a) A permanent dwelling, v.1

We should notice, first of all, two simple but important expressions: "we know…we have". "For *we know* that if our earthly house of this tabernacle were dissolved, *we have* a building of God, an house not made with hands, eternal in the heavens". There is no mistaking the assurance and certainty with which Paul writes.

"We know." This assurance rests, not on speculation or wishful thinking, but on the resurrection of the Lord Jesus. "Knowing that he which raised up the Lord Jesus shall raise up us also by Jesus.…" (4: 14). In the darkest hours of persecution, Paul and his colleagues trusted in "God which raiseth the dead" (2 Cor. 1 :9). He had already dealt with the subject in his First Epistle to the Corinthians: "But now is Christ risen from the dead, and become the firstfruits of them that slept" (1 Cor. 15: 20). It has to be said that Old Testament believers had similar confidence. Job was among them: "For I know that my redeemer liveth, and that he shall stand at the latter day upon the earth: and though after my skin worms destroy this body, yet in my flesh shall I see God: whom I shall see for myself, and mine eyes shall behold, and not another; though my reins be consumed within me" (Job 19: 25-27). David was another: "As for me, I will behold thy face in righteousness: I shall be satisfied, when I awake, with thy likeness" (Psalm 17: 15).

"We have." "We have a building of God." Paul mentions several things that we possess in this epistle: "seeing then that *we have* such hope", (3: 12); "seeing *we have* this ministry" (4: 1); "*we have* this treasure" (4: 7); now "*we have* a building of God" (5: 1). These things are part of Paul's treasured possessions "having nothing, and yet possessing all things" (6: 10).

He therefore begins:

"For we know that if our earthly house (we have already compared this with the "earthen vessels", 4: 7) of this tabernacle were dissolved, we have a building of God, an house not made with hands, eternal in the heavens." We should notice:

i) The present state of the body is called "our earthly house of this *tabernacle*". The word "tabernacle" means 'tent'. See 2 Peter 1 verse 14, "Shortly I must put off this my tabernacle". A tent is an impermanent residence.

ii) The resurrection body is called "a *building* of God, an house not made with hands…" That is, it is a permanent structure. Paul is referring here, *not* to heaven itself, but to living in a body suited for heaven. He calls it "our house which is *from* heaven", by which he does not mean a *new* body provided by heaven, but a body that has been *changed* by divine power. "Far more can be done in a building than can be done in a tent!...God has designs on our bodies which beggar imagination!" (David Gooding).

It is necessary to remember that it will be the same body. See 1 Corinthians 6 verses 13-14, "Now the body...is for the Lord; and the Lord for the body. And God hath both raised up the Lord, and will also raise us up by his own power". When Lazarus died and was subsequently raised by the Lord Jesus, the body that went into the tomb was the body that came out of the tomb. The body that was placed in Joseph's tomb was the body in which the Lord Jesus left the tomb. The bodies of believers down through the ages will be raised. It will be the same body, otherwise it would not be resurrection at all! It will be a *changed* body! He will "*change* our vile body ('body of humiliation') that *it* (so it is the same body) may be fashioned like unto *his* glorious body" (Phil. 3: 21).

So we have:

- *Two houses.* One of which is *impermanent*, we might say, temporary: a "tabernacle". One of which *is permanent*: a "building".

- *In two places.* One on *earth*: "our earthly house". One in *heaven*: "eternal in the heavens".

- *Of two qualities.* One *can* be *"dissolved"* or 'destroyed' (*kataluo*). The same word is used by the Lord Jesus in connection with the destruction of the temple: "There shall not be left here one stone upon another, that shall not be *thrown down*" (Matt. 24: 2). "Our earthly house" can be 'thrown down' by men: the word indicates a violent death. One *cannot* be *destroyed*. It is "eternal in the heavens". It is said to be "an house not made with hands". Compare Hebrews 9 verse 11, "But Christ being come an high priest of good things to come, by a greater and more perfect tabernacle, *not made with hands*, that is to say, not of this building"; Colossians 2 verse 11, "the circumcision *made without hands*". That is, not physical, but spiritual: not human, but divine.

This should be compared with 1 Corinthians 15 verses 42-44: "It (the believer's body) is *sown* in corruption; it is *raised* in incorruption: It is *sown* in dishonour; it is **raised** in glory: It is **sown** in weakness; it is **raised** in power; It is sown a natural body; it is raised a spiritual body. There is an natural body, and there is a spiritual body." We should notice:

i) Paul does not say '**when** our earthly house', but "**if** our earthly house". That is, death is by no means certain. The passage therefore bears this out.

ii) Paul therefore emphasises the proper hope of the believer: "**not** for that we would be unclothed, **but** clothed upon, that mortality might be swallowed up of life" (v.4). It is, **not** so much to being "absent from the body", as later in the passage (see v.8), **but** the possession of the resurrection of body.

In this connection it is import to notice that Paul does **not** say that 'corruption might be swallowed up of life', **but** that "mortality might be swallowed up of life". 'Corruption' refers to those who have died: 'mortality' refers to those who are alive. See 1 Corinthians 15 verses 51-54.

So for the believer, death is passing from temporary residence on earth with a view to permanent residence in heaven in a body suited to that new environment. It is passing from temporary uncertainty to permanent glory.

b) The passing from suffering, vv.2-4

These verses describe three phases of life for the believer: *(i)* the present phase; *(ii)* the final phase; *(iii)* the interim phase.

i) **The present phase.** "In this (tabernacle) we groan" (v.2); "we that are in this tabernacle do groan" (v.4); "at home in the body" (v.6).

ii) **The final phase.** "Clothed upon *(ependuo)* with our house which is from heaven" (v.2); "being clothed *(enduo)*..." (v3.); "clothed upon *(ependuo)*..." (v.4).

iii) **The interim phase**. That is, for believers who 'fall asleep'. "The earthly house...dissolved" (v.1); "found naked *(gumnos)*..." (v.3): that is, the soul without the body; "unclothed *(ekduo)*..." (v.4); "absent from the body" (v.8). "Naked" is the result of dying"; "unclothed" is the act of dying.

When the Lord returns, those who are "alive and remain" will not experience the interim phase ("naked...unclothed...absent from the body"). They will enter the final phase immediately without dying: they will be "clothed upon". This section of the chapter (vv.2-4) repeats the word "groan" ("for in this we **groan**…we that are in this tabernacle do **groan**", vv.2,4), and the repetition emphasises the reality of suffering. But not only so: it also emphasises that suffering deepens desire for the day when we will pass beyond its sphere:

> *Though He may send some affliction,*
> *'Twill but make me long for home.*

"For in this (i.e. 'this tabernacle') we groan earnestly desiring (*epipotheo*, from *potheo*, 'to yearn' or 'to long for') to be clothed upon with our house which is from heaven". The words "from heaven" indicate its origin. Compare 1 Corinthians 15 verses 42-44, where there is a different emphasis: it is 'out of the grave' or "raised".

It has often been pointed out that Paul does not say 'moan', but "groan!" The word "groan" (*stenazo*) conveys the idea of inward grief: 'an inward, unexpressed feeling of sorrow' (W.E.Vine). Mark uses the word twice in connection with the Lord Jesus: "And looking up to heaven, he **sighed**" (Mark 7: 34); when the Pharisees sought a sign, the Lord Jesus "**sighed** deeply" (Mark 8: 12)." The word is used of believers in Romans 8 verse 23, "even we ourselves **groan** within ourselves…"

Paul refers here, primarily, to circumstances causing grief, and creating desire for our "house which is **from heaven**". Doubtless he has in mind what he calls his "light affliction" (4: 17).

We, too, groan when we see the ravages of sin around us. See, again, Romans 8 verse 23: "And not only (they), but ourselves also, which have the first-fruits of the Spirit, even we ourselves groan within ourselves, waiting for the adoption, to wit, the redemption of our body". The fact too that "our outward man perish" also makes us earnestly desire "to be clothed upon with our house which is from heaven".

Solomon describes the deterioration of the "outward man" quite vividly. See Ecclesiastes 12 verses 3-5: "In the day when…

- "the keepers of the house shall tremble" (the hands).

- "the strong men shall bow themselves" (the legs).

- "the grinders shall cease because they are few" (not so many teeth).

- "those that look out of the windows be darkened" (eyesight failing).

- "the doors shall be shut in the streets when the sound of grinding is low" (a hearing aid is needed).

- "he shall rise up at the sound of a bird" (old people get up early: not teenagers!)

- "all the daughters of music shall be brought low" (cannot sing too well).

- "they shall be afraid of that which is high" ('better live on the flat dear: can't climb hills at our age!')

- "and the almond tree shall flourish" (hair as white as snow).

- "and the grasshopper shall be a burden" (referring to the staggering gait of the grasshopper).

- "and desire shall fail" (physical appetites decline).

And finally, "Man goeth to his long home, and the mourners go about the streets" (the end of life's journey).

No wonder Paul repeats, "For we that are in this tabernacle do groan, being **burdened"** (v.4). The word "burdened" (from *baras,* a weight) indicates something pressing, and Paul is no doubt referring here, primarily, to the persecution he faced. See Chapter 1 verse 8, "we were pressed (*bareo*) out of measure" or "we were weighed down exceedingly"(RV). The word is also used in Chapter 4 verse 17, "a far more exceeding and eternal **weight** of glory". When we are "clothed upon with our house which is from heaven" we shall no longer be "burdened" for "God shall wipe away all tears from their eyes and there shall be no more death, neither sorrow, nor crying, neither shall there be any more pain, for the former things have passed away" (Rev. 21: 4).

Paul therefore looked forward primarily, not to being "unclothed" (to dying), but to being "clothed upon" (to meeting the Lord apart from dying), so "that mortality (meaning 'liable to death and decay') might be swallowed up of

111

life". "Life" here ("swallowed up of life") refers to the life of God Himself. For "swallowed up" see also 1 Corinthians 15 verse 54, "then shall be brought to pass the saying that is written, Death is swallowed up in victory". He makes it clear he welcomed ("willing" meaning 'to be well pleased') being "absent from the body" (v.8) even though it meant being "found naked" (v.3). He makes it equally clear that he welcomed **even more** being "clothed upon" and "mortality" being "swallowed up of life" (v.4).

c) The promise fulfilled, v.5

"Now he that hath wrought us for the selfsame thing is God, who also hath given unto us the earnest of the Spirit." We should notice:

i) "Now he that hath **wrought** us…" According to the scholars, the word "God" is in a position of emphasis: 'But it is God who fashioned us for this very thing'. There is no hint of human accomplishment: this is God's crowning act of grace. Compare Ephesians 2 verse 10, "For we are his workmanship": *poiema* here has given rise to our English word 'poetry'. It has the idea of beauty and symmetry.

ii) "The **earnest** of the Spirit". See also 2 Corinthians 1 verse 22, "who hath also sealed us, and given the earnest of the Spirit in our hearts"; Ephesians 1 verse 14: "that Holy Spirit of promise, which is the earnest of our inheritance until the redemption of the purchased possession, unto the praise of his glory". "The term "earnest" (*arrabon*) means a deposit which is in itself a guarantee that the full amount will be paid later" (P.E.Hughes). According to W.E.Vine the word originally meant "earnest-money deposited by the purchaser and forfeited if the purchase was not completed". It was probably a Phoenician word, introduced into Greece. "In general usage it came to denote a pledge or earnest of any sort. In modern Greek, *arrabona* is an engagement ring" (W.E.Vine). So, we have the **pledge now** in anticipation of the fulfilment.

d) The presence of the Lord, vv.6-8

"Therefore we are always confident, knowing that, whilst we are at home in the body, we are absent from the Lord: (for we walk by faith, not by sight): we are confident, I say, and willing rather to be absent from the body, and to be present (*endemeo*, 'to be at home', W.E.Vine) with the Lord", or 'at home with the Lord' (RV).

"Therefore we are always **confident** ('of good courage', RV)", that is, **in view of death,** knowing that it is passing from our temporary home in the body, where we are absent from the Lord, to our permanent home with the Lord.

Whilst we are "at home in the body" and "absent from the Lord", we walk by **faith,** but when "absent from the body" and "present with the Lord", it will by **sight:** we shall be with Him.

> *"For ever with the Lord", Amen, so let it be.*
> *Life from the dead is in that word. 'Tis immortality.*
> *Here in the body pent, absent from Him I roam*
> *Yet nightly pitch my moving tent a day's march nearer home.*
>
> *So when my latest breath shall rend the veil in twain*
> *By death I shall escape from death, and life eternal gain.*
> *Knowing as I am known, how shall I love that word,*
> *And oft repeat before the throne. "For ever with the Lord".*

2 CORINTHIANS

"We must all appear before the judgment seat of Christ"

Read Chapter 5:9-15

We have noted that the chapter can be divided in the following way: **(1)** passing into the presence of Christ (vv.1-8); **(2)** appearing before the judgment seat of Christ (vv.9-10); **(3)** serving in view of the love of Christ (vv.11-15); **(4)** preaching reconciliation by Christ (vv.16-21).

1) PASSING INTO THE PRESENCE OF CHRIST, vv.1-8

Paul describes death for the believer in four ways: the believer can face even death with the utmost confidence because:

i) It means a **permanent dwelling** (v.1): "For we know that if our earthly house of this tabernacle were dissolved, we have a building of God, an house not made with hands, eternal in the heavens".

ii) It means **passing from suffering** (vv.2-4): "For in this we groan, earnestly desiring to be clothed upon with our house which is from heaven".

iii) It means the **promise fulfilled** (v.5): "Now he that hath wrought us for the selfsame thing is God, who also hath given unto us the earnest of the Spirit".

iv) It means the **presence of the Lord** (vv.6-8): "we are confident, I say, and willing rather to be absent from the body, and to be present (*endemeo*, 'to be at home') with the Lord".

These verses describe three phases of life for the believer: *(i)* the present phase; *(ii)* the final phase; *(iii)* the interim phase.

i) **The present phase.** "In this (tabernacle) we groan" (v.2); "we that are in this tabernacle do groan" (v.4); "at home in the body" (v.6).

ii) **The final phase.** "Clothed upon *(ependuo)* with our house which is from heaven" (v.2); "being clothed *(enduo)*…" (v.3); "clothed upon *(ependuo)*…" (v.4).

iii) The interim phase. That is, for believers who 'fall asleep'. "The earthly house…dissolved" (v.1); "found naked *(gumnos)*…" (v.3): that is, the soul without the body; "unclothed *(ekduo)*…" (v.4); "absent from the body" (v.8). "Naked" is the result of dying"; "unclothed" is the act of dying.

Paul now applies this to present conduct, which reminds us that the Bible never refers to future events in a vacuum. It has been said that the Old Testament prophets addressed the present in the light of the future, and this is equally true of New Testament teaching. See for example, 2 Peter 3 verse 11, "Seeing then that all these things shall be dissolved, what manner of persons ought ye to be in all holy conversation and godliness"; 1 John 3 verse 3, "And every man that hath this hope in him ('set upon him', Christ) purifieth himself, even as he (Christ) is pure". See also 1 Corinthians 15 verse 58; Philippians 4 verse 1; 1 Thessalonians 4 verse 18. This brings us to:

2) APPEARING BEFORE THE JUDGMENT SEAT OF CHRIST, vv.9-10

"Wherefore we labour, that, whether present or absent, we may be accepted of him ('well-pleasing to him'), for we must all appear before the judgment seat of Christ; that every one may receive the things done in his body, according to that he hath done, whether it be good or bad." We can consider these verses as follows; *(a)* the practice of being well-pleasing to Him (v.9); *(b)* the proof of being well-pleasing to Him (v.10).

a) The practice of being well-pleasing to Him, v.9

The opening word, "Wherefore", establishes the connection with the preceding verses. In view of the fact that believers are bound for heaven where they will be 'at home with the Lord' (v.8), and having received the divinely-given pledge that God will honour His promise (v.5), Paul now describes the effect in his life. We must notice the following: "Wherefore…

i) **"We labour".** Or "we make it our aim" (RV) with a margin note, 'ambitious'. The word (*philotimeomai*) is also used in 1 Thessalonians 4 verse 11 (AV "**study to** be quiet": 'aim to be quiet'). To "be quiet" means 'to be at rest.' It means to have orderly and peaceful lives. It means that we cause no disturbance to other people. We are not to be excitable and unstable people. It is also used in Romans 15 verse 20, "so have I **strived** to preach the gospel, not where Christ was named", or "making it my aim so to preach the gospel…" (RV). We are therefore to be ambitious to preach the gospel.

Having substituted the word 'ambitious' for "labour", "study", and "strived", we must review **our** ambitions! Are **we** ambitious for God? That is, ambitious to be well-pleasing to the Lord (2 Cor. 5: 9), to have orderly and peaceful lives (1 Thess. 4: 11), to preach the gospel (Rom. 15: 20). It is good to be ambitious in this way!

ii) ***"Whether present (at home) or absent".*** That is, in or out of the body. But if the meaning is 'in or out of the Lord's presence' there is no alteration to the sense of the verse! However, it does seem that we should take the former meaning: P.E.Hughes quotes F.G.Filson as follows: "it is not important whether the final day (the day of the Lord's coming) finds us *at home* in the physical body *or away*, i.e., already separated from that body by death; what counts is that while we have time we should make every effort *to please* the Lord".

iii) ***"We may be accepted of him"*** or "be well-pleasing (*euarestos*) to him" (RV). Thus (v.9) Paul was ambitious **now** so that **now** and in the **future** he might be well-pleasing to the Lord. Are **we?** The following should also be considered: Romans 12 verses 1-2, "present your bodies a living sacrifice, holy, **acceptable** (*euarestos*) unto God which is your reasonable service. And be not conformed to this world: but be ye transformed by the renewing of your mind, that ye may prove what is that good, and **acceptable** (*euarestos),* and perfect will of God"; Ephesians 5 verse 10, "walk as children of light… proving what is **acceptable** (*euarestos)* unto the Lord"; Philippians 4 verse 18, "a sacrifice acceptable, **well-pleasing** (*euarestos*) to God"; Colossians 3 verse 20, "Children, obey your parents in all things: for this is **well-pleasing** (*euarestos*) unto the Lord".

b) The proof of being well-pleasing to Him, v.10

Whether or not we have been well-pleasing to Him will be seen at a given point in the future: "For we must all appear before the judgment seat of Christ; that every one may receive the things done in his body, according to that he hath done, whether it be good or bad".

This subject, the judgment seat of Christ, is dealt with in Romans 14 (loving the brethren); 1 Corinthians 3 (labouring in building); 2 Corinthians 5 (living in the body). It is called "the judgment seat of God" in Romans 14 verse 10, RV. It is called "the judgment seat of God" because Christ will act on behalf of God, since He has committed all judgment into the hands of the Son (John 5: 22).

It is important to distinguish between various sessions of judgment. *(i)* 2 Corinthians 5 verse 10: "For we must all appear before the judgment seat of Christ"; *(ii)* Matthew 25 verse 31: "When the Son of man shall come in his glory, and all the holy angels with him, then shall he sit upon the throne of his glory"; *(iii)* Revelation 20 verse 11: "And I saw a great white throne, and him that sat on it".

As to people:	2 Cor 5, it is the church.
	Matt 25, it is the living nations.
	Rev 20, it is the unregenerate.
As to place:	2 Cor 5, it is in heaven.
	Matt 25, it is on earth.
	Rev 20, it is in space.
As to period:	2 Cor 5, it is after the rapture.
	Matt 25, it is prior to the millennium.
	Rev 20, it is after the millennium.
As to purpose:	2 Cor 5, it is in view of reward.
	Matt 25, it is in view of millennial blessing.
	Rev 20: it is in view of eternal judgment

We must now examine this verse in detail. It can be demonstrated that each word is significant:

i) *"We must".* Divine righteousness requires it. True values must be displayed. Time does not always enable us to see things in perspective, or enable us to rightly value them. There must be a time when all is assessed by one standard, something that is not always possible here on earth. Different people judge by different standards.

ii) *"All".* It is not optional. Every believer, without exception, "must... appear before the judgment seat of Christ".

iii) *"Appear".* Or "be manifested (*phaneroo*)" (RV). W.E.Vine points out that the word "appear" does not do justice to the original text: "A person may appear in a false guise or without a disclosure of what he truly is; to be manifested is to be revealed in one's true character". Possibly, Paul had in mind the false teachers here. 'Be manifested' means, obviously, 'to uncover, lay bare, reveal'. The same word in its noun form (*phanerosis)* occurs in 2 Corinthians 4 verse 2, "by manifestation of the truth commending ourselves to every man's conscience in the sight of God". See also 1 Corinthians 3 verse 13, "Every man's work shall be made manifest (*phaneros*)"; 1 Corinthians 4 verse 5, "make manifest (*phaneroo*) the counsels of the hearts". Compare Luke 12 verses 2-3, "For there is nothing covered that shall not be revealed". Bear in mind 1 Samuel 16 verse 7; Hebrews 4 verse 13.

iv) *"Before the judgment seat of Christ".* The word used here (*bema)* denotes a raised place or platform from which tribunals were conducted. The word is used of:

- *Pilate's* judgment seat, Matthew 27: 19.

- *Herod's* throne, Acts 12: 21.

- *Gallio's* judgment seat, Acts 18: 12, 16, 17. Note: "drave them from the judgment seat...beat him (Sosthenes) before the judgment seat...Gallio cared for none of those things".

- *Festus'* judgment seat, Acts 25: 6, 17.

- *Caesar's* judgment seat, Acts 25: 10. Paul was actually standing at Festus' judgment seat, but he calls it "Caesar's judgment seat".

Notice that in four out of the five cases, judgment was perverted. But this cannot possibly be said about the "judgment seat of Christ": He will be "the *righteous judge"* (2 Tim. 4: 8).

The "judgment seat of Christ" will take place "at that day" (2 Tim. 4: 8), that is, "the day of Christ" (Phil. 1: 10; 2: 16), elsewhere called "the day of the Lord Jesus" (1 Cor. 5: 5; 2 Cor. 1: 14) and "the day of our Lord Jesus Christ" (1 Cor. 1: 8). These passages all refer to the Lord's coming and to His review and reward of our work for Him. This will take place in heaven. For further reading see 1 Thessalonians 2 verse 19; Hebrews 13 verse 17; 1 Peter 5 verse 4, 2 John 8; Revelation 3 verse 11.

v) *"That every one".* It will be personal. Not a 'team award'. The work of each individual believer will be assessed and rewarded, or not rewarded, as the case may be.

vi) *"May receive the things done in the body, whether good or bad".* It will be appropriate and just. The word "receive" (*komizo*) means to 'receive back" as in Ephesians 6 verse 8, "Whatsoever good thing any man doeth, the same shall he receive (*komizo*) of the Lord" or "receive again from the Lord" (RV); as in Colossians 3 verse 25, "But he that doeth wrong shall receive (*komizo*) for the wrong which he hath done" or 'shall receive again for the wrong that he hath done" (RV).

3) SERVING IN VIEW OF THE LOVE OF CHRIST, vv.11-15

In these verses, Paul speaks the impact of the judgment seat of Christ on *(a)* his ministry (vv.11-12) and on *(b)* his motives (vv.13-15).

a) His ministry, vv.11-12

That is, his ministry *(i)* in relation to his opponents (v.11a); *(ii)* in relation to God (v.11b); *(iii)* in relation to the Corinthians (vv.11c-12).

i) *In relation to his opponents, v.11a.* "Knowing therefore the terror of the Lord, we persuade men..." The word "terror" *(phobos)* means fear and is so translated in the RV, "Knowing therefore the fear of the Lord..." It is usually rendered "fear" in the New Testament. (It is also translated "terror" in 1 Peter 3: 14 AV: the RV has 'fear').

As P.E.Hughes observes, 'By "the fear of the Lord", then, the apostle does not mean that terror...which the ungodly will experience when they stand before God's judgment throne (cf. Rev. 6: 15ff), but that reverential awe which the Christian should feel towards the Master whom he loves and serves and at whose hand he will receive "the things done in the body'". Paul is therefore referring here, not to the necessity of warning the ungodly of the wrath to come, but to the necessity, forced upon him, of persuading certain members of the church at Corinth of his personal integrity (see 1: 12; 4: 1-2; 6: 3; 7: 2). The word "persuade" (*peitho*) means 'to prevail upon or win over, to persuade' (W.E.Vine)'. See Acts 17 verse 4: "And some of them (at Thessalonica) were persuaded ("believed", AV), and consorted with Paul and Silas" (RV). Compare Acts 19 verse 8, "disputing and persuading the things concerning the kingdom of God".

ii)   In relation to God, v.11b. "But we are made manifest unto God." The words translated "manifest" (here) and "appear" (v.10, AV) are the same (*phaneroo*). If Paul was obliged to persuade men of his personal uprightness and apostolic authority, there was no need to persuade God. "Paul possessed that priceless and unassailable bulwark of the soul, the testimony of a clear conscience before God" (P.E.Hughes). Compare Chapter 1 verse 12. See Acts 23 verse 1, "I have lived in all good conscience before God until this day"; Acts 24 verse 16, "And herein do I exercise myself, to have always a conscience void of offence toward God, and toward men"; 1 Thessalonians 2 verse 5, "For neither at any time used we flattering words, as ye know, nor a cloke of covetousness; God is witness"; 1 Thessalonians 2 verse 10, "Ye are witnesses, and God also, how holily, and justly and unblameably we behaved ourselves among you that believe".

iii)   In relation to the Corinthians, v.11c. "But we are made manifest unto God; and I trust ***also*** are made manifest (*phaneroo*) in your consciences." The Corinthians, above all people, were in a position to recognise and acknowledge his integrity.

Paul now explains why he had written in this way: "For we commend not ourselves again unto you, but give you occasion to glory on our behalf, that ye may have somewhat to answer them which glory in appearance and not in heart" (v.12). Compare Chapter 3 verse 1. Paul is not indulging in self-glory here. The false charges of his opponents could not harm him personally. He had a clear conscience before God. But they could harm the assembly at Corinth by robbing them of his apostolic ministry. In the words of John Calvin, "Christ's servants ought to be concerned for their own reputation only in so far as it is for the advantage of the church". With this in mind, he gave the Corinthians ground on which to speak on his behalf when he was falsely charged. The false teachers gloried "in appearance, and not in heart". Paul ever sought to serve in the fear of the Lord and with the consciousness that his motives and methods were acceptable to Him.

The words "them which glory in appearance, and not in heart" recall Matthew 6 verses 1-18: "When thou doest alms... when thou prayest... when ye fast". The Lord commanded His disciples to do all these things "in secret". The Lord does not even refer to the religious leaders by name: he simply calls them "hypocrites" in saying that they did these things "that they might have glory of men... be seen of men... appear unto men".

Having spoken about men "which glory in appearance, and not in heart", Paul now speaks about his own heart. This brings us to:

b) His motives, vv.13-15

Paul reveals his motives here in two ways *(i)* "for your cause" (v.13); *(ii)* "for the love of Christ" (vv.14-15).

i) *"For your cause", v.13.* "For whether we be beside ourselves, it is to God: or whether we be sober, it is for your cause" (v13). This is a verse of contrasts.

- *Godward.* The words, "beside ourselves" are, literally, 'to be put out of position' or 'displaced'. Here 'to be out of one's mind'. Compare Mark 3 verses 20-21: "And the multitude cometh together again so that they could not so much as eat bread. And when his friends heard of it, they went out to lay hold on him, for they said, He is beside himself".

This paints the picture of a man of tremendous zeal in unrelenting service for God. It was not a case of zeal in a good cause, or zeal in promoting himself or his own interests, but in God's interests. He did not spare himself in service for God. The language suggests that he was being charged with extremism, but if this is the case, then a further charge follows, this time of extremism in the opposite direction:

- *Manward.* "Whether we be sober, it is for your cause". If the words "besides ourselves" means 'to be out of one's mind, then "sober" (*sophroneo*) means the opposite: to be sober-minded or 'of a sound mind', as in Romans 12 verse 3, "not to think of himself more highly than he ought to think; but to think soberly"; Titus 2 verse 6, "Young men likewise exhort to be sober minded"; 1 Peter 4 verse 7, "But the end of all things is at hand: be ye therefore sober, and watch unto prayer".

The words "whether we be sober" describe the soundness of Paul's ministry and in particular, his sober assessment of things at Corinth. It therefore appears that Paul was charged with extremism: with excessive zeal on one hand, and excessive heaviness in ministry on the other, doubtless referring to his corrective teaching. But the charges were completely unfounded.

There was no extremism or fanaticism in his preaching and teaching at Corinth. Whether it was his zeal in gospel preaching or his sober teaching, "it is for your cause". Paul had the good of the assembly in view and both aspects of his service flowed out of his love for them. This was the motive of Paul's unremitting service for God, and thoughtful, sober attitude to the Corinthians. But this derived from "the love of Christ": "For the love of Christ constraineth us..." This brings us to:

ii) *"For the love of Christ", vv.14-15.* In this connection we must notice the source, the power, and the effect of "the love of Christ":

- *The source.* It is "the love of *Christ*" (v.14). This is not so much his love for Christ - though that inevitably is involved - but rather Christ's love for him. This is clear from what follows, the "love of Christ" was seen in His death: "he died for all". His service, whether in unremitting gospel zeal or sober teaching, flowed out of his deep appreciation of the love of Christ for him. The effect of the "love of Christ" for him is next described:

- *The power.* "The love of Christ *constraineth us*" (v.14). The word constrain (*sunecho*) means, literally, 'to hold together'. It has the idea of being confined between two walls. See Philippians 1 verse 23, "I am in a *strait betwixt two* (one word, *sunecho*)"; Luke 22 verse 63, those "that *held* (*sunecho*) Jesus". The love of Christ held Paul fast.

- *The effect.* "Because we thus judge, that if one died for all, then were all dead: and that he died for all, that they which live should *not* henceforth live unto themselves, but *unto him* which died for them and rose again" (vv.14-15).

The overall teaching is clear: "the love of Christ" for us means that we should "live… unto him". There is, however, a difference of opinion over the words, "if one died for all, then were all dead", since "then were all dead" is, literally, 'therefore all died'. It is argued that the apostle is referring here to the **effect** of Christ's death ('therefore all died', RV) rather than the **cause** of His death ("then were all dead", AV). On this basis the "all" must refer, not to mankind generally, but to believers particularly. Against this, there is evidently a clear distinction between "all" and "they which live", and this leads to the conclusion that the AV has it right! The New Translation (JND) has "having judged this: that if one died for all, then all have died" with a footnote "or 'had died'. It is the aorist, and refers to the state Christ's death proved them to be in, in a state of nature. To apply it as a consequence is, I judge, an utter blunder".

How then will the love of Christ in His death for all be demonstrated in the lives of His people? "That they which live should not henceforth live unto themselves, but unto him which died for them and rose again." It will become evident in the selfless Christ-filled life of His people: they will "live…unto him". But it is "unto him which died for them **and rose again**". His death without resurrection would have been defeat. A dead Saviour is a contradiction in terms. How could we "live unto him" if it was His death only that took place? Believers can sing:

> He is Lord, He is Lord,
> He is risen from the dead and He is Lord.
> Every knee shall bow, every tongue confess
> That Jesus Christ is Lord.

Can **we** really say that 'we live…unto him which died for us and rose again'? Only in this way can we be 'well-pleasing unto him' (v.9).

2 CORINTHIANS

"We are ambassadors for Christ"

Read Chapter 5:16-21

We have noted that the chapter can be divided in the following way: **(1)** passing into the presence of Christ (vv.1-8); **(2)** appearing before the judgment seat of Christ (vv.9-10); **(3)** serving in view of the love of Christ (vv.11-15); **(4)** preaching reconciliation by Christ (vv.16-21).

1) PASSING INTO THE PRESENCE OF CHRIST, vv1-8

Paul describes death for the believer in four ways: the believer can face even death with the utmost confidence because:

i)　It means a **permanent dwelling** (v.1): "For we know that if our earthly house of this tabernacle were dissolved, we have a building of God, an house not made with hands, eternal in the heavens".

ii)　It means **passing from suffering** (vv.2-4):　"For in this we groan, earnestly desiring to be clothed upon with our house which is from heaven".

iii)　It means the **promise fulfilled** (v.5): "Now he that hath wrought us for the selfsame thing is God, who also hath given unto us the earnest of the Spirit".

iv)　It means the **presence of the Lord** (vv.6-8): "we are confident, I say, and willing rather to be absent from the body, and to be present (*endemeo*, 'to be at home') with the Lord".

We then noticed that the Bible never refers to future events in a vacuum, and that Paul brings the teaching in verses 1-8 to bear upon present conduct, which brings us to:

2) APPEARING BEFORE THE JUDGMENT SEAT OF CHRIST, vv.9-10

"Wherefore we labour, that, whether present or absent, we may be accepted of him ('well-pleasing to him'), for we must all appear before the judgment seat of Christ; that every one may receive the things done in his body, according to that he hath done, whether it be good or bad." We considered these verses as follows; *(i)* the practice of being well-pleasing to Him (v.9); *(ii)* the proof of being well-pleasing to Him (v.10).

i) **The practice of being well-pleasing to Him, v.9.** This involves spiritual ambition: "Wherefore we make it our aim (margin 'ambitious')..." (RV). The words, "whether present (at home) or absent" mean whether in or out of the body. P.E.Hughes quotes F.G.Filson as follows: "it is not important whether the final day (the day of the Lord's coming) finds us at home in the physical body or away, i.e., already separated from that body by death; what counts is that while we have time we should make every effort to please the Lord".

(ii) **The proof of being well-pleasing to Him, v.10.** Whether or not we have been well-pleasing to Him will be seen at the judgment seat of Christ, when we will 'receive the things done in the body'.

3) SERVING IN VIEW OF THE LOVE OF CHRIST, vv.11-15

In these verses Paul speaks of the impact of the judgment seat of Christ on *(i)* his ministry (vv.11-12) and *(ii)* his motives (vv.13-15):

i) **His ministry, vv.11-12.** This was threefold: in relation to his **opponents** ("knowing therefore the terror of the Lord, we persuade men" of his personal integrity); in relation to **God** ("But we are made manifest unto God"); in relation to the **assembly** at Corinth ("I trust also are made manifest in your consciences").

ii) **His motives, vv.13-15.** These were twofold: *"For your cause"* ("For whether we are beside ourselves, it is to God: or whether we be sober, it is for your cause"); *"For the love of Christ constraineth us"*. In this connection, we noted:

- the **source.** It is "the love of Christ": not 'our nice thoughts of Him', but remembrance of His death at Calvary.

- the **power.** "The love of Christ **constraineth** us", meaning 'to hold together, confirm, secure, hold fast'. See Acts 18 verse 5, "pressed in the spirit" (AV); '**constrained** by the word' (RV). For "constraineth" see Philippians 1 verse 23, "**Strait** betwixt two"; Luke 19 verse 43 (of the siege of Jerusalem), "thine enemies shall... **keep thee in** on every side"; Luke 22 verse 63, "the men that **held** Jesus".

- the **effect.** "Because we thus judge, that if one died for all, then were all dead: and that he died for all, that they which live should **not** henceforth live unto themselves, but **unto him** which died for them and rose again."

This brings us to:

4) PREACHING RECONCILIATION BY CHRIST, vv.16-21

Having said that believers "live unto him which died for them, and rose again", Paul spells out the consequences in terms of **(a)** people (vv.16-17) and **(b)** preaching (vv.18-21)

a) People, vv.16-17

What does 'living unto him' mean in terms of people? Having said that believers no longer "live unto themselves, but unto him which died for them, and rose again" (v.15), Paul now explains that this is a totally new relationship, not based on anything in the past (v.16), but on a new and living relationship with the risen Christ (v.17). He describes the first as "old things", and second as "all things are become new".

i)   "Old things." These are summed up in the words "after the flesh" (v.16). "Wherefore henceforth know we no man after the flesh: yea, though we have known Christ after the flesh, yet now henceforth know we him no more."

- "We know no man after the flesh." The word "know" is used in the sense of appraising and evaluating: it refers to the judgment and understanding of people. Paul no longer evaluated men "after the flesh", that is, in the way unregenerate men, and the world in general, appraises people. Because Christ was everything to Paul, he was no longer swayed by what men are or have been, or have seen, or have done.

This is the complete reverse of the false teachers who "glory in appearance and not in heart" (v.12). Sadly the assembly at Corinth had become infected by this attitude, and in consequence Paul was obliged to say, "For ye are yet carnal (having the nature of flesh): for whereas there is among you envying, and strife, and divisions, are ye not carnal, and walk as men? For while one saith, I am of Paul; and another, I am of Apollos; are ye not carnal?" (1 Cor. 3: 3-4). Rather than this, "He that glorieth, let him glory in the Lord" (1 Cor. 1: 31).

- "Yea, though we have known Christ after the flesh, yet now henceforth know we him no more." It is certainly possible that when Paul was a disciple of Gamaliel in Jerusalem (Acts 22: 3) he actually heard the Lord and even met Him. However, the immediate context makes it clear that prior to his conversion, "Paul's knowledge of Christ has been after the flesh, formed in accordance with human and mistaken standards" (P.E.Hughes). This is precisely true of countless multitudes today. They think only in terms of a historical Jesus, and frequently do so without any knowledge of the historical facts recorded in the Gospels.

Paul could well be referring here to the Jewish party at Corinth who said, "I am of Christ", possibly claiming that they had known Him in His earthly ministry. That guaranteed nothing. He can only be known on the basis of His death and resurrection. True enlightenment was only possible after the coming of the Holy Spirit on the day of Pentecost.

ii) New things. "Therefore if any man be in Christ, he is a new creature: old things are passed away; behold all things are become new." Paul's conversion meant the transformation of his knowledge of Christ. As P.E.Hughes observes, "A man in Christ is a creature entirely renewed, for whom the old judgments after the flesh have become a thing of the past. He now knows Christ as he truly is". A number of important things should be noticed here:

- "Therefore if any man be in Christ." This describes our new position: once "in Adam", having Adam's fallen nature with all its consequences, we are now "in Christ", with all the blessings that attach to this new relationship. These include the security of the believer, his acceptance with God, his assurance of the future, and his inheritance of glory.

- "He is a new creature." Literally, 'there is a new creation'. Both expressions are comprehended in Ephesians 2 verse 10, "Created in

Christ Jesus unto good works..." See also Ephesians 4 verse 24, "the new man which after God hath been created in righteousness and holiness of truth" (RV); Galatians 6 verse 15, "For neither is circumcision anything, nor uncircumcision, but a new creation" (RV).

- "Old things have passed away." Aorist tense is used here, signifying that at a definite moment the "old things" passed away.

- "Behold." P.E.Hughes calls this "an unmistakeable note of spontaneous jubilation" or "a sudden note of triumph"'. Compare Isaiah 43 verse 18, "Remember ye not the former things, neither consider the things of old. Behold , I will do a new thing". See Revelation 21 verse 5, "And he that sat upon the throne said, Behold, I make all things new".

- "All things have become new." The perfect tense is used here: "all things" became and continue to be new.

In verses 14-17, Paul explains why he was both 'out of his mind' and 'sober-minded' (v.13). It was because the "love of Christ" had revolutionised his life: old things had given place to new things. But Paul was not content to enjoy his blessing alone:

Have you found the heavenly light?
Pass it on!
Souls are groping in the night,
Daylight gone;
Hold thy lighted lamp on high,
Be a star in someone's sky;
He may live who else would die;
Pass it on!

Paul now describes the way in which he discharged his responsibility as "a new creature" in Christ. We therefore come now to Paul's service:

b) Preaching, vv.18-21

What does 'living unto him' mean in terms of preaching? We should notice that the words "reconciled...reconciliation...reconciling" occur five times in these verses. See verse 18 (twice), verse 19 (twice), verse 20. The section can be outlined as follows: (i) the enjoyment of reconciliation (v.18); (ii) the ministry of reconciliation (vv.18-19); (iii) the word of reconciliation (v.19); (iv) the preaching of reconciliation (vv.20-21).

It is worth pointing out that justification has to do with the guilt of sin; sanctification with the filth of sin, redemption with the bondage of sin, and reconciliation with the alienation of sin. Furthermore, "reconciliation" has to do with persons, whereas "propitiation" has to do with sins. The word "reconciliation" means, basically, to change: of persons, to change from enmity to friendship. Man needs to be reconciled: "For if when we were enemies, we were reconciled to God by the death of his Son..." (Rom. 5: 10). The need for reconciliation arises out of man's hostile attitude. The enmity lies with man. Reconciliation therefore means to change from enmity to amity. "Primarily, reconciliation is what God accomplishes, exercising His grace toward sinful man on the ground of the death of Christ. On the basis of this, men are invited to be reconciled, that is, to change their attitude, and accept God's provision" (W.E.Vine). Not once is God said to be reconciled. The enmity is alone on our part: we to Him, not Him to us. So:

i) The enjoyment of reconciliation, verse 18. "And all things are of God, who hath reconciled us to himself by Jesus Christ." It has been accomplished entirely by God. "And all things are of God..." That is, just as the first creation was by Christ, so the new creation is by Him. But it must be shared with others. Thus:

ii) The ministry of reconciliation, verses 18-19. "And hath given to us the ministry of reconciliation; to wit, that God was in Christ, reconciling the world unto himself, not imputing their trespasses unto them."

Notice: "hath reconciled us...hath given to us the ministry of reconciliation". Compare Colossians 1 verses 21-29. The "ministry of reconciliation" is now defined: "To wit, that God was in Christ, reconciling the world unto himself, not imputing their trespasses unto them". We should notice:

- "That God was in Christ". As P.E.Hughes observes "there has never been unanimity as to how the opening clause of this verse should be understood". Some say that it means that 'God was in Christ, reconciling the world to Himself': others say that it means that 'in Christ God was reconciling the world to Himself'. The past tense supports the latter. God, at a historical moment was reconciling the world unto Himself. Compare Romans 5 verse 10, "Much more then, being now justified by his blood, we shall be saved from wrath through him. For if, when we were enemies, we were reconciled to God through the death of his Son, much more, being reconciled, we shall be saved by his life".

- "Reconciling the world unto himself." See also Colossians 1 verse 20, "By him to reconcile all things unto himself, by him, I say, whether they be things in earth, or things in heaven". Compare "hath reconciled us" here (v.18). Not that God needed to be reconciled because of His enmity and hostility towards us. But His holiness demanded satisfaction for man's sin.

- "Not imputing their trespasses unto them." "Imputing" has sense of 'reckoning'. We might be inclined to say that "them" are believers, but the context ("reconciling the world unto himself") suggests otherwise. The words, "not imputing their trespasses unto them", mean that God has not yet reckoned with men in connection with their sins.

Thus reconciliation had been made available to all: His work is sufficient: but only actual in the case of believers.

iii)   The word of reconciliation, verse 19. "Word" here is *logos.* Compare Ephesians 1 verse 13, "the word of truth, the gospel of your salvation"; Colossians 1 verse 5, "the word of the truth of the gospel"; 1 Corinthians 1 verse 18, "the word of the cross" (RV): "the preaching of the cross" (AV).

The Greek word *logos* indicates what is true and trustworthy, as opposed to *mythos* which indicates what is fictional and spurious.

iv)   The preaching of reconciliation, verses 20-21. In undertaking the "ministry of reconciliation" and in conveying the "word of reconciliation", Paul and his companions acted as ambassadors. "Now then we are ambassadors for Christ, as though God did beseech (you) by us: we pray (you) in Christ's stead, be ye reconciled to God" or 'We are ambassadors therefore on behalf of Christ, as though God were intreating by us..." (RV). See Proverbs 13 verse 17, "A wicked messenger falleth into mischief but a faithful ambassador is health". We should notice:

- The character of the preaching. An ambassador acts and speaks, not only on behalf of, but also in the place of, the sovereign from whom he receives his commission. An ambassador is a representative of another country and another monarch. He is a citizen of another country. He promotes the interests of another country. He seeks to enhance the reputation of another country. He knows the mind and will of that country.

There is therefore a need for faithfulness and precision. This is not a figure of speech or an analogy, but quite factual. God speaks through Christ's ambassadors.

- The entreaty by the preachers. "As though God did beseech (you) by us: we pray (you) in Christ's stead, be ye reconciled to God" or 'We are ambassadors therefore on behalf of Christ, as though God were intreating by us…" (RV).

Note: the word of reconciliation to the world at large is in view here, omitting "you", "as though God did beseech by us: we pray in Christ's stead".

In verse 19, we have God's initiative in reconciliation: "reconciling the world unto himself". In verse 20, we have the preacher's involvement in reconciliation. "Beseech…pray." "The message of reconciliation is not something which Christ's ambassador announces with impersonal detachment" (P.E.Hughes). "Beseech" (*parakaleo*) is a stronger word than 'ask'. "Pray" (*deomai*) is sometimes rendered 'beseech' and has the meaning 'to desire' or 'long for. In verse 20, we have the sinner's invitation: "be ye reconciled to God".

> *I am a stranger here within a foreign land:*
> *My home is far away upon a golden strand.*
> *Ambassador to be, of realms beyond the sea:*
> *I'm here on business for my King.*
>
> *This is the message that I bring,*
> *A message angels fain would sing,*
> *'Oh be ye reconciled',*
> *Thus saith my Lord and King,*
> *'O be ye reconciled to God'.*

- The basis of the preaching, verse 21. "For he hath made him to be sin for us, who knew no sin; that we might be made the righteousness of God in him."

The invitation, "Be reconciled", is therefore accompanied by a declaration of the ground on which reconciliation has been effected, and is available. It is a continuation of "be ye reconciled to God". We should notice:

- "Made him (to be) sin for us". Not 'made a sinner for us'. A sinless one must die. Not made a sin-offering (true elsewhere as the "lamb of God") for us. But here "made sin for us". But in what sense? He was made the subject of God's wrath and judgment for us. He was reckoned to be sin for us. God treated His beloved son as sin must be treated

- "Who knew no sin". Compare Hebrews 4 verse 15; 1 Peter 2 verse 22; 1 John 3 verse 5; Hebrews 7 verse 26. Here, He "knew no sin" in His own consciousness.

As God, it goes without saying. As man, it is of vital importance that it should be equally true. Note: His own consciousness bore testimony: John 8 verse 46 ("Which of you convinceth me of sin?"); heaven bore testimony (Matthew 3: 17: 17: 5); the Roman governor bore testimony: ("I find no fault in this man", Luke 23: 4: also Luke 23: 14, 22); people at Calvary bore testimony (Luke 23: 41, 47). Compare 1 Peter 3 verse 18, "Christ also hath once suffered for sins, the just for the unjust" ('the righteous for the unrighteous') that he might bring us to God".

- "That we might be made the righteousness of God in him" or "that we might become God's righteousness in him" (JND). Not "righteous", but "the righteousness of God". It should be noted that "just as Paul does not say that Christ was not made sinful, but sin, for us, so also he does not say that in Him we are made righteous… but *righteousness*, indeed, even more expressly, the righteousness of God" (P.E.Hughes).

The Lord Jesus took our place with its consequences ("He was "made… sin for us") that we might have His place and its consequences ("that we might be made the righteousness of God in him"). Our sin was reckoned to Christ. His righteousness is reckoned to us. We have 'become God's righteousness in him'.

We are reconciled to God only because of the death of Christ. Reconciliation cannot be separated from His sacrifice at Calvary.

> *Oh, wondrous cross! Oh, precious blood!*
> *Oh, death by which I live!*
> *The sinless One, for me made sin,*
> *Doth now His wondrous heart within*
> *Eternal refuge give!*

2 CORINTHIANS

"Receive not the grace of God in vain"

Read Chapter 6:1 - 7:1

This chapter may be divided into four paragraphs as follows: *(1)* a united appeal (vv.1-3); *(2)* an unqualified commendation (vv.4-10); *(3)* an unrequited love (vv.11-13); *(4)* an unequal yoke (vv.14-18). The last paragraph ends with Chapter 7 verse 1.

1) A UNITED APPEAL, vv.1-3

Notice the connection with Chapter 5: "We **then,** as workers together with him, beseech you also that ye receive not the grace of God in vain". We may divide this sub-section as follows: *(a)* the unity of the appeal; *(b)* the burden of the appeal; *(c)* the example of the appeal; *(d)* the power for the appeal.

a) The unity of the appeal

"We then, as workers together with him." Note the italicised words ("with him"). The text should therefore read, "We then as workers together (*sunergeo*)". The word is employed in Mark 16 verse 20, "the Lord working with them (*sunergeo*)"; in 1 Corinthians 16 verse 16, "every one that helpeth (*sunergeo*) with us and laboureth"; Romans 16 verse 21, "Timotheus my workfellow (*sunergos*)"; Colossians 4 verse 11, "These only are my fellowworkers (*sunergos*)unto the kingdom of God, which have been a comfort unto me".

Compare 1 Corinthians 3 verse 9, "we are labourers together (*sunergos*) with God" or "we are God's fellow-labourers" (RV). That is, Paul and Apollos, fellow-workers, both belong to God: they are nothing in themselves.

The reference to "workers together" here could be to "me and Silvanus and Timotheous" (2 Cor. 1: 19).

b) The burden of the appeal

"That ye receive not the grace of God in vain." This is explained by reference to the subject matter at the end of Chapter 5, where he speaks of *reconciliation:*

- "And all things are of God, who hath *reconciled* us to himself by Jesus Christ" (v.18).

- "And hath given to us the ministry of *reconciliation*" (v.18).

- "God was in Christ, *reconciling* the world unto himself" (v.19).

- "And hath committed unto us the word of *reconciliation"* (v.19).

- "We pray (you) in Christ's stead, be ye *reconciled* to God" (v.20).

But in particular, the "grace of God" is displayed in the final verse, "For he hath made him to be sin for us, who knew no sin: that we might be made the righteousness of God in him" (5: 21). The Lord Jesus took our place, with all its consequences, that we might have His place, with all its consequences. What grace!

How could they "receive...the grace of God in vain?" By failing to live in a manner consistent with their reconciliation to God. That is, in the words of verse 15, by living "unto themselves", rather than "unto him which died for them and rose again". Or, in the words of Chapter 6 verse 17, by failing to "come...out from among them, and be ye separate, saith the Lord".

To "receive...the grace of God in vain" does not imply loss of salvation, but loss of the object for which that grace has been extended to us. Compare 1 Corinthians 15 verse 10, "his grace which was bestowed upon me was not in vain (*kenos*)".

We rejoice in "the grace of God", but has there been an appropriate change in our lives? See Titus 2 verses 11-12, "For the grace of God that bringeth salvation hath appeared to all men, teaching us, that, denying ungodliness and worldy lusts, we should live soberly, righteously, and godly, in this present world". Else, we have "received...the grace of God in vain". The word "vain" *(kenos)* has the sense of the hollowness of anything.

Hence, in view of the implications of this, the strong word employed: "we... beseech you". It means 'to entreat' *(parakaleo)*. In Chapter 5 verse 20, it is used in connection with Gospel preaching: in Chapter 6 verse 1, it is used in connection with the Lord's people.

c) The example of the appeal

Verse 1 leads directly to verse 3. So verse 2 is a parenthesis. We therefore read as follows: "We then, as workers together with him, beseech you also that ye receive not the grace of God in vain...giving no offence in any thing, that the ministry be not blamed".

The sense of the passage is therefore:

i) "We beseech you that ye receive not the grace of God in vain", and

ii) We "give no offence in anything that **our** (see RV) ministry be not blamed".

So Paul tells the Corinthians that he gave them no occasion to stumble, incurring blame on himself, and thus causing them to "receive...the grace of God in vain". Note the words: "**offence**" *(proskopos),* meaning a stumblingblock. There was no reason in Paul and his companions for the Corinthians to stumble. The word "**blamed**" *(momaomai)* means 'to find fault with'. It occurs again in Chapter 8 verse 20. It could also convey the suggestion of mockery and ridicule.

To summarise: there was no discrepancy between the standard Paul enjoined on the Corinthians, and his own standard of conduct.

d) The power for the appeal

This brings us to the parenthesis in verse 2: "For he saith, I have heard thee in a time accepted, and in the day of salvation have I succoured thee: behold, now is the accepted time; behold, now is the day of salvation".

This cites Isaiah 49 verse 8, "Thus saith the LORD, In an acceptable time have I heard thee, and in a day of salvation have I helped thee". The passage refers to the blessing of the Gentiles through Christ. See verse 6: "I will also give thee for a light to the Gentiles..." Paul now says that 'time' is *'now'*, thus adding to the citation of Isaiah 49 verse 8 the words, "Behold, now is the accepted time; behold, now is the day of salvation".

But the actual words quoted in verse 2, from Isaiah 49, speak of divine help: "In the day of salvation I have **helped** thee". The parenthesis therefore teaches that there was help available so that they need not "receive...the grace of God in vain". (Isaiah 49: 8 answers Isaiah 49: 4: "I have laboured in **vain**, I have spent my strength for nought, and in **vain**").

Having said, "giving no offence in any thing that the (our) ministry be not blamed", Paul now shows that the reverse was true. So in verse 3, it is "giving no offence", and verse 4 it is "approving (commending) ourselves". If in verse 3, the ministry was not to be blamed, then in verse 4, the ministers were to be commended. This brings us to:

2) AN UNQUALIFIED COMMENDATION, vv.4-10

We should carefully note the following in connection with the words "commending ourselves":

i)   That this commendation was necessary in view of his adversaries. See Chapter 3 verse 1; Chapter 4 verse 2; Chapter 5 verse 12.

ii)   That this commendation was not so much by word, but by deed and character.

iii)   That this commendation concerned their status "*as the ministers (servant)s of God*". They were demonstrated to be the servants of God through what follows. Note: Paul is not making grandiose claims here. He describes himself and his colleagues simply 'servants of God'.

Paul's commendation involves three things *(a)* the endurance of hardships in their lives (vv.4-5); *(b)* the spiritual qualities in their lives (vv.6-8a); *(c)* the paradoxes in their lives (vv.8b-10)

a) The endurance of hardships commended them, vv.4-5

"But in all things approving ourselves as the ministers of God" or "but in everything commending ourselves as the ministers (servants) of God in **much endurance** ('patience', AV)" (JND), in the following circumstances. (Note: it is "patience" in circumstances" and "longsuffering" with people). Three triplets follow: *(i)* their hardships in **general terms** (v.4): "afflictions… necessities…distresses"; *(ii)* Their hardships **at the hands of men** (v.5a): "stripes…imprisonments…tumults"; *(iii)* their hardships which they accepted **voluntarily** (v.5b): "labours…watchings…fastings".

i)   Their hardships in general terms, v.4

"In afflictions." The word *thlipsis* means 'a pressing, pressure. It is found in Acts 14 verse 22, "we must through much tribulation (*thlipsis*) enter into the kingdom of God", and Acts 20 verse 23, "bonds and afflictions (*thlipsis*) abide me".

"In necessities." The word "necessities" means 'what must needs be' (W.E.Vine). That is, 'what must needs be' because they were servants of God. This is illustrated in 1 Corinthians 4 verse 11, "Even to this present hour we both hunger and thirst, and are naked, and are buffeted, and have no certain dwelling place…"

"In distresses." The word *stenochoria* means 'narrowness of place - straits - anguish'. Situations of utter perplexity without apparent deliverance. See Chapter 4 verse 8, "We are troubled on every side, yet not **distressed** (i.e. there is a way out); we are perplexed, but not in despair". See also Chapter 6 verse 12, "Ye are not **straitened** in us, but ye are **straitened** in your own bowels".

ii)   Their hardships at the hands of men, vv.5a

"In stripes." See also Chapter 11 verse 23, "In stripes above measure"; Chapter 11 verse 24, "Of the Jews five times received I forty stripes save one"; Chapter 11 verse 25, "Thrice was I beaten with rods".

"In imprisonments." See Chapter 11 verse 23, "In prisons more more frequent".

"In tumults." Meaning 'disturbances/commotions. As at Pisidian Antioch (Acts 13: 50), Iconium (Acts 14: 5), Lystra (Acts 14: 19), Philippi (Acts 16: 22), Thessalonica (Acts 17: 5), Corinth (Acts 18: 12), Ephesus (Acts 19: 23).

iii)   Their hardships which they accepted voluntarily, v.5b

"In labours." Laborious toil, involving weariness.

"In watchings." Sleeplessness: doubtless in devotion to work and to prayer.

"In fastings." Not formal fastings, but voluntary fastings to enable uninterrupted work and devotion.

b) The spiritual qualities in their lives commended them, vv.6-8a

Paul now enumerates the spiritual qualities and resources that enabled them to be "in much patience (endurance)" in the circumstances described. So it was "by..." (AV). However "by" should be "in" as in verses 4-5. The Greek preposition in still *'en'*.

i)   "By pureness." That is, "pureness" of life and motive. The word *hagnotes* means pure from defilement: not contaminated.

ii)   "By knowledge." That is, knowledge of the truth.

iii)   "By longsuffering." The word "longsuffering" (*makrothumia*) comes from *macros*, meaning 'long', and *thumos*, meaning 'temper'. It has been defined as 'the forebearance which endures injuries and evil deeds without being provoked to anger and vengeance'.

iv)   "By kindness." The word means 'good' or 'pleasant'.

v)   "By the Holy Spirit." A seemingly unusual inclusion with the spiritual qualities listed. The teaching, surely, is that the Holy Spirit cannot be separated from the gifts and graces which He imparts. Here, in particular, it is holiness of character.

vi)   "By love unfeigned." Unhypocritical love. See 1 Peter 1 verse 22, "Ye have purified your souls in obeying the truth through the Spirit unto unfeigned love of the brethren..."

vii)   "By the word of truth." See Ephesians 1 verse 13, "The word of truth, the gospel of your salvation".

*viii) **"By the power of God."*** The power displayed in his preaching. See 1 Corinthians 2 verse 3-5.

ix) **"By the armour of righteousness on the right hand and on the left."** (Note the preposition here, *'dia'*, meaning 'through'). The word "armour" translates *hoplon* meaning 'weapon.' Compare 2 Corinthians 10 verse 4, "For the weapons of our warfare are not carnal, but mighty through God to the pulling down of strongholds". Paul may refer here to the **right** hand for offence, and the **left** hand for defence. But he probably means prepared for attack from any quarter.

x) **"By honour and dishonour."** The preposition is again *'dia'*. He must be careful to commend himself as the servant of God whether **popular** or **despised** by others.

xi) **"By evil report and good report."** The preposition is again *'dia'*. This refers to what is said in his absence, hence the word "report". As opposed to "honour and dishonour" which refer to **personal** treatment.

c) The paradoxes in their lives commended them, vv.8b-10

A series of paradoxes follows, prefixed by "as". Note: We should notice that the first phrase refers to Paul and his colleagues as seen by men: the second phrase refers to them as seen by God.

i) **"As deceivers and yet true."** "As **deceivers**": this is what men perpetrated, and how men branded him. (See, for example, Romans 3: 8). It refers, doubtless, to his calumniators. "And yet ***true***": see Chapter 4 verse 2, "By manifestation of the truth commending ourselves to every man's conscience in the sight of God"; Chapter 2 verse 17, "In the sight of God speak we in Christ".

ii) **"As unknown, and yet well known."** "As **unknown.**" possibly referring, ironically to Chapter 3 verse 1, "Do we begin again to commend ourselves? or need we, as some others, epistles of commendation to you, or letters of commendation from you?" "And yet **well known".** See 2 Timothy 2 verse 19, "The Lord knoweth them that are his".

iii) **"As dying, and, behold, we live."** "As **dying.**" See Chapter 1 verse 8-9. See also 1 Corinthians 15 verse 31, "I die daily". "And, behold, we *live*". See Chapter 1 verse 10. "Behold" - there is a sense of wonder here - "Behold, we live!"

iv) *"As chastened, and not killed."* This is possibly a reference to Psalm 118 verse 17, "I shall not die, but live, and declare the works of the LORD. The LORD hath chastened me sore, but he hath not given me over unto death". "As *chastened.*" We need to bear in mind that this does not imply sinfulness on the part of the recipient, but training. Thus the circumstances through which he passed were part of a divine process to develop character. "And not *killed*". God was not intent on his destruction - as may have been suggested - but on his good.

v) *"As sorrowful, yet alway rejoicing."* "As *sorrowful.*" Compare Chapter 2 verses 13-14, which refer to sorrow over conditions at Corinth. "Yet alway *rejoicing.*" Paul and his colleagues rejoiced none the less in the progress of the gospel.

vi) *"As poor, yet making many rich."* Not 'as poor...yet rich', but "yet *making* many rich". Compare Revelation 2 verse 9; 3 verse 17. "As *poor*". Paul counted all loss for Christ. See 1 Corinthians 4 verse 11-13, "We both hunger and thirst, and are naked, and are buffeted, and have no certain dwelling place". "Yet making many *rich.*" See Acts 20: 20, "I kept back nothing that was profitable unto you, but have shewed you, and have taught you publickly, and from house to house".

vii) *"As having nothing, yet possessing all things."* "As having *nothing*". See, again, 1 Corinthians 4 verses 11-13. Humanly speaking, without home, money, possessions: hated, hunted and despised. "Yet possessing *all things.*" *"*All things are yours" (1 Cor. 3: 21); "How shall he not with him also freely give us all things" (Rom. 8: 32); "His divine power hath given unto us all things that pertain unto life and godliness" (2 Pet.1: 3); "Heirs of God, and joint-heirs with Christ" (Rom. 8: 17).

Note these paradoxes in the perfect Servant

i) *"As deceivers, and yet true."* "Sir, we remember that that deceiver said..." (Matt. 27: 63). See also John 7 verses 12, 47.

ii) *"As unknown, and yet well known."* "We know that God spake unto Moses, but as for this fellow, we know not whence he is" (John 9: 29).

iii) ***"As dying, and, behold, we live."*** "I am he that liveth, and was dead; and, behold I am alive for evermore" (Rev. 1: 18).

iv) ***"As chastened, and not killed."*** "Though he were a son, yet learned he obedience by the things which he suffered" (Heb. 5: 8).

v) ***"As sorrowful, yet always rejoicing."*** "A man of sorrows, and acquainted with grief" (Isaiah 53: 3). "These things have I spoken unto you, that my joy might remain in you" (John 15: 11).

vi) ***"As poor, yet making many rich."*** "For ye know the grace of our Lord Jesus Christ, that, though he was rich, yet for your sakes he became poor, that ye through his poverty might be rich" (2 Cor. 8: 9).

vii) ***"As having nothing, and yet possessing all things."*** "The foxes have holes, and the birds of the air have nests; but the Son of man hath not where to lay his head" (Matt. 8: 20). "Appointed heir of all things" (Heb. 1: 2).

> *It is the way the Master went:*
> *Should not the servant tread it still?*

Thus in all circumstances, favourable or otherwise, Paul and his companions 'commended themselves as the servants of God'.

3) UNREQUITED (or UNREWARDED) LOVE, vv.11-13

Paul now seeks a response of love from those he loved. Paul is deeply moved here: "O ye Corinthians, our mouth is open unto you, our heart is enlarged" (v. 11). Compare "O Philippians" (Philippians 4: 15, JND: "Now ye Philippians", AV); "O foolish (Galatians" 3: 1). Paul was deeply stirred: hence the intensity of his language. Compare Psalm 45, "My heart is inditing a good matter: I speak of the things which I have made touching the King; my tongue is the pen of a ready writer". Paul speaks about "mouth" and "heart": the Psalmist speaks about "heart" and "tongue".

Paul spoke freely to them out of, literally, a 'broad' heart. That is, out of great affection. "Ye are not straitened in us" (v. 12). The word "straitened" (*stenochoreo*) derives from two words *steno*, meaning 'narrow', and *choros*, meaning 'a space'. Hence 'to be pressed for room'. There was no restriction in Paul's heart so far as the Corinthians were concerned.

There was evidently restriction on the part of the Corinthians towards Paul: "But ye are straitened in your own bowels" (v.12). The word "bowels" has the idea of affections. Paul did not squeeze them out of his affections, even though they did so to him. But he desired a similar disposition on the part of his spiritual children: "Now for a recompence in the same...be ye also enlarged" (v.13). The word "recompence" means 'a reward', or 'requital'. That is, he requested an affection from them equivalent to his own. He makes this request as a father who should enjoy a primary place in the affections of his children (v.13). See 1 Corinthians 4 verses 14-15, "In Christ Jesus I have begotten you through the gospel". See also 2 Corinthians 12 verse 15, "And I will very gladly spend and be spent for you; though the more abundantly I love you, the less I be loved".

We should notice that while Paul's love from them did not depend on their love for him, he was far from satisfied with the situation.

4) THE UNEQUAL YOKE, 6: 14 - 7: 1

This section is bounded on either side by sections stressing his love and affection for them. See Chapter 6 verses 11-13 and Chapter 7 verses 2-3. The warning against the unequal yoke, and compromise, is thus set against the context of Paul's affection for them, and flows from that affection. But there is another connection: on the one hand Paul has asked for open hearts towards him, but now he asks for closed hearts towards evil.

These verses set out both sides of separation: it is *(a)* negative (6: 14-16a) and *(b)* positive (6: 16b - 7: 1)

(a) Negative separation, 6: 14-16a

"Be ye not unequally yoked together with unbelievers." (In the Old Testament, see the relationship between Jehoshaphat and Ahab: note the word "affinity".) The idea is of a double yoke under which two animals work side by side, possibly referring here to Deuteronomy 22 verse 10, "Thou shalt not plough with an ox and ass together". The walk is different, and the height is different. See Amos 3 verse 3, "Can two walk together, except they be agreed?"

Whilst this statement is applicable in principle to a wide variety of situations, it is, quite clearly, a warning in the first instance, against participation in idolatry. We should notice the words employed:

i)   *"Fellowship"*. This translates *metoche,* meaning a partnership. See Luke 5 verse 7, "they beckoned unto their partners". We should add that three verses later, where the word "partners" appears again, the underlying word is *koinonos* (Luke 5: 10).

ii)   *"Communion"*. This translates *koinonia,* a having in common.

iii)   *"Concord"*. This translates *sumphonesis*, whence our English word 'symphony'. It means 'a sounding together'. It is rendered "music" in Luke 15 verse 25.

iv)   *"Part"*. This translates *meros*, meaning 'a portion'.

v)   *"Agreement"*. This translates *sunkatathesis*, with the idea of being 'well-minded' or 'well disposed towards'.

Thus the passage does not command monasticism, or the seclusion of the cloister. It demands, not no contact, but no participation. Separation is not isolation. It is not 'no **contact***,* but 'no **contract***'* with evil.

There are five references to things which are mutually exclusive: they can be grouped as follows:

i)   **Different principles.** "Righteousness" and "unrighteousness", then "light" and "darkness".

ii)   **Different authorities.** "Christ" and "Belial". In the Old Testament, we read of the 'sons of Belial' (Judges 19: 22) and the 'children of Belial' (Judges 20: 13). In Nahum 1 verse 11, the word translated 'the wicked one', is 'Belial'.

iii)   **Different people.** "He that believeth" and "an infidel" (i.e. an unbeliever).

iv)   **Different places.** "The temple of God" and "idols".

(b) Positive separation, 6: 16b - 7: 1

Having said "And what agreement hath the temple of God with idols", Paul continues, "for ye are the temple of the living God". That is, they are in fellowship with "the *living* God" as opposed to *lifeless* idols. We should notice the following:

i)   *The holiness of the temple*. In saying "ye are the temple of the living God" Paul refers to the *assembly* at Corinth. See 1 Corinthians 3 verses 16-17, "Know ye not that ye are the temple (RV 'a temple') of God, and that the Spirit of God dwelleth in you? If any man defile the temple of God, him shall God destroy; for the temple of God is holy, which temple ye are". The believers at Corinth were therefore to have the character of those in fellowship with God, and this is clearly stated in the words "ye are the temple of the living God; *as God hath said*, I will dwell in them, and walk in them; and I will be their God, and they shall be my people". The words, "as God hath said", refer to Leviticus 26 verses 11-12, "And I will set my tabernacle among you: and my soul shall not abhor you. And I will walk among you, and will be your God, and ye shall be my people". See also, for example, Ezekiel 37 verse 26. Note Psalm 78 verse 41, "Yea, they turned back, and tempted God, and limited the Holy One of Israel".

ii)   *The separation from idolatry.*   "Wherefore come out from among them, and be ye separate, saith the Lord, and touch not the unclean thing, and I will receive you..." (v.17). Paul now refers to Isaiah 52 verse 11, referring to return from captivity: "Depart ye, depart ye, go ye out from hence, touch not the unclean thing". Israel were to leave Babylon with all its idolatry, and the believers at Corinth were ensure that they were not defiled by idolatrous Corinth. Do notice the words, "Come ye out....I will receive you". So He is *already outside!*

iii)   *The relationship with God*. Should it be thought that separation from evil means a lonely pathway ahead, Paul makes clear that the reverse is true! The God who says "come out from among them, and be ye separate, saith the Lord, and touch not the unclean thing, and I will receive you" (v.17) continues by saying, "And (I) will be a Father unto you, and ye shall be my sons and daughters, saith the Lord Almighty" (v.18). Paul now refers to Isaiah 43 verse 6, a passage which refers, again, to return from captivity: "bring my sons from far, and my daughters from the ends of the earth". Compare 2 Samuel 7 verse 14, "I will be his father, and he shall be my son". Compare Jeremiah 31 verse 1. "At the same time, saith the Lord, I will be the God of all the families of Israel, and they shall be my people".

We should note that the words "And I will be a Father unto you" do not mean that if we "come out from among them" then He will **become** our Father, but that we will **enjoy** Him as Father in all His fatherly care and provision.

iv)   *The purity of life.* "Having therefore *these* promises, dearly beloved (one word "beloved"), let us cleanse ourselves from all filthiness of the flesh and spirit, perfecting holiness in the fear of God" (7: 1).   We should note the following:

- "Having therefore these promises". That is, having them on a continuing basis. What promises? "I will dwell in them...I will be their God...I will receive you...I will be a Father unto you".

- "Let us cleanse ourselves". The tense here is cleanse ourselves once and for all. Notice too that Paul does not say 'do *you* cleanse yourselves', but, "let *us* cleanse ourselves". The preacher should always put his teaching into practice in his own life

- "Filthiness" means a soiling or defilement. "Flesh and spirit" refers to "all defilement of every possible kind, both external and the internal: both seen and unseen, both public and private" (P.E.Hughes).

- "Perfecting holiness in the fear of God". The word *epiteleo* means 'to bring to the end' (W.E.Vine). Compare Galatians 3 verse 3; Philippians 1 verse 6. In the words of P.E.Hughes, "We are intended to press on towards the goal of perfection (Heb. 6: 1). And this is to be done 'in the fear of God' - that is, in reverence and devotion towards Him to whom we owe everything, in awe of Him at whose judgment-seat we shall have to give an account of the things done in the body (5: 10)".

2 CORINTHIANS

"Ye sorrowed to repentance"

Read Chapter 7:2-16

In introducing the teaching in this chapter, we should notice the following. It is most important to look at any section of the Scriptures in its proper context.

a)   Paul begins with an appeal: "We...beseech you also that ye receive not the grace of God in vain" (6: 1). The "grace of God" here describes the "word of reconciliation" (5: 19). To "receive not the grace of God in vain" is to rest on the work of Christ, and to live appropriately (5: 15; 7: 1).

b)   Paul and his fellow-labourers were no stumblingblock to them in this regard: "giving no offence in anything" (6: 3). He continues by drawing attention to his moral right to say "in all things approving ('commending', JND) ourselves as the ministers of God" (6: 4). Paul and his colleagues were in a position to commend themselves: *(i)* in view of the hardships they endured (6: 4-5); *(ii)* in view of their spiritual qualities (6: 6-8a); *(iii)* in view of the paradoxes in their lives (6: 8b-10).

c)   Paul's desire that they should not "receive the grace of God in vain" flowed out of deep affection for them, even though their own affection for him was limited (6: 11-12).

d)   Out of that deep affection for them, Paul urges them to live as people who had received the grace of God. Relationships were to be regulated, and holiness achieved, all this in the context of idolatry, and its attachments (6: 14-18). If they continued with idolatrous associations, they would 'receive the grace of God in vain'.

Now Paul appeals to them: "Receive us; we have wronged no man, we have corrupted no man, we have defrauded no man" (7: 2). Sadly, the appeal was necessary in view of their attitude towards him: "Ye are not straitened in us, but ye are straitened in your own bowels. Now for a recompence (I speak as unto my children) be ye also enlarged" (6: 12-13).

The chapter may be divided as follows: *(1)* the request for fellowship (vv.2-3): "Receive us" (v.2); *(2)* the rejoicing in tribulation (vv.4-7): "I am exceeding joyful...I rejoiced the more" (vv.4, 7); *(3)* the response to his letter (vv.8-11): "For though I made you sorry with a letter...the same epistle hath made you sorry" (v.8); *(4)* the reason for his letter (v.12): "I wrote...that our care for you in the sight of God might appear unto you"; *(5)* the result of their obedience (vv.13-16): "he (Titus) remembereth the obedience of you all" (v.15). Paul's rejoicing in this chapter should be noted:

- He rejoiced at the report of Titus (vv.4-7); "I am exceeding joyful" (v.4); "I rejoiced" (v.7). In this, he experienced the help of the "God of all comfort" (1: 3-4): "we are troubled (pressed) on every side, yet not straitened (in despair)" (4: 8). Paul rejoiced, not only on account of his personal satisfaction, but also on account of the satisfaction of Titus. Paul was encouraged because Titus was encouraged.

- He rejoiced at the response to his letter (vv.8-12). "Now I rejoice, not that ye were made sorry, but that ye sorrowed to repentance". He had made them sorry: he was sorry that he made them sorry: but he was not sorry that he made them sorry unto repentance! He rejoiced "that ye might receive damage ('suffer loss') by us in nothing" (v.9), that is, at the judgment seat. But it should be said that we can 'suffer loss' by our negligence in not dealing with a matter.

- He rejoiced at the reception of Titus (vv.13-16): "exceedingly the more joyed we for the joy of Titus" (v.13). "I rejoice, therefore that I have confidence in you in all things" (v.16).

1) THE REQUEST FOR FELLOWSHIP, vv.2-3

We should notice *(a)* the nature of the appeal (v.2); *(b)* the grounds of the appeal (v.2); *(c)* the atmosphere of the appeal (v.3).

a) The nature of the appeal, v.2

"Receive us; we have wronged no man..." This refers back to Chapter 6 verse

12. "Receive us" is, literally, 'make room for us' or "Open your hearts to us" (RV). This is the very opposite to their attitude towards him, necessitating him to say, "ye are straitened in your own bowels" (6: 12). It is the appeal of a man who loved them, and who longed for their fellowship. He felt deeply the resistance to him on the part of some at Corinth, especially as they had no ground on which to exclude him. He fears that they were still keeping him at a distance.

b) The grounds of the appeal, v2

"We have wronged no man, we have corrupted no man, we have defrauded no man". This covers the practical, doctrinal and financial relationship between Paul and the Corinthians.

i) **"Wronged no man."** This expresses his relationship with them practically and in general terms. The word "wronged" means to act unjustly towards someone.

ii) **"Corrupted no man."** This expresses his relationship with them doctrinally. The word "corrupted" means to destroy by means of corrupting. Not **adding** anything of a corrupting nature. It covers dishonourable dealing with people, resulting in the worsening of their condition. The word is used in 1 Corinthians 3 verse 17, "If any man defile (corrupt) the temple of God, him shall God destroy (corrupt)".

iii) **"Defrauded no man."** This expresses his relationship with them financially. Not **taking** anything from them. The word is used in Chapter 12 verses 17-18, "make a gain of you". So, Paul did not seek personal or financial advantage: "we took advantage of no man" (RV). He had not enriched himself at their expense.

These three statements probably rebutted accusations that Paul actually did these things. "Did I make gain of you by any of them whom I sent unto you? I desired Titus, and with him I sent a brother. Did Titus make a gain of you? walked we not in the same spirit? walked we not in the same steps?" As to "defrauded no man", see Acts 20 verse 33 ("I coveted no man's silver, or gold, or apparel"); 1 Thessalonians 2 verses 5, 10 ("neither at any time used we flattering words... nor a cloke of covetousness; God is witness... Ye are witnesses, and God also, how holily and justly and unblameably we behaved ourselves among you that believed").

Paul had moral grounds on which to say, "Open your hearts to us" (RV). The aorist tense (in v.2) points back to a specific time. That is, to Paul's visit to Corinth. They knew Paul's manner of life. See Chapter 1 verse 12, "in simplicity and godly sincerity, not with fleshly wisdom, but by the grace of God, we have had our conversation in the world, **and more abundantly to you-wards**".

c) The atmosphere of the appeal, v.3

"I speak not this to condemn you: for I have said before, that ye are in our hearts to die and to live with you." (Like Ittai: "As the LORD liveth, and as my lord the king liveth, surely in what place my lord the king shall be, whether in death or in life, even there also will thy servant be", 2 Sam. 15: 21). That is, he was willing to share their ills and their joys. Are **we** like this in the assembly? "'Whatever their lot, he was willing to share it with them" (A.McShane). There were no restraints in his love for them. Compare 1 John 3 verse 16, "we ought to lay down our lives for the brethren".

Quite evidently, Paul could have spoken in **recrimination** ("condemn you"), but his appeal was out of love and affection. In assembly life, we need to bear this in mind: our reaction to unjust and unwarranted attitudes should not be an aggrieved spirit - and censure - but the absence of these things, because of our love for the saints.

"For as I said before, that ye are in our hearts". See Chapter 6 verses 11-12: "O ye Corinthians, our mouth is open unto you, our heart is enlarged. Ye are not straitened in us, but ye are straitened in your own bowels". See 1 Thessalonians 3 verse 8, "For now we live, if ye stand fast in the Lord". This a 'nursing mother' attitude (1 Thess. 2: 7).

2) THE REJOICING IN TRIBULATION, vv.4-7

In these verses we should notice: *(a)* Paul's rejoicing in them (v.4); *(b)* Paul's rejoicing in adversity (vv.4-5); *(c)* the reason for Paul's rejoicing (vv.6-7).

a) Paul's rejoicing in them, v.4

Here is supporting evidence for Paul's statement, "ye are in our hearts" (v.3): "Great is my boldness of speech toward you, great is my glorying of you: I am filled with comfort, I am exceeding joyful in all our tribulation". Do note what he said **to them** ("towards you") and what he said **to others** ("great is my glorying of you"). There was no discrepancy between the two: no 'double-talk'.

"Boldness of speech" means outspokenness of speech. Compare Hebrews 4 verse 16, "Let us come boldly…" Paul speaks boldly with reference to *his love* for them. He stresses this in the epistle. See, for example, Chapter 2 verse 4: "For out of much affliction and anguish of heart I wrote unto you with many tears; not that ye should be grieved, but that ye might know *the love* which I have more abundantly unto you". His boldness in expressing his love for them is perhaps something that he could not have shown before.

His "boldness of speech" is accompanied by his glorying in them: "great is my glorying of you". He did this to Titus, see verse 14, and to the Macedonian believers in Chapter 9 verses 1-4. But why? Very clearly, it was the result of the great encouragement *they had given him* (vv.5-16). Just listen to him: "I am filled with comfort (encouragement), I am exceeding joyful (overabounding, see Romans 5 verse 20: "grace did much more abound") in all our tribulation". Do *we* give one another joy in this way? The reason for Paul's joy follows (vv.6-7), but notice first:

b) Paul's rejoicing in adversity, vv.4-5

"I am exceeding joyful in all our *tribulation.*" His rejoicing in them enabled him to rejoice in adversity. Is *our* conduct, like the conduct of the Corinthians, an *encouragement* to fellow-believers under pressure? Compare Hebrews 13 verse 17, "Obey them that have the rule over you, and submit yourselves: for they watch for you souls, as they that must give an account, that they may do it (that is, do the work - "watch for your souls") with joy, and not with grief: for that is unprofitable for you".

Paul refers to his adversity in sayng, "For, when we were come into Macedonian, our flesh had no rest, but we were troubled on every side; without were fightings, within were fears". The words, "our flesh had no rest", suggest persecution: "we were troubled on every side". "*Without* were fightings": that is, strifes, contentions. "*Within* were fears": that is, concerning the state of things at Corinth. In this connection, we must notice Paul's deep concern:

- When writing the First Epistle from Ephesus. See Chapter 2 verse 4, "for out of much affliction and anguish of heart I wrote unto you with many tears".

- After dispatching the letter, at Troas. See Chapter 2 verses 12-13, "Furthermore, when I came to Troas... I had no rest in my spirit, because I found not Titus my brother..."

- When arriving in Macedonia. See Chapter 7 verse 5, "For, when we were come into Macedonia, our flesh had no rest, but we were troubled on every side; without were fightings, within were fears". Using different words, Paul says virtually the same thing later in the epistle: "Besides those things that are without, that which cometh upon me daily, the care of all the churches" (11: 28).

c) The reason for Paul's rejoicing, vv.6-7

"Nevertheless God, that comforteth those that are cast down, comforted us by the coming of Titus". The word translated "coming" (*parousia*) means the arrival and presence of Titus. For reference to "comfort" see Chapter 1 verses 3-4. The coming of Titus, and its result for Paul, in his adversity, illustrates Chapter 4 verse 8, "we are pressed ('troubled', AV) on every side, yet not straitened ('in despair', AV)" (RV).

The word "**comforteth**" (God habitually comforts) means 'to encourage'. The words "**cast down**" mean, literally, humbled, with the idea of being downcast. So God brought relief to beleaguered Paul at just the right moment.

But Paul's rejoicing was not just the personal joy in meeting up with Titus (we rightly sing, 'Great the joy when Christians meet'), but in **the news that he carried.** "And not by his coming only, but by the consolation wherewith he was comforted in you, when he told us your earnest desire, your mourning, your fervent mind toward me; so that I rejoiced the more". We must notice:

i) **Titus himself was encouraged.** "The consolation wherewith he was comforted in you." The words "consolation" and "comfort" are the same (*paraklesis*), meaning 'a calling to one's side'.

ii) **Paul was encouraged because Titus was encouraged.** "God... comforted us by the coming of Titus; and not by his coming only, but by the consolation wherewith he was comforted in you."

iii) **Paul was encouraged by their "earnest desire...mourning...your fervent mind" toward him.** As always in Scripture, words are well-worth careful attention. We should notice here:

- "Your **earnest desire**", that is, their longing to see him.

- "Your **mourning**": the word here (*odurmos*) means 'to bewail'. Compare 1 Corinthians 5 verse 2, "Ye have not rather mourned (*pentheo*)". The other occurrence in the New Testament of *odurmos* is in Matthew 2 verse 18.

- "Your **fervent mind toward me**": the word "fervent" means 'zeal' *(zelos* akin to *zeo*, to be hot). It occurs in Acts 18 verse 25 (of Apollos, "fervent in the spirit"); Romans 12 verse 11 ("fervent in spirit").

But Paul's rejoicing was not based on: sentiment: it was based on:

3) THE RESPONSE TO HIS LETTER, vv.8-11

Paul did not rejoice in their change of attitude, gratifying though that certainly was: he rejoiced rather in the effect of his epistle. Wrongs had been righted. We should now notice: *(a)* Paul's twofold view of their sorrow (vv.8-9); *(b)* Paul compares two kinds of sorrow, v.10; *(c)* Paul describes their sorrow (v.11).

a) Paul's twofold view of their sorrow, vv.8-9

The Revised Version is helpful here: "For though I made you sorry (*lupeo*) with my epistle, I do not regret (*metamelomai*) it. Though I did regret (*metamlomai*), for I see that the epistle made you sorry (*lupeo*), though but for a season. Now I rejoice, not that ye were made sorry (*lupeo*), but that ye were made sorry (*lupeo*) unto repentance (*metanoya*): for ye were made sorry (*lupeo*) after a godly sort, that ye might suffer loss by us in nothing". So:

i)　Paul's epistle grieved them. It made them sorry: "I made you sorry with my epistle".

ii)　Paul did not regret this. His epistle made them sorry unto repentance. "I do not regret it…but that ye were made sorry unto repentance."

iii)　Paul did regret this. Because it was no joy to him that they were made sorry. "Now I rejoice, not that ye were made sorry…"

So, when Paul considered the effect of the First Epistle, he found no joy in their sorrow in itself, but he found great joy in *what their sorrow produced - repentance.*

There is a lesson for us here. It should give us no joy to see distress when wrong ways are pointed out, but only when that sorrow leads to the righting of wrongs committed. There is an attitude which says – 'That's told him where to get off' - and we feel that we've achieved something worthwhile!

Genuine love feels the distress of the saints. There should be no pleasure in inflicting pain - only pleasure in what is beneficial at the end. It was not sorrow - but the fruit of sorrow that caused his joy. Paul's words, "sorrowed after a godly manner" mean 'in a manner agreeable to the mind of God'.

The words, *"that ye might suffer loss by us in nothing"*, mean 'that ye might not suffer loss by our negligence in not dealing with the matter'. They would have suffered loss - that is, at the judgment seat of Christ (1 Cor. 3: 15) - had Paul not written. The purpose of godly leaders should be to ensure that the saints do not suffer loss: they must therefore act responsibly in adverse circumstances.

b) Paul compares two kinds of sorrow, v.10

"For godly sorrow worketh repentance to salvation not to be repented of ('which bringeth no regret', RV): but the sorrow of the world worketh death."

i)   Godly sorrow: this is "to salvation". That is, "to salvation" as described in Philippians 2 verse 12, "work out your own salvation". Here (v.10), it refers to a repentance not to be regretted. It is sorrow because of the *nature* of sin, causing repentance.

ii)   The sorrow of the world: this "worketh death". That is, bearing in mind James 1 verse 15, ("when lust hath conceived it bringeth forth sin, and sin when it is finished bringeth forth death"), the sorrow of the world has its fulfilment in death. Better, "anguish, so common in fallen man, only hastens his end which is death" (A.McShane). It is sorrow because of the painful *consequences* of sin.

c) Paul describes their sorrow, v.11

"For behold this selfsame thing, that ye sorrowed after a godly sort" or "ye were made sorry after a godly sort" (RV). Once again, the word study is absorbing:

i) **"Behold".** They were eager to deal with the matter after previous apathy.

ii) **"What carefulness".** This refers to diligence in the sense of earnestness.

iii) **"Clearing of yourselves".** The word "clearing" (*apologia*) signifies a defence against an accusation.

iv) **"Indignation".** That is, displeasure with themselves (anger) at previous conduct.

v) **"Fear".** Compare Acts 5 verse 11, "And great fear came upon all the church".

vi) **"Vehement desire".** This is one word *(epipothesis)* meaning 'a longing for, an earnest desire'.

vii) **"Zeal".** The word means 'fervency' *(zeelos).*

viii) **"Revenge".** Or "avenging" (RV). Not vindictiveness, but vindication of that which is right in dealing with the guilty party. See 1 Corinthans 5 verse 13.

All this leads Paul to say, "In every way ye have proved (approved: established) yourselves to be pure (*hagnos* - not contaminated) in the matter" (JND). It is important to notice that Paul does not go into detail - he simply refers to "**the matter**".

4) THE REASON FOR HIS LETTER, v.12

"Wherefore, though I wrote unto you, I did it not for his cause that had done the wrong, nor for his cause that suffered wrong, but that our care (*spoude*, translated elsewhere 'diligence', 'haste', 'forwardness') for you in the sight of God might appear unto you."

It could be said, following the Revised Version, that Paul does not deny that he had in mind the perpetrator of the offence, and of the one who had suffered because of the offence, but that the major reason was that the Corinthians might be reminded of the affection and loyalty which bound them to him as their spiritual father. Here is the RV text: "So although I wrote unto you, I wrote not for his cause that did the wrong, nor for his cause that suffered the wrong, but that your *earnest care for us* might be made manifest unto you in the sight of God". However, the AV makes better sense! Compare 1 Corinthians 4 verses 14-15, "I write not these things to shame you, but as my beloved sons I warn you. For though ye have ten thousand instructors in Christ, yet have ye not many fathers: for in Christ Jesus I have begotten you through the gospel".

We should notice the reasons given in the Second Epistle for writing the First Epistle: see Chapter 2 verses 3, 4 & 9 and here, Chapter 7 verse 12.

5) THE RESULT OF THEIR OBEDIENCE, vv.13-16

We should notice: *(a)* the result for Paul (v.13): he was encouraged; *(b)* the result for Titus (vv.14-15): his love for them was enhanced.

a) The result for Paul, v.13

i) **Paul rejoiced.** "Therefore we were comforted (encouraged) in your comfort." So the way in which the Corinthians had responded to his First Epistle brought Paul encouragement. But more follows:

ii) **Paul rejoiced because the Corinthians had encouraged Titus.** This brought Paul even more *joy:* "yea, and exceedingly the more joyed we for the joy of Titus, because his spirit was refreshed by you all".

The language here is more emphatic. Paul found greater joy in the fact that another brother had been blessed through them! The word *"refreshed"* means 'to give rest'. Compare 1 Corinthians 16 verse 18, "For they have refreshed my spirit and your's".

We should notice that "his spirit was refreshed by you *all*" See also verse 15, "he remembereth the obedience of you *all*". What greater joy to a servant of God than to see united obedience to God's word!

b) The result for Titus, vv.14-15

Titus had been sent to Corinth with good impressions of them. Paul's confidence in them had been impressed upon him. "For if I have boasted any thing to him of you, I am not ashamed; but as we spake all things to you *in truth* (the assembly at Corinth was founded on the truth of the gospel), even so our boasting, which I made before Titus, is found *a truth.*" Paul had no cause to eat his words of confidence!

What a good way to send a brother off to visit the saints - expecting the best! See 1 Corinthians 13 verse 7, "Love...beareth all things, believeth all things, hopeth all things..."

We should notice the link between the words, "even so our boasting is found in truth", and "as we spake all things to you in truth". There was a reality about the work of grace in their hearts - they really had been founded on the truth of the gospel - else they would not have recognised the need to act as they did.

Titus' love for the saints (his "inward affection") was promoted by their obedience, and the manner in which he was received by them. "And his inward affection (so it was not cosmetic!) is more abundant toward you, whilst he remembereth the obedience of you all, how with fear and trembling ye received him" (v.15). The lesson is clear: our submission to the word of God will encourage the love for each other.

It was not acceptance of tyranny, but "fear and trembling" in view of what their misdemeanours might entail. We too are to tremble at the word of God: "To this man will I look, even to him that is poor and of a contrite spirit, and trembleth at my word" (Isaiah 66: 2). We all need to bow to its counsel, and fear to transgress its commands.

The conclusion follows: "I rejoice therefore that I have confidence in you in all things" or "I rejoice that in everything (that is, in their obedience and love) I am confident as to you" (v.16, JND).

Paul is therefore emboldened to appeal in connection with the stewardship of the believers at Corinth (Chapters 8-9), and then to embark on the stern denunciation of false apostles (Chapters 10-13). He has set the atmosphere for what follows, particularly in Chapters 8-9.

2 CORINTHIANS

"For ye know the grace of our Lord Jesus Christ"

Read Chapter 8:1-24

The way in which the assembly at Corinth had responded to his First Epistle, enabled Paul to raise a further matter.

i) They had not only addressed the serious matter raised in 1 Corinthians 5, but had exhibited what Paul describes as "your fervent mind toward me; so that I rejoiced the more" (7: 7). In view of the good news from Titus, he concludes that section of the Epistle on a happy note; "I rejoice therefore that I have confidence in you in all things" (7: 16). The atmosphere was right to broach the matter of their support for the needy saints in Judaea.

ii) Rather than censuring them for their tardiness in the matter, Paul refers to the example of the believers in Macedonia. With this twofold background, he now deals with the subject of their gift, from which we may learn a great deal to help us in our own stewardship.

It is fitting that Titus, who brought good news from Corinth (7: 6), who obviously enjoyed their confidence (7: 7, 13) and loved them dearly (7: 15), should be the man who returned, with others, to collect and carry the gift to Jerusalem (8: 16-18).

This chapter may be divided as follows: *(1) The example of the churches in Macedonia, (vv.1-6).* Note the expressions, "the grace of God bestowed on the churches of Macedonia" (v.1), and "praying us with much intreaty" (v.4); *(2) The appeal to the church at Corinth (vv.7-15).* Note the expressions, "abound in this grace also" (v.7), and "perform the doing of it" (v.11); *(3) The administration of the funds for Judea (vv.16-24).* Note the expressions, "travel with us with this grace" (v.19), and "providing for honest things" (v.21).

The word "grace" (vv.1, 7, 19) is a very big word in the New Testament. It is rendered "benefit" in 2 Corinthians 1 verse 15.

1) THE EXAMPLE OF THE CHURCHES IN MACEDONIA, vv.1-6

We must notice the following: *(a)* it was the result of the grace of God (v.1); *(b)* it was the result of great sacrifice, vv.2-4; *(c)* it was the result of devotion to Christ, vv.5-6.

a) It was the result of the grace of God, v.1

"Moreover, brethren, we do you to wit ('make known to you', JND) of the grace of God bestowed on the churches of Macedonia." Notice that in spite of the attitude towards him at Corinth (see 6: 12), he still calls them "brethren!"

Giving is called a 'grace' (8: 1); a 'fellowship' (8: 4); an 'abundance' (8: 20); a 'ministration' (9: 1, 13), a 'bounty' (9: 5).

We should emphasise Paul's reference here to the "grace of God". The sacrificial fellowship exhibited by the Macedonian churches was produced, not by natural generosity, but by "the grace of God bestowed" on them. Most certainly, to use an earlier statement in the Epistle, the believers at Corinth had not received "the grace of God in vain" (6: 1). This reminds us that:

> *Every virtue we possess,*
> *And every victory won,*
> *And every thought of holiness,*
> *Are His alone.*

We should also notice that it is "the church**s** of Macedonia", **not** 'the Macedonian church'. Compare Galatians 1 and the expressions, "the churches of Galatia" (v.2) and "the churches of Judaea" (v.22). While there was obviously fellowship between local churches, there was no such thing as 'church federation'.

The assembly at Thessalonica, in Macedonia, had been an example in another way. See 1 Thessalonians 1 verses 6-7, "And ye became followers of us, and of the Lord, having received the word in much affliction, with joy of the Holy Ghost: so that ye were **examples** (*tupos:* a model) to all that believe in Macedonia and **Achaia**".

b) It was the result of great sacrifice, vv.2-4

How was "the grace of God" (v.1) displayed? The answer follows: "How that in a great trial of affliction (they could have excused themselves from helping on this ground!) the abundance of their joy and their deep poverty abounded unto the riches of their liberality (see definition below)" (v.2). This is a verse of contrasts:

i) "*Great trial of affliction...abundance of their joy*". The word "*trial*" means 'proof' or 'trying': "*affliction*" (*thlipsis*) means 'pressure': "*abundance*" (*perisseia*) means 'an exceeding measure - something above the ordinary', as in Romans 5 verse 17, "For if by one man's offence death reigned by one; much more they which receive abundance of grace and of the gift of righteousness shall reign in life by one, Jesus Christ".

ii) "*Deep poverty... riches of their liberality*". The word "*poverty*" is found again in verse 9 "that ye through his poverty might be rich"); "*abounded*" is the verb of "abundance"; "*liberality*" means 'simplicity' or 'single-mindedness', as opposed to duplicity (*haplous* - simple - as opposed to *diplous* - double): hence, true open-heartedness and generosity towards others, in which there is no duplicity of motive. The word occurs again Chapter 9 verse 11 ("bountifulness") and Chapter 9 verse 13 (liberal").

Only the grace of God can bring joy out of affliction, and liberality out of poverty. The assembly at Thessalonica (in Macedonia) had "received the word in much affliction with *joy* of the Holy Ghost" (1 Thess.1: 6). They had not changed! Here, it is the "abundance of their *joy*".

"Their deep poverty" and the "riches of their liberality" are discussed in verse 3: "For to their power, I bear record, yea, beyond their power they were willing of themselves..." The word "power" (*dunamis*) means 'ability', so they gave:

- *According* to their ability: "to their power (ability)". They gave until they were down to the 'bread-line'.

- *Beyond* their ability: "beyond their power (ability)". They gave until they were below the 'bread-line'.

That is, not only up to the level available after meeting basic needs, but actually over that level to the point at which those basic needs were at risk.

Compare Mark 12 verses 41-44, "Of her want did cast in all that she had". They went that far to meet the needs of fellow-believers they had never seen! They did this voluntarily: "willing of themselves" means, 'willing of one's own accord'. Compare verse 17: "of his (Titus) own accord". The value of willingness to give sacrificially in this way is greater than the actual monetary value involved.

It was certainly not a grudging willingness: "Praying us with much intreaty that we would receive the gift, and take upon us the fellowship of ministering to the saints" or "Beseeching us with much intreaty in regard to this gain, and the fellowship in the ministering" (RV). In the words of Chrysostom, "It was they, not Paul, who did the begging!" Every word is full of meaning: "**Praying**" (*deomai*) means 'beseeching': "**intreaty**" (*paraklesis*) means 'appeal': "**gift**" (*charis*) means 'grace', as in verse 6: "**fellowship**" (*koinoneo*) means 'sharing': "**ministering**" (*diakonia*) means 'serving'.

c) It was the result of devotion to Christ, vv.5-6

Giving is an integral part of our devotion to the Lord. It is the product of a life surrendered to Him, and thus to the interests of His people. We should note the order in what follows:

"And (this they did), not as we had hoped, but *(i)* first gave their **own selves** to the Lord, and *(ii)* unto us, by the will of God" (v.5). Here was the secret of their generosity. "Once the heart is surrendered, the hand will instinctively be opened" (A.McShane). The Levites "were wholly **given unto him** (Aaron) out of the children of Israel" (Num. 3: 9). But the Macedonian believers **gave themselves!** We are to 'present our bodies a living sacrifice, holy, acceptable unto God, which is our reasonable service' (Rom.12: 1).

> But we never can prove
> The delights of His love,
> Until all on the altar we lay;
> For the favour He shows,
> And the joy He bestows,
> Are for them who will trust and obey.

The **first** gift given by the Macedonians, was themselves: the **second** was their substance.

In view of this, Paul was now sending Titus to Corinth to complete the matter of their own stewardship. "Insomuch ('so that', JND) we desired Titus, that as he had begun, so he would also finish in you the same grace also" (v.6). We should read Ecclesiastes 5 verses 4-6 in this connection. The words, "as he had begun" evidently refer to 1 Corinthians 16 verses 1-4, "Now concerning the collection for the saints, as I have given order to the churches of Galatia, even so do ye. Upon the first day of the week let every one of you lay by him in store, as God hath prospered him, that there be no gatherings when I come. And when I come, whomsoever ye shall approve by your letters, them will I send to bring your liberality unto Jerusalem". Titus had evidently carried the First Epistle to Corinth.

Attention is drawn to he repetition of the word "grace": "the **grace** of God bestowed on the churches of Macedonia" (v.1); "begging of us with much intreaty (to give effect to) the **grace** (that is, the grace of giving) and fellowship of the service... to the saints" (v.4, JND); "that... he (Titus) would also finish in you the same **grace** also" (v.6).

Following the example of the Macedonians believers (vv.1-6), we come now to:

2) THE APPEAL TO THE CHURCH AT CORINTH, vv.7-15

Attention is drawn to five things in these verses: *(a)* the exhortation to the church (v.7); *(b)* the example of the Macedonians (v.8); *(c)* the example of the Lord Jesus (v.9); *(d)* the execution of their intention, vv.10-11; *(e)* the explanation of the purpose, vv.12-15.

a) The exhortation to the church, v.7

"Therefore as ye abound in every thing, in faith, and utterance, and knowledge, and in all diligence, and in your love to us, see that ye abound in this grace also." Once again, the words are absorbing: "**abound**", occurring twice here, and in verse 2 ("abundance... abounding") means 'an exceeding measure'; "**every thing**": compare 1 Corinthians 1 verse 7, "ye come behind in no gift"; 1 Corinthians 1 verse 5, "in every thing ye are enriched by him, in all utterance, and in all knowledge"; "**diligence**" *(spoude,)* meaning 'earnestness': "**love to us**" or "in love from you to us" (JND).

His appeal, "see that ye abound in this grace also", was consistent with their 'abounding' in other ways. This emphasises the necessity for balance. It is possible to be zealous in one direction, and forget the necessity for zeal in other directions.

b) The example of the Macedonians, v.8

"I speak not by commandment, but by occasion of the forwardness of others, and to prove the sincerity of your love."

Paul does not insist on a collection for the needy saints in Judaea (compare 1 Corinthians 16: 1). But just as the Macedonian believers had displayed great earnestness, so he calls on the Corinthians to "prove the sincerity of their love". The word "**prove**" (*dokimazo*) is used in the sense of 'putting to the test'; "**sincerity**" (*gnesios,* not *eilikrines* here) means 'true' or 'genuine'. We should notice *(i)* that the zeal of others should be a lesson for us; *(ii)* that giving should be out of love, not out of obligation. In this connection we should note 1 Corinthans 13 verse 3, "And though I bestow all my goods to feed the poor, and though I give my body to be burned, and have not charity, it, profiteth **me** nothing". It might 'profit' others, but **not** "me".

c) The example of the Lord Jesus, v.9

"For ye know the grace of our Lord Jesus Christ, that though he was rich, yet for your sakes he became poor, that ye, though his poverty might be rich." **He** proved the sincerity of His love!

Thus, Paul has referred to the example of the Macedonians – "the forwardness of others (v.8). Now he adduces the supreme example. The Macedonians, marked by "deep poverty", "abounded unto the riches of their liberality". The Lord Jesus "became poor", "that ye through his poverty might be rich".

The Macedonian believers had made others rich by their poverty. They had impoverished themselves in so doing: but none had impoverished themselves to the extent of the Lord Jesus Christ. From highest heaven, He descended to Calvary (Philippians 2) and the grave. None was richer than He; none became poorer than He.

We should notice that the passage does not say that He became poor when He had been rich, but that He became poor when He was rich. He assumed poverty, yet did not lose His riches. And what riches for ourselves! "He raiseth up the poor out of the dust, and lifteth up the beggar from the dunghill, to set them among princes, and to make them inherit the throne of glory" (1 Sam. 2: 8). See also, for example Romans 8 verse 17.

In this connection it is worth pointing out that while the Lord Jesus "took upon him the form of a servant", He did not cease to be "in the form of God" (Phil. 2: 6-7). Similarly, while "learned he obedience by the things which he suffered", He did not cease to be the "Son" (Heb. 5: 8).

d) The execution of their intention, vv.10-11

"And herein I give my advice, for that is expedient for you, who have begun before, not only to do, but also to be forward a year ago" (v.10), or "And herein I give my judgment: for this is expedient for you, who were the first to make a beginning a year ago, not only to do, but also to will" (RV). The word "*expedient*" means 'profitable'. In saying "herein I give my judgment", Paul refers to Christ's example. Again, Paul does not command (see v.8), but gives his judgment in view of the Lord's example.

They 'were the first to make a beginning' in the matter. Now Titus was coming to "finish in you the same grace also" (v.6). So: "**Now therefore** perform the doing of it, that as there was a readiness to will, so there may be a performance also out of that which ye have" (v.11). We should notice that Paul does not say, 'out of that which ye *own*', but 'out of that which ye *possess*'.

> Naught that I have my own I call,
> I hold it for the Giver:
> My heart, my strength, my life, my all,
> Are His, and His for ever.

In this connection we should notice *(i)* that 'After all is said and done, there's more that's said than done!' Christians are expected to be people of their word. Compare Acts 11 verses 29-30, "Then the disciples, every man according to his ability, *determined* to send relief unto the brethren which dwelt in Judaea: which also they *did,* and sent it to the elders by the hands of Barnabas and Saul". We should also notice *(ii)* that it is "out of that which ye have". But the Macedonians did *more* than that: "*beyond* their power they were willing of themselves" (v.3).

163

e) The explanation of the purpose, vv.12-15

In these verses, Paul emphasises that in appealing to them, he was not creating an unfair burden, and asking them to do the impossible. So:

"For if there be first a willing mind, it is accepted according to that a man hath, and not according to that he hath not. For I mean not that any other man be eased, and ye burdened. But by an equality: that now at this time your abundance may be a supply for their want, and that their abundance also may be a supply for your want, that there may be equality" (vv.12-14).

Whilst he knew that the Corinthians, with their earthly wealth, were in a position to help the poor saints in Judaea, "it was no part of his plan that the burden of the Jews should be transferred to the Corinthians, and that by relieving one distress, another would be created" (A.McShane). First of all, there must be willingness to help, for as A.McShane points out, "not even the hungry at Jerusalem would want to eat bread supplied by unwilling hands".

The words, "that now at this time your abundance may be a supply for their want, and that their abundance also may be a supply for your want, that there may be equality", may mean one of two things:

i) That in the present circumstances ("now at this time") when the Corinthians were enjoying a measure of material prosperity, they were to help less favoured brethren in Judaea, so that if the positions were reversed, help could flow from Judaea to Corinth.

ii) That Paul is referring to the abundance at Corinth of material things, and to the abudance in Judea of spiritual things. See Romans 15 verses 25-27, "But now I go unto Jerusalem, to minister unto the saints. For it hath pleased them of Macedonia and Achaia to make a certain contribution for the poor saints which are at Jerusalem. It hath pleased them verily, and their debtors they are. *For if the Gentiles have been made partakers of their spiritual things, their duty is also to minister unto them in carnal things*".

If we adopt the second explanation, then, as noted above, "your abundance" (at Corinth) is in *material* things, and "their abundance" (in Judea) is in *spiritual* things. It should be noted that the poverty of the Judean saints had become the opportunity for help from non-Jewish believers, thus demonstrating the oneness of the body, and reducing division between Jewish and non-Jewish believers.

The principle "that there may be equality" is illustrated by reference to the gathering of the manna. "As it is written, He that gathereth much had nothing over, and he that gathered little had no lack" (v. 15). See Exodus 16 verse 18. Israel was commanded, "Gather of it every man according to his eating". We know that it was *God-given,* but here emphasis is placed on its *distribution.* A.McShane puts it like this: "Some of the people were more energetic than others and were able to gather more than they needed, so that they were instructed to share their abundance with the more feeble, and in some cases with those who were unable to gather any. At the end, all had plenty, and there was no possibility of hoarding it up, for it would not keep. Thus, those who shared their surplus were nothing poorer in so doing". There was 'an equality'. Selfishness would bring corruption: it "bred worms and stank". Selfishness in material things brings the same result, albeit in a different way.

This brings us to the final section of the chapter. The keynote is in verse 21, "Providing for honest things, not only in the sight of the Lord, but also in the sight of men". So:

3) THE ADMINISTRATION OF THE FUNDS FOR JUDEA, vv.16-24

We should notice *(a)* the people involved in the administration (vv. 16-19); *(b)* the principle involved in the administration (vv.20-21); *(c)* the personal godliness involved (vv.22-24).

a) The people involved in the administration, vv.16-19

"But thanks be to God which put the same earnest care (diligent zeal', JND) into the heart of Titus for you" (v.16). The "same earnest" care as *who?* Paul himself! "Earnest care" in *what?* That they should abound in liberality as in other spiritual graces. See verse 7. Note that *God* had "put the same earnest care into the heart of Titus". It was not so much the collection at Corinth, but the spiritual stature of the saints at Corinth that Titus and Paul desired. It was God-given "earnest care" (*spoude*, meaning 'zeal'). Do *we* have the same concern for God's people?

Titus displayed his "earnest care" by willingness to return to Corinth. "He accepted the exhortation, but being more forward, of his own accord he went unto you" (v.17). People like this are most valuable. There is a saying that 'One volunteer is worth ten pressed men!'

But "in the mouth of two or three witnesses shall every word be established", and Paul therefore says "we have sent with him the brother, whose praise is in the gospel, throughout all the churches" (v.18), or "whose praise in the gospel is spread though all the churches" (RV). Tradition favours Luke, but Paul does not name him. There are many suggestions. It is worth saying that there are often lessons to be learned by the very absence of information! The point is simply that Titus was accompanied by a man of recognised spiritual worth, and was therefore an acceptable witness to the financial integrity of Paul and Titus. *This is an abiding principle.*

"And not that only, but who was also chosen of the churches (the Macedonian churches) to travel with us *with this grace* (*charis*: gift) which is administered *by us* to the glory of the (same) Lord, and declaration of your ready mind" (v.19). For the words, "declaration of your ready mind", some read 'and to show all readiness'. These additional words emphasise that while the gift was for the Lord's glory, it was also an indication of the willingness of the believers at Corinth to demonstrate their whole-hearted fellowship with needy saints in Judea.

b) The principle involved in the administration, vv.20-21

The coming of Titus and the unnamed brother was a safeguard: "Avoiding this, that no man should blame us in this abundance (in the matter of this bounty) which is administered *by us:* providing for honest things, not only in the sight of the Lord, but also in the sight of men" or "for we take thought for things honourable, not only in the sight of God, but also in the sight of men" (RV). See Proverbs 3 verse 4, "So shalt thou find favour and good understanding in the sight of God and man". This is most important: the way in which we deal with financial matters, and other matters too, must not only be right, it must be seen to be right!

The word "*abundance*" here (*hadrotes*) differs from its use in verses 2 and 14. It comes from *hadros* meaning "thick, fat, full-grown, rich." The word "*providing*" means 'to take thought for' and "*honest*" (*kalos*) means 'honourable' or 'becoming'.

c) The personal godliness involved, vv.22-24

Continuing the need for "things honourable", a third brother, also unnamed, is mentioned. "And we have sent with them our brother, whom we have oftentimes proved diligent (again, *spoude*, meaning 'earnest') in many things, but now much more diligent, upon the great confidence which I have in you" (v.22) or "the great confidence which *he* hath in you" (RV). Confidence promotes earnestness. Compare Acts: 6 verse 3, "Look ye out among you seven men of honest report, full of the Holy Ghost and wisdom, whom we may appoint over this business…"

To emphasise the reliability of Titus, and the two unnamed brothers, Paul adds, "Whether any do enquire of Titus, he is my partner and fellow-helper concerning you: or our brethren be enquired of, they are the messengers of the churches, and the glory of Christ" (v.23).

- Paul describes Titus as "my partner and my fellow-worker toward you". The word partner (*koinonos*, meaning 'having in common') occurs in Luke 5 verse 10, where "James and John, the sons of Zebedee" are described as "partners with Simon".

- Paul describes the two unnamed brothers as "messengers ('apostles') of the churches and of the glory of Christ". We should notice three things about them: *(i)* they are "our brethren"; *(ii)* they are "messengers of the churches"; *(iii)* they were to "the glory of Christ". In the connection with the last of these, compare verse 19, "To the glory of the (omit 'same') Lord", perhaps meaning, simply, 'a credit to Christ'. In the words of J.M.Davies, "They were His (Christ's) trophies and by their ministry brought Him glory". The New Translation (JND) is not easily followed here: "or our brethren, [they are] deputed messengers of the assembly, Christ's glory".

They were to be given a warm welcome at Corinth: "Wherefore shew ye to them, and before the churches (whom they represented), the proof of your love, and of our boasting on your behalf" (v.24). The word translated "proof" here (*endeixis*), means 'make a declaration' or 'show forth'. Compare 7 verse 14.

2 CORINTHIANS

"Thanks be unto God for his unspeakable gift"

Read Chapter 9: 1-15

As we have already noticed, 2 Corinthians chs.8-9 deal with the collection for the needy saints in Judaea. The assembly at Corinth had expressed their intention to help, but failed to implement the collection urged in 1 Corinthians 16 verses 1-4, whereas the saints in Macedonia had responded nobly.

In Chapter 8, we noted the following: *(1)* the example of the churches in Macedonia (vv.1-6); *(2)* the appeal to the church at Corinth (vv.7-15); *(3)* the administration of the funds for Judaea (vv.16-24).

- In connection with the example of the churches in Macedonia (vv.1-6), we noticed: *(a)* that it was the result of the grace of God (v.1); *(b)* that it was the result of great sacrifice (vv.2-4): it flowed from open-hearted generosity, without duplicity of motive, the meaning of "liberality" (*haplous* not *diplous*); *(c)* that it was the result of devotion to Christ (vv.5-6). We could write over theses verses, they "***first gave their own selves to the Lord***" (v.5).

- In connection with the appeal to the church at Corinth (vv.7-15), we noticed *(a)* the exhortation to the church (v.7): "abound in this grace also"; *(b)* the example of Macedonia (v.8), reminding us that the zeal of others should be a lesson to us; *(c)* the example of the Lord Jesus (v.9): an example without parallel!; *(d)* the execution of their intention (vv.10-11): "Now therefore perform the doing of it": the Macedonians had completed the task, and the Lord Jesus had completed the work: they had proved "the sincerity of their love": now the Corinthians must follow suit; *(e)* the explanation of the purpose (vv.12-15): "that there may be equality". We could write over these verses, "***Now...perform the doing of it***" (v.11).

- In connection with the administration of the funds for Judaea (vv.16-24), we noticed *(a)* the people involved in the administration (vv.16-19): men known to the assembly at Corinth: a plurality of people so that "in the mouth of two or three witnesses shall every word be established"; *(b)* the principle involved in the administration (vv.20-21): "providing for honest things, not only in the sight of God, but also in the sight of men"; *(c)* the personal godliness involved (vv.22-24): whether named or unnamed, Paul attests their worthiness to be involved in carrying funds. We could write over these verses the words quoted above: ***"providing for honest things, not only in the sight of the Lord, but also in the sight of men" (v.21).***

Chapter 8 ends, like the previous chapter, with Paul boasting in the Corinthians, first of all to Titus (7: 14), and now to those who were to carry the funds (8: 24).

Now, in Chapter 9, Paul explains *(1)* the reason for writing (vv.1-5); *(2)* the requirements in giving (vv.6-11); *(3)* the results of giving (vv.12-15).

1) THE REASON FOR WRITING, vv.1-5

It was not to condemn them, but to save them from embarrassment. There is certainly a lesson here! In this paragraph, we should notice the following: *(a)* the result of his boasting (vv.1-2): see Chapter 8 verse 24; *(b)* the vanity of his boasting (vv.3-4); *(c)* the fulfilment of his boasting (v.5). The words "boast" or "boasting" occur three times in this section (vv.2, 3, 4). The word "ready" also occurs three times (vv.2, 3, 5).

a) The result of his boasting, vv.1-2

"For as touching the ministering to the saints, it is superfluous for me to write unto you… your zeal hath provoked very many". The expression, "ministering (*diakonia*) to the saints", is illustrated in Acts 6: "their widows were neglected in the daily ***ministration***" (v.1); "It is not reason that we should leave the word of God, and ***serve*** tables" (v.2).

The word "***superfluous***" *(perissos)* means 'abundant, more than sufficient', and the words, "it is superfluous for me to write unto you", therefore mean 'there is no real need for me to write unto you'. He did not doubt their willingness to relieve the poverty of the needy saints in Judaea, and had no reason to doubt their sincerity. It was, as we shall see, a case of fulfilling their expressed intention.

The reason for this statement follows: "For I know the **forwardness** (*prothumia*) of your mind, for which I boast of you to them of Macedonia, that Achaia was ready a year ago, and your zeal hath provoked very many" (v.2) or "For I know your readiness…" (JND). *Prothumia* means 'readiness' in sense of 'eagerness' and 'willingness'. For other occurrences of the word "zeal" (*zelos*, akin to *zeo*, to be hot, to boil), see John 2 verse 17 ("zeal for thine house"); Romans 10 verse 2 ("zeal of God"); 2 Corinthians 7 verse 7 ("zeal for me" JND); 2 Corinthians 7 verse 11. ('zeal' in dealing with immorality). See also Philippians 3 verse 6: "Concerning zeal, persecuting the church".

The word "**provoked**" (*erethizo*) means 'to excite' or 'to stir up', and refers to provocation in best sense! The same word is used in a bad sense in Colossians 3 verse 21, "Fathers, provoke not your children to anger, lest they be discouraged". A different word (*paroxusmos*) is used in Hebrews 10 verse 24.

These verses should lead us to ask ourselves at least two questions: firstly, 'What about our zeal?' We should all be spiritual 'zealots'! Secondly, 'What effect are we having on other people?'

b) The vanity of his boasting, vv3-4

Since they were prepared a year ago, and many had been stirred by their stated intention, Paul now says, "Yet have I sent the brethren, lest our boasting of you should be in vain in this behalf, that, as I said, ye may be ready (that is, prepared)" (v.3).

So, a year ago, they were prepared, that is, in **intention**: now they were to be prepared in **fulfilling that intention**, as urged in the previous chapter: "And herein I give my advice, for this is expedient for you, who have begun before, not only to do, but also to be forward a year ago. Now therefore perform the doing of it (so supporting their stated intention), that as there was a readiness to will, so there may be a performance also out of that which ye have" (8: 10-11).

Otherwise, what embarrassment! "Lest haply if they of Macedonia come with me, and find you unprepared, we (that we say not, you) should be ashamed in this same confident boasting" (v.4). The Corinthians needed to consider Paul's possible embarrassment before others, through their neglect, and we must remember that our failure could cause others embarrassment. We do need to consider one another's interests, shall we say, for example, in avoiding behaviour which might embarrass the assembly to which we belong.

c) The fulfilment of his boasting, v.5

"Therefore I thought it necessary to exhort the brethren, that they would go before unto you, and make up beforehand your bounty, whereof ye had notice before ('your aforepromised bounty', RV) that the same might be ready, as a matter of bounty, not of covetousness". Paul refers here to the "brethren" already mentioned (v.3), namely, Titus and his colleagues. See Chapter 8 verses 16-24. He had 'exhorted' these brethren to "go before unto you, and make up beforehand your bounty, whereof ye had notice before, that the same might be ready, as a matter of bounty, and not as of covetousness". As always, the wording merits careful examination:

- "As a matter of **bounty**". That is, 'as a matter of blessing'. The Greek word here (*eulogia*) means a blessing. A different word (*hadrotes*) is used in Chapter 8 verse 20, "this abundance ('bounty'. RV) which is administered by us". The word *hadrotes* means 'thick' or 'well-grown'. Another word is used in Chapter 9 verse 11, where Paul uses the expression "bountifulness" (*haplotes*), meaning 'simple' or 'single', which carries the idea of liberality without duplicity. The same word is used in Chapter 8 verse 2 and Chapter 9 verse 13.

Eulogia means 'to speak well of', or 'to praise'. In the Septuagint Version, *eulogia* is used of a bountiful gift in Genesis 33 verse 11: "Take, I pray thee, my blessing (the cattle), that is brought to thee...and he urged him, and he took it" (Jacob to Esau), and in Joshua 15 verse 19: "Give me a blessing... and he gave her the upper springs, and the nether springs" (Achsah to Caleb). In 1 Corinthians 16 verse 1, the word "collection" translates *logia*.

- "And not as of covetousness *(pleonexia)*" or "not of extortion" (RV): "not as got out of you" (JND). That is, a gift which betrays the giver's unwillingness to bestow what is due, or, regretting what was given. So the gift was to be prepared out of an expansive, and not a grudging spirit. This leads on to the second section, where we learn about:

2) THE REQUIREMENTS IN GIVING, vv.6-11

They were to give *(a)* bountifully (v.6); *(b)* purposefully (v.7); *(c)* cheerfully (v.7); *(d)* confidently (vv.8-11).

a) Bountifully, v.6

"But this I say, He which **soweth** sparingly shall reap sparingly, and he which **soweth** bountifully shall reap bountifully" or "he that sows in [the spirit of blessing] blessing shall reap also in blessing" (JND). "Bountifully" translates, again, *eulogia,* meaning a bountiful gift.

This recalls the oft-occuring law of sowing and reaping. See, for example, Galatians 6 verse 7: "Be not deceived; God is not mocked: for whatsoever a man soweth, that shall he also reap. For he that soweth to his flesh, shall of the flesh reap corruption; but he that soweth to the Spirit, shall of the Spirit reap life everlasting". We must notice that what is given is not lost. To give is to **sow**, and while in the present context the 'reaping' is not necessarily financial reaping, we should not forget that Paul did say, in view of the material support given sent to him at Rome, "my God shall supply all your need according to his riches in glory by Christ Jesus" (Phil. 4: 19). See also, Proverbs 19 verse 17, "He that hath pity upon the poor lendeth to the LORD; and that which he hath given will he pay him again".

But it is not quantity, but **quality** of giving. The poor widow in Mark 12 verses 43-44 "cast more in, than all they which have cast into the treasury: for all they did cast in of their abundance; but she of her want did cast in all that she had, even all her living". Sowing bountifully does not necessarily involve vast amounts! The widow gave "two mites": she could have kept one! But she sowed "bountifully".

The verse (v.6) is illustrated in Proverbs 11 verse, "There is that scattereth, and yet increaseth; and there is that withholdeth more than is meet, but it tendeth to poverty. The liberal soul shall be made fat: and he that watereth shall be watered also himself". See also Proverbs 3 verses 9-10, "Honour the LORD with thy substance, and with the firstfruits of all thine increase: so shall thy barns be filled with plenty, and thy presses shall burst out with new wine". Turning to the New Testament: "let us not be weary in well doing: for in due season we shall reap, if we faint not" (Gal. 6: 9).

But it is not giving for the sake of gain: that is the principle of covetousness in verse 5. The verse stresses giving "bountifully" - a gift freely and spontaneously bestowed, and thus constituting a blessing to the recipient. The word "bountifully" translates the Greek *ep' eulogiais,* meaning, "literally, 'with blessings' (RV margin), that is, that blessings may accrue" (W.E.Vine). How will this be displayed? This follows:

b) Purposefully, v.7

"Every man according as he purposeth *in his heart,* so let him give, not grudgingly, or of necessity: for God loveth a cheerful giver". The state of heart is all-important: "as he hath *purposed* in his heart". The word *proaireo* ("purposed") means 'to take by choice', literally, 'to bring forth or forward' (W.E.Vine). Compare 1 Corinthians 16 verse 2, "On the first day of the week let every one of you lay by him in store, as God hath prospered him".

This leads us to say, importing a 'little extra' from 1 Corinthians 16 verse 2, that we are to give *proportionately*: "On the first day of the week let every one of you lay by him in store, *as God hath prospered him*". Then we are to give:

c) Cheerfully, v.7

"Every man according as he purposeth *in his heart,* so let him give, not grudgingly, or of necessity: for God loveth a *cheerful giver*." We should note the following:

- "*Not grudgingly*". Literally, 'not out of sorrow'. That is, grieving at parting with money.

- "*Or of necessity*". Literally, 'what must need be'. That is, out of a sense of compulsion in view of what others are doing, or what might be said if we desist in our giving.

- "*For God loveth a cheerful giver*". The word rendered "cheerful" (*hilaros*), has its English counterpart in 'hilarious'. A joy in doing something. As a brother once said, "When the offering is announced, we should say 'Hallelujah, here comes the bag!'"

It has been suggested that Paul may have had in mind that way in which

Israel was to give for the tabernacle: "every man that giveth it willingly with his heart" (Exod. 25: 2).

d) Confidently, vv.8-11

Paul gives four excellent reasons why we may exercise our stewardship with confidence.

i) Because willing and sacrificial giving (v.7) will bring the ability to do more. "And God is able to make all grace abound to you; that ye, always having all sufficiency in all things, may abound to every good work" (v.8).

Of the churches in Macedonia, Paul had written: "Moreover, brethren, we do you to wit (we make known unto you) of the grace of God bestowed on the churches of Macedonia" (8: 1). It was the operation of His grace in their hearts that promoted their sacrificial giving. Now, to the saints at Corinth, Paul observes (following "he that soweth bountifully shall reap also bountifully", and "God loveth a cheerful giver"), that "God is able to make all grace abound toward you". That is, "His boundless giving will ensure that the good work of generosity will continue. He not only gives the grace to give, but supplies the means to do it. Where there is a generous spirit, there will be funds to disperse" (A.McShane). By our giving, we place ourselves in receipt of divinely-given ability to be in a position to continue "to every good work".

This is a marvellous verse! Do notice: ***(i) unlimited ability***: "God is ***able***"; ***(ii) unequalled provision***: "***all*** grace": compare the Lord's words to Paul, "my grace" (12: 9); ***(iii) unfailing guarantee***: "***always*** having all sufficiency in all things". All grace - at all times (always) - for all need (every good work). This is illustrated perfectly in 1 Kings 17 verses 8-16 where the widow made Elijah "a little cake first", and then enjoyed unceasing provision from God! The same principle is observable in verse 10: "Now he that ministereth seed to the sower both minister bread for your food, and multiply your seed sown, and increase the fruits of your righteousness". The second reason why we should give confidently is:

ii) Because willing and sacrificial giving is an indication of moral righteousness. "As it is written, He hath dispersed abroad; he hath given to the poor: his ***righteousness*** remaineth for ever" (v.9).

Paul cites Psalm 112 verse 9 here: "He (the man "that feareth the LORD, that delighteth greatly in his commandments", v.1) hath dispersed ('he scattereth abroad', RV), he hath given to the poor; his righteousness endureth for ever". Here, again, we have the figure of the sower at work. Psalm 112 displays **practical righteousness** in action, especially in regard to money matters. See verse 3, "Wealth and riches shall be in his house: and his righteousness endureth for ever". See also verse 5, "A good man showeth favour and lendeth...the righteous shall be in everlasting remembrance".

In the next verse (v.10), Paul develops this, and we have the third reason why we should give confidently:

iii) *Because willing and sacrificial giving must have a beneficial result.* "Now he that ministereth (*choregeo*, meaning 'supplies') seed to the sower both minister bread for (omit 'your', see JND) food ('eating', JND) and multiply your seed sown, and *increase* the fruits of your righteousness" (v.10), or "And he that supplieth seed to the sower, and bread for food, shall supply and multiply *your* seed for sowing, and increase the fruits of your righteousness" (RV). The words, "seed...bread", reflect natural cause and effect. See Isaiah 55 verse 10. The words, "seed sown...increase the fruits of your righteousness", reflect spiritual cause and effect. The RSV reads, "He who supplies seed to the sower and bread for food will supply and multiply your resources and increase the harvest of your righteousness."

The words, "Now *he* that *ministereth* seed to the sower" remind us that all that we can give comes from God in the first place. After all, like David we have to say, "Of thine own we have given thee" (1 Chron. 29: 14). The fourth reason why we should give confidently is:

iv) *Because willing and sacrificial giving will bring honour to God.* So, leaving out the AV's brackets, "being enriched in every thing to all bountifulness, which causeth through us *thanksgiving to God*" (v.11).

This verse links the second and third sections of the chapter. The verse concludes the exhortation and instruction so far as the givers are concerned, and then shews the result.

In sowing financially, not only is the practical righteousness of the saints displayed, but they themselves are enriched - *not* impoverished by giving, but *enriched!* That is, enriched spiritually. With what result? "To all bountifulness" (*haplos*, as in 8: 2) - liberality - open-hearted generosity. And the result?: "which causeth, *through us* (as the vehicles through which the generosity is bestowed) thanksgiving to God".

Having considered *(1)* the reason for writing (vv.1-5) and *(2)* the requirements in giving (vv.6-11), we come, finally, to:

3) THE RESULTS OF GIVING, vv.12-15

Our stewardship has four results: *(a)* it promotes the welfare of the saints (v.12a); *(b)* it promotes thanksgiving to God (vv.12b-13); *(c)* it promotes prayer (v.14); *(d)* it promotes fellowship (v.14).

a) It promotes the welfare of the saints, v.12a

"For the administration of this service (*leitourgia*, ministration of this *priestly* service: the word is used in Luke 1: 23, Hebrews 8: 6; 9: 21) not only *supplieth the want of the saints*, but is abundant also ('aboundeth also', RV) through many thanksgivings to God."

So the saints are helped. Compare Philippians 4 verse 18, "I have all, and abound: I am full, having received of Epaphroditus the things which were sent from you".

b) It promotes thanksgiving to God, vv.12b-13

"For the administration of this service not only supplieth the want of the saints, but is abundant also ('aboundeth also') *through many thanksgivings to God.* Whiles by the experiment of this ministration they *glorify God* for your professed subjection unto the gospel of Christ, and for your liberal distribution unto them, and unto all men."

So God is glorified. Compare, again, Philippians 4 verse 18: "an odour of a sweet smell, a sacrifice acceptable, wellpleasing *to God".* He is glorified in two ways:

- *Through the evidence thus supplied of Gentile conversions:* "whiles by the experiment of this ministration they *glorify God* for your professed subjection unto the gospel of Christ" or "seeing that through the proving (*dokime:* so it is a proving) of you by this ministration (*diakonia*) they glorify God for the obedience of your confession unto the gospel of Christ" (RV). The last words here are elsewhere rendered, "by your obedience in acknowledging the gospel of Christ" or "for the obedience of your confession unto the gospel of Christ". That is, the Judaean saints would see in the collection, the reality and genuineness of their obedience to the gospel. Thus the circumstances, harrowing though they must have been, gave opportunity for the Jewish saints to posess evidence of the reality of the grace of God in their Gentile brethren. Compare James 2 verses 14-18, "What doth it profit, my brethren, though a man say he hast faith, and have not works...?"

- *Through the meeting of their needs.* They glorify God "for your liberal distribution unto them, and unto all men".   The word "***liberal***" translates, again, *haplos,* meaning, as we have seen, liberality, open-hearted generosity. The word "***distribution"*** (*koinonia)* means fellowship or sharing.

c) It promotes prayer, v.14

"And by ***their prayer for you,*** which long after you for the exceeding grace of God in you" or "while they themselves also, with supplication on your behalf, long after you by reason of the exceeding grace of God in you" (RV).

d) It promotes fellowship, v.14

"And by ***their prayer for you,*** which long after you for the exceeding grace of God in you". We cannot miss Paul's confidence in the believers at Corinth. As a result of the anticipated gift from them, the believers in Judea were praying for them and longing after them on account of the "exceeding grace of God" in them. We know that Paul's confidence was fully justified: see Romans 15 verse 25: "But now I go to Jerusalem to minister to the saints".

Thus this section of the epistle ends as it begins, with reference to the "grace of God" (8: 1; 9: 14). But not quite. Having spoken about the thanksgiving to God in Judea for the gift to be sent by the Corinthian believers, Paul goes further - much further - in saying, "Thanks be unto God for his unspeakable gift" (v.15).

Here is the evidence of the grace of God - in His "unspeakable gift". When speaking about the Macedonians, he emphasises the poverty of the Lord Jesus (8: 9): when exhorting the Corinthians, He speaks about the riches of the Lord Jesus. There was never a gift so rich as Christ Himself! It has been said that in 2 Corinthians 8 verse 9 we have the grace in His **coming down**, and in 2 Corinthians 9 verse 15 we have the praise that **goes up!**

The word "unspeakable" (*anekdiegetos*) is only used here, and means 'inexpressible', it cannot be declared or related (W.E. Vine). Compare 1 Peter 1 verse 8, "ye rejoice with joy unspeakable (*aneklaletos*, meaning 'unable to be told, or spoken, out') and full of glory".

The **outcome** of Paul's ministry in these chapters is seen in Romans 15 verse 26. "It hath pleased them of Macedonia and Achaia to make a certain contribution for the poor saints which are at Jerusalem."

2 CORINTHIANS

"He that glorieth, let him glory in the Lord"

Read Chapter 10: 1-18

With this chapter we reach the third major division of the epistle. By way of revision we should recall that the epistle may be divided as follows: *(i)* **Suffering** (Chapters 1-7): although "without were fightings, within were fears" (7: 5), the power of God enabled him to persevere in His service and to maintain godly principles of conduct. *(ii) Giving* (Chapters 8-9): the secret of stewardship is made clear: "they first gave themselves to the Lord". The supreme example was the Lord Jesus. He "became poor" but was none other than God's "unspeakable gift". This gift cannot be expounded. *(iii) Glorying* (Chapters 10-13). The slander of his detractors obliges Paul to vindicate his ministry. Religious slander is the worst. Chapters 10-13 are very personal, and this note is struck with the opening verse: "Now I Paul myself beseech you…" (10: 1).

It has been suggested that Chapters 10-13 can be entitled: *ch.10*, the conflict of the servant; *ch.11*, the counterfeit of the servant; *ch.12,* the communion of the servant; *ch.13*, the confirmation of the servant.

Paul now turns from the defensive to the offensive. He deals with the party at Corinth who were evidently bent on discrediting him. See 1 Corinthians 9 verses 1-3, "Am I not an apostle? am I not free? have I not seen Jesus Christ our Lord? Are ye not my work in the Lord…Mine answer to them that do examine me, is this…"

The chapter may be divided as follows: *(1)* the authority of Paul's ministry (vv.1-11); *(2)* the assessment of Paul's ministry (vv.12-18). A.Wiseman (Eastbourne Bible Readings, May 2006) divided the chapter thus: *(1)* declaring his position to the assembly (vv.1-6); *(2)* defending himself against criticism (vv.7-12); *(3)* defining his territory (vv.13-18).

In verses 1-11 (*the authority of his ministry*), Paul discusses his authority and its effect. See verse 8: "For though I should boast somewhat more of our authority, which the Lord hath given us for edification, and not for your destruction, I should not be ashamed". His enemies poured scorn upon his authority, virtually accusing him of being a 'paper tiger'. See verse 1: "Who in presence am base among you, but being absent am bold toward you". See verse 10: "For his letters, say they, are weighty and powerful; but his bodily presence is weak, and his speech contemptible".

In fact, the passage is locked together by reference to his presence and absence. "Now I Paul myself beseech you by the meekness and gentleness of Christ, who in *presence* am base among you, but being *absent* am bold toward you" (v.1). He refers to his presence and his absence. "Let such an one think this, that, such as we are in word by letters when we are *absent*, such will we be also indeed when we are *present*" (v.11) He refers to his absence and his presence.

The fact that Paul did not make a practice of asserting his authority when present with the Lord's people, for very good reasons, did not mean that he was incapable of doing so. But there is far more to authority than righting wrongs! This follows:

In verses 12-18 (*the assessment of his ministry*), having reminded them of his authority, Paul emphasises that this was not a matter of self-commendation. The false teachers did that: "For we dare not make ourselves of the number, or compare ourselves with some that commend themselves" (v.12). True commendation was the Lord's prerogative: "For not he that commendeth himself is approved, but whom the Lord commendeth" (v.18).

In fact the passage is locked together by reference to commendation. "For we dare not make ourselves of the number, or compare ourselves with some that *commend* themselves" (v.12): "For not he that *commendeth* himself is approved, but whom the Lord *commendeth*" (v.18).

We must now consider the details in these sections of the chapter

1) THE AUTHORITY OF PAUL'S MINISTRY, vv.1-11

This section of the chapter may be divided into two main paragraphs. It is clear that Paul is rebutting an attack on his authority, and is evidently quoting his opponents in saying, "who in presence am base among you, but being absent am bold toward you" (v.1). His authority *(A)* enabled him to be bold (vv.1-6) and *(B)* enabled him to boast (vv.7-11).

A) It enabled him to be bold, vv.1-6

Although Paul had no wish to be bold amongst them (vv.1-2a), he was nevertheless ready to be bold amongst them (vv.2b-6).

a) He had no wish to be bold amongst them, vv.1-2a

The possession of authority did not mean that he wished to use it come what may. The man with apostolic authority appeals to them, rather than commands them: "Now I Paul myself beseech you by the meekness and gentleness of Christ". Notice the language here:

i) "Now I Paul myself". (There is no trace of Saul here!) This emphasises his deep personal interest. It stresses his personal connection with Corinth.

ii) "Beseech". Meaning 'intreat', as in Chapter 6 verse 1, "We then as workers together with him, *beseech* you also that ye receive not the grace of God in vain". He employs the word *parakaleo* here - a stronger word than 'ask'.

iii) "By the meekness (inward: He took no offence) and gentleness (outward: He gave no offence) of Christ." Paul besought them with affection. The spirit and disposition of Christ should characterise us at all times: even when faced with exasperating circumstances, as here. Paul keeps in mind the example of the Lord Jesus. He had unlimited power and authority, but was "meek and lowly in heart" (Matt. 11: 29). Paul does not censure the Corinthians vehemently for tolerating the party bent on defaming him. He entreats them with Christ-like meekness and gentleness. Such features are not incompatible with stern denunciation of false teachers. See Chapter 11 verses 3-15.

Paul was evidently well aware of the way in which he was misrepresented by some at Corinth: "Who in presence am base among you, but being absent am bold toward you". The word "base" (*tapeinos*) means 'humble' or 'low'. The word "bold" means 'of good courage'. It has been pointed out that Paul means 'little', and in this he was unlike Saul the son of Kish. See 1 Samuel 10 verse 23. Saul was impressive to the natural mind, but Paul, though unimpressive in this way, was a man of spiritual stature.

This was evidently an echo of a slander against him by his enemies at Corinth. Perhaps referring to his first visit. See 1 Corinthians 2 verses 3-4, "And I was with you in weakness, and in fear, and in much trembling". The slander, however, ignored the fact that his speech and preaching was "in demonstration of the spirit and of power".

Paul was thus accused of cowardice. They inferred that 'he says things from a distance which he cannot carry out in practice'.

The purpose of his appeal in verse 1 is given in verse 2. "But I beseech you, that I may **not be bold** when I am present with that confidence, wherewith I think to be bold against some which think of us as if we walked according to the flesh." His opponents had accused him of being "base" when with them, and "bold" when absent. Very well, but he had no desire to be "bold" when with them!

We should notice his words here, "I beseech". The entreaty of verse 1 now becomes more appealing. He employs the Greek word *deomai*. He makes an earnest appeal for the saints at Corinth to put things right, so that there would be no need for him to demonstrate, as he intended, that he was capable not only of writing stern letters, but of acting with severity.

b) He was nevertheless prepared to be bold amongst them, vv.2b-6

"That I may **not be bold** when I am present with that confidence wherewith I think to be bold against some, which think of us as if we walked according to the flesh." The party at Corinth (note "some": not all were involved at Corinth) to whom Paul refers, were those whose opinion it was ('which count of us', RV) "as if we walked according to the flesh". They accused him of a double standard: one when present at Corinth, and another when absent. Compare Chapter 1 verse 17, "When I therefore was thus minded, did I use lightness? or the things that I purpose, do I purpose according to the *flesh*, that with me there should be yea yea, and nay nay". That is, they implied, that he wrote one thing, but did another.

But we must remember that Paul did not delight in the prospect of demonstrating the consistency between his letters, and his personal presence. Hence "But I *beseech* you". We must note the lesson for ourselves here. Paul had no desire to engage in self-vindication.

The accusation that he walked "according to the flesh" is the first of four references to "the flesh", viz:

i) Verse 2. "As if we walked according to **the flesh**", that is, with a double standard. See, again, Chapter 1 verse 17.

ii) Verse 3. "For though we walk in (not 'according to' now) **the flesh**", that is, being subject to the laws and limitations of humanity: as the "earthen vessel" (4: 7). Compare the expression, "to abide in the flesh" (Phil. 1: 24).

iii) Verse 3. "We do not war after **the flesh**", meaning that the believer does not use the weapons of the unregenerate. See, for example, 2 Corinthians 4 verse 2, "but have renounced the hidden things of dishonesty ('shame'), not walking in craftiness, nor handling the word of God deceitfully". Hence:

iv) Verse 4. "For the weapons of our warfare are not **carnal** ('are not of **the flesh**')." Compare, 2 Corinthians 1 verse 12, "For our rejoicing is this, the testimony of our conscience, that in simplicity and godly sincerity, not with **fleshly** wisdom, but by the grace of God, we have had our conversation, in this world, and more abundantly to you-ward".

How much we need the whole panoply of God (Eph. 6: 11-17). Such weapons are, "mighty **through God** to the pulling down of strongholds". This is a **warning:** nothing else will be effective against "strongholds" (fortresses). See Jericho! Only spiritual weapons will be sufficient in casting them down. It is a **promise**. They **will be** divinely powerful, though scorned by the world, and by carnal believers. The following two verses describe the 'holy war' in which Paul was engaged: *(i)* in the world (v.5): *(ii)* in the assembly (v.6).

i) **In the world, v.5.** We should notice:

- **The opposition.** Here are the "strongholds" of verse 4. "Casting down imaginations, and every high thing that exalteth itself against the knowledge of God." Such opposition will become 'full-blown' at the end-time. See 2 Thessalonians 2 verses 3-12.

The word "imaginations" means 'reasonings'. See 1 Corinthians 1 verses 22-24, "For the Jews require a sign, and the Greeks seek after wisdom, but we preach Christ crucified (here is Paul's weaponry), unto the Jews a stumblingblock, and unto the Greeks foolishness: but unto them which are called, both Jews and Greeks, Christ, the power of God, and the wisdom of God". In the words of A.McShane: "Whether we think of the Greek philosopher, the Roman imperialist, or the Jewish ritualist, they each had this in common, that they resisted the message of the cross".

- **The object.** "Bringing into captivity every thought to the obedience of Christ". The whole of verse 5 concerns the will and intellect. Through the Gospel, man's rebellious thoughts are brought "into captivity to the obedience of Christ" (RV). Mind and thought becomes subject to Him. This is continued in verse 6:

ii) In the assembly, v.6. "And being in readiness to avenge all disobedience, when your obedience is ('shall have been', JND) fulfilled."

The extension suggests that if in verses 4-5, Paul had ability to bring into "captivity every thought to the obedience of Christ" through gospel preaching, he was able to use that same authority in relation to those in the assembly at Corinth who would not bow to the authority of Christ. Thus Paul asserts that far from being "base among you", he will "avenge all disobedience", but only *after* "*your* obedience is fulfilled". Thus:

- Paul would not act indiscriminately. He would not censure the whole assembly: only the disobedient.

- He anticipated that the assembly generally would respond obediently. The reason for this is in Chapter 7 verses 15-16, "He remembereth the obedience of you all, how with fear and trembling ye received him. I rejoice therefore that I have confidence in you in all things." That is, they had responded obediently to the First Epistle: they would also do so in the Second Epistle.

B) It enabled him to boast, vv.7-11

We should notice that he refers *(a)* to their boast (v.7) and *(b)* to his boast (vv.8-11).

a) Their boast, v.7

"Do ye look on things after the outward appearance? If any man trust to himself that he is Christ's, let him of himself think this again, that, as he is

Christ's, even so are we Christ's" or "Ye look at the things that are before your face" (RV). That is, superficially: 'You accept things as they appear - accept statements people make without giving thought to them or testing them'. Paul's opponents claimed authority, and placed themselves in the highest positions. In fact, higher even than Paul himself. But the Corinthians had not fully investigated the validity of that claim. If they had given careful thought to the matter, they would have concluded that Paul was equal to every claim they asserted for themselves.

This evidently refers to the people described in verse 12: "For we dare not make ourselves of the number, or compare ourselves with some that commend themselves" or "For we are not bold to number or compare ourselves with certain of them that commend themselves" (RV). Paul refers to them in Chapter 11 verses 22-23, "Are they Hebrews? So am I. Are they Israelites? So am I. Are they the seed of Abraham? So am I. Are they ministers of Christ? I more..."

Quite obviously, some were making claims for themselves which gave them alleged superiority. Perhaps those who dared to say "I am of Christ" (1 Corinthians 1 verse 12). Possibly people who claimed to have seen and heard Him. But Paul had too! See, for example, 1 Corinthians 9 verse 1. But Paul could boast beyond them of his authority, so:

b) Paul's boast, vv.8-11

Paul could boast in divinely-given authority. Verse 8 substantiates the closing statement of verse 7, "Even so are we Christ's". "For though I should boast (glory) somewhat more of our authority, which the **Lord hath given** (note) us for edification, and not for your destruction, I should not be ashamed" or "For though I should glory somewhat abundantly concerning our authority (which the Lord gave for building you up, and not for casting you down), I shall not be put to shame" (RV). Paul's authority was:

- *"For edification",* that is, building up, and not for

- *"Destruction",* that is, casting down. Certainly for casting down imaginations, and every high thing that exalteth itself against the knowledge of God", but not for 'casting down' the saints!

The last words, "I should not be ashamed", mean that Paul would not be proved wrong in glorying in his authority. The idea is - following the RSV

– "even though I boast a little too much of our authority…I should not be ashamed". Paul, however, acknowledges his own precept: "He that glorieth, let him glory in the Lord". Hence the important words, "Which the Lord gave".

The words, "I should not be ashamed", are explained in verses 9-11: "That I may not seem as if I terrify you by letters. For his letters, say they, are weighty and powerful; but his bodily presence is weak (it doesn't look like it from 11: 23-28!), and his speech contemptible (it doesn't look like it from Acts 14: 12!). Let such an one think this, that, such as we are in word by letters when we are absent, such will we be also in deed when we are present". By this, Paul means that he would not be ashamed of the authority in which he gloried, since the people who slanderously asserted that although he terrified by letters, but was totally different when present, would find him exactly the same in presence as his letters. The accusation that he was inconsistent would be proven false. The accusation was:

- His letters. They were "weighty and powerful". But:

- His presence. It was "weak" and "contemptible". That is, of no account. Compare 1 Corinthians 2 verse 1: "not with excellency of speech or wisdom" and 1 Corinthians 2 verse 4: "not with enticing words of man's wisdom".

"Terrify" means 'to frighten away'. But his presence would be as powerful as his letters.

2) THE ASSESSMENT OF PAUL'S MINISTRY, vv.12-18

Note again how the section *commences*, "some that *commend* themselves", and how the section *concludes*: "For not he that *commendeth* himself is approved, but whom the Lord *commendeth*". We must notice *(A)* how others measured their ministry (v.12); *(B)* how Paul measured his ministry (vv.13-16); *(C)* the conclusion (vv.17-18).

A) How others measured their ministry, v.12

In connection with those that commend themselves, Paul speaks of the criterion by which they do this: "measuring themselves by themselves". The whole emphasis is on "themselves" throughout. The word occurs five times in this verse!

Paul, bold to avow his authority in absence or presence, is not so bold as to rest his authority on self-commendation. In commending themselves, his detractors had only failed to discredit Paul, and shown their true colours.

In connection with himself and his fellow-labourers, Paul used another measure: "But we will not glory beyond our measure, but according to the measure of the province which God apportioned to us as a measure to reach even unto you" (v.13, RV).

B) How Paul measured his ministry, vv.13-18

We may notice four things here:

i) **Its source, v.13a.** It was given by God. "But we will not boast of things without our measure, but according to the measure of the rule which **God hath distributed to us.**" That is, he recognised that God had allotted to him a certain sphere or area of service - which included Corinth. So:

ii) **Its scope, v.13b-14.** It extended to them. It extended to Corinth. "A measure to reach even unto you. For we stretch not ourselves beyond our measure, as though we reached not unto you: for we are come as far as to you also in preaching the gospel of Christ." In visiting Corinth in "the gospel of Christ", Paul had not overstepped the bounds of the sphere allotted to him. He had laid the foundation at Corinth (see 1 Cor. 3: 10): he was their spiritual father (1 Cor. 4: 15).

But now others had come to Corinth who had no authority to do so: they were not appointed by God at all.

iii) **He did not seek gain from the labour of others, v.15a.** "Not glorying beyond our measure, that is, in other men's labours." That is, he, not the false apostles had been responsible for founding the work at Corinth. Evidently, his opponents had been boasting and taking credit for work that was not theirs at all. Compare Romans 15 verse 18, "For I will not dare to speak of any of those things which Christ hath not wrought by me, to make the Gentiles obedient, by word and deed".

iv) **Enlargement through them, vv.15b-16.** "But having hope, when your faith is increased, that we shall be enlarged by you according to our rule abundantly." In speaking about 'enlargement', Paul has in mind preaching "the gospel in the regions beyond you, and not to boast in another man's line of things made ready to our hand". He expresses the hope that "as your faith groweth, we shall be magnified in you according to our province unto further abundance, so as to preach the gospel even unto parts beyond you" (RV).

The spiritually unsettled state of affairs at Corinth was a hindrance to further progress. Compare Romans 15 verse 20, "So have I strived to preach the gospel (making it my aim so to preach the gospel), not where Christ was (already) named, lest I should build upon another man's foundation". He continues "having a great desire these many years to come unto you; whensoever I take my journey into Spain I will come to you…I will come by you into Spain" (Rom. 15: 23-24, 28).

C) The conclusion, vv.17-18

Paul had said a great deal about himself of necessity, in view of those who were bent on destroying his stature in the eyes of the Corinthians. Far, however, from desiring glory and praise for all that had been accomplished, Paul now states: "But he that glorieth let him glory in the Lord. For not he that commendeth himself is approved, but whom the Lord commendeth". Compare 1 Corinthians 4 verse 5, "Then shall every man have praise of God". Looking back over verses 13-18, we will notice that Paul employs the formula "not…but" three times:

i)   "We will **not** glory beyond our measure, **but** according to the measure of the province which God appointed to us" (v.13).

ii)   "**Not** glorying beyond our measure, that is, in other men's labours; **but** having hope…" (v.15).

iii)   "**Not** to glory in another's province in regard of things ready to our hand, **but** he that glorieth let him glory in the Lord" (vv.16-17).

2 CORINTHIANS

"False apostles"

Read Chapter 11: 1-33

As already noted, the final section of the Epistle (Chapters 10-13) addresses the attempts of "false apostles" (11: 13) to undermine Paul's authority, and therefore to discredit his ministry. In Chapter 10 verses 1-11, the apostle firmly rebuts the charge that he was just a 'paper tiger': "Let such an one think this, that, such as we are in word by letters when we are absent, such will we be also in deed when we are present" (10: 11). In passing, this reminds us that the Lord's people should be 'men of their word'. All too often, things 'go wrong' in assembly life, and good men stay silent.

Unlike his detractors, Paul studiously avoided self-commendation: "we dare not make ourselves of the number, or compare ourselves with some that commend themselves: but they measuring themselves by themselves, and comparing themselves among themselves are not wise" (10: 12). Paul recognised that that God had given him "the measure of the rule" (10: 13), and therefore gloried in the Lord's commendation (10: 14-18).

The word *kanon*, translated "rule" (10: 13, 15) means, literally, "a straight rod, used as a ruler or measuring implement" (W.E.Vine), and refers to the extent of responsibility given by God. The same word is translated "line" (10: 16). Paul always moved within that area, that is, within the appointed limits marked out for him by God. This included Corinth, see Chapter 10 verse 14.

Quite obviously, Paul was being accused, by those who commended themselves, of having no credence or authority at Corinth.

While Chapter 11 may be broadly divided as follows *(1)* the plans of Satan (vv.1-15); *(2)* the pretensions of men (vv.16-33), we will follow a more detailed analysis: *(1)* their espousal to Christ (vv.1-6); *(2)* the exclusion of their support (vv.7-12); *(3)* the exposure of his opponents (vv.13-15); *(4)* the explanation of his folly (vv.16-33).

1) THEIR ESPOUSAL TO CHRIST, vv.1-6

"Would to God you could bear with me a little in my folly, and indeed bear with me" (v.1). Paul explains his "folly" in Chapter 12 verse 11: "I am become a fool in glorying, ye have compelled me". They had "compelled" him by their acceptance of false teachers with their self-commendation and boasting, making it necessary for Paul to draw attention to himself - something he described as 'a little folly' (v.1, JND). He employs the very weapons of his adversaries. They had made progress at Corinth by their boasting and self-commendation. Very well: Paul will do the same, and prove that while they had no grounds for boasting, he had every reason to do so.

We must remember that Paul indulged in this 'little folly' for the best of reasons: see Chapter 12 verse 19, "We do all things, dearly beloved, *for your edification*". It was this that enabled him to say, "For though I should boast somewhat more (over much) of our authority, which the Lord hath given us for edification, and not for your destruction, I should not be ashamed" (10: 8).

While the words "and indeed bear with me" could serve to emphasise Paul's desire ("bear with me... indeed bear with me"), it seems more likely that they are an appeal to the Corinthians: "but indeed bear with me" (JND). Paul now explains why he said "bear with me". Two reasons follow *(a)* his desire for them (v.2); *(b)* his disquiet over them (vv.3-6).

a) His desire for them, v.2

"For I am jealous over you with godly jealousy: for I have espoused you to one husband, that I may *present you as a chaste virgin to Christ.*"

In saying, "I have espoused (betrothed) you", Paul is speaking as their spiritual father. See 1 Corinthians 4 verse 15: "For though ye have ten thousand instructors in Christ, yet have ye not many fathers: for in Christ Jesus I have begotten you through the gospel". We should notice:

i)   There was no selfish motive in this: it was "*godly jealousy*". The wording, "I have espoused you to one husband, that I may present you as a chaste virgin to Christ" recalls Genesis 2 verse 22: "And the rib, which the LORD God had taken from man, made he a woman, and **brought her unto the man**". God gave Eve to Adam, and to him alone.

ii) Paul was not primarily concerned, in the midst of personal attacks upon him, with his own position, but with the spiritual welfare of the Corinthians. He was concerned with their exclusive loyalty to Christ. Hence "one husband". He was therefore concerned with their love, devotion and affection - with all that is involved in loyalty to Christ. Paul speaks in this respect as their spiritual parent: "I have espoused you..." The servant of God should be concerned with the affection of the saints Christward.

b) His disquiet over them, vv.3-6

"But I fear lest by any means, as the serpent beguiled Eve through his subtilty, so your minds (thoughts, JND) should be corrupted from the simplicity that is in Christ." This recalls Genesis 3 verse 1, "Now the serpent was more subtle than any beast of the field which the LORD God had made. And he said unto the woman, Yea, hath God said, Ye shall not eat of every tree of the garden?" Satan attacked and misdirected her thoughts. The word "subtilty" (*panourgia*) means craftiness or 'all working': as in 2 Corinthians 4 verse 2 ("not walking in craftiness").

The word "beguiled" (*exapateo*) means 'thoroughly beguiled' (W.E.Vine). Compare 1 Timothy 2 verse 14: "And Adam was not deceived, but the woman being deceived, was in the transgression". That is, Satan offered something seemingly so attractive. See Genesis 3 verse 5. We must remember that error can be alluring and attractive. False teachers, with their boastful claims, can appear so appealing. We must heed the warning, "Whoso transgresseth ('goes forward', JND: with the footnote 'this is what is called development: he does not abide in what was from the beginning'), and abideth not in the doctrine of Christ, hath not God" (2 John 9).

Paul's desire to present them "as a chaste virgin to Christ" was under threat. He describes the threat as follows: that "your minds should be corrupted from the simplicity that is in (towards) Christ" or "from simplicity as to the Christ" (JND). That is, "from wholeheartedness, singleness of devotion, freedom of duplicity...of a faithful bride" (P.E.Hughes). While the RV has "from the simplicity **and the purity** that is towards Christ", J.N.Darby is not convinced: 'but it seems to me a gloss' (margin).

Eve, the first bride, was deceived by Satan's "subtilty". Now the saints at Corinth - also viewed as a bride - were in danger from the same source. We must not be unmindful of the **ongoing strategy of Satan.** The words "from the simplicity that is in Christ" mean from the 'singleness that is in Christ', with the idea of whole-heartedness. Paul uses the word *haplous,* meaning no duplicity. The opposite word is *diplous,* meaning 'double'.

The statement in verse 3 most clearly implies that the false teachers were tools of Satan, and this is categorically stated in verses 13-15.

Verses 4-6 shew us *(i)* how believers can be "corrupted from the simplicity that is in Christ", and *(ii)* how believers are preserved as "a chaste virgin to Christ".

i)   Believers are corrupted by false teaching, v.4. "For if he that cometh preacheth another Jesus, whom we have not preached, or if ye receive another spirit, which ye have not received, or another gospel, which ye have not accepted, ye might well bear with him." Compare Galatians 1 verses 6-7, "But though we, or an angel from heaven, preach any other gospel unto you than that which we have preached unto you, let him be accursed. As we said before, so say I now again, If any man preach any other gospel unto you than that ye have received, let him be accursed". We should notice:

- That the words, "he that cometh", are probably used in an *ironic* sense. The false teachers were the very opposite to an apostle – 'one who is sent'. These teachers had no divine commission or authority: they simply came.

- That the words, "ye might well bear with him", are perhaps better translated, 'you bare well enough with him'. Again, the sense is *ironical.*

- That the words, "another Jesus", mean another of the same kind (*allos*). That is, speaking of the same Person, but erroneously - not speaking of one whose sacrifice alone could deal with sin. We have "another Jesus" today: He is said to be man, but not God. He is said to be crucified, but not risen from the dead. The false teachers at Corinth certainly have their modern counterparts.

- That the words, "another spirit" and "another gospel" translate, not *allos* (meaning another of the same kind), but *heteros,* meaning another of a different kind. In saying "another spirit", Paul refers, not to the liberty and power of the Holy Spirit, but to bondage. See Romans 8 verse 15: "For ye have not received the spirit of bondage again to fear; but ye have received the Spirit of adoption, whereby we cry, Abba, Father". In saying "another gospel", Paul refers to a totally different message. See Galatians 1 verses 6-7, "I marvel that ye are so soon removed from him that called you into (in) the grace of Christ unto another (*heteros*) gospel (that is, a gospel which is not of the same kind): which is not another (*allos*)" (that is, a gospel of the same kind).

ii) Believers are preserved by pure teaching, vv.5-6. In this connection we must notice two matters: Paul's position (v.5) and) Paul's preaching (v.6).

- His position, v.5. "For I suppose I was not a whit behind the very chiefest apostles" or "For I reckon that I am not a whit behind the very chiefest apostles" (R.V). The point of the statement is this: in view of the fact that they were disposed to bear with "he that cometh", there was every reason for them to bear with him (see v.1) in view of the fact that he was "not a whit behind the very chiefest apostles". P.E.Hughes puts it as follows; "You bear well enough with an intruder such as I have just described (v.4); then I ask you at least to bear with me".

But who were the "very chiefest apostles?" See also Chapter 12 verse 11. It could be argued that the reference is to Peter, James and John. Paul would be thus saying that if the Corinthians were prepared to bear with the deceivers, they could well bear with him as comparable with the very chief apostles in view of his calling, labours and gifts. But it seems highly likely that the irony continues from verse 4, and that reference is being made, in fact, to the false teachers, who with all their self-recommendation and glory, are described as 'extra-super-apostles' (P.E.Hughes). W.E.Vine explains that the word *huperlian* derives from "*huper*, over, and *lian,* exceedingly, pre-eminently, very much". They were in fact, "False apostles, deceitful workers, transforming themselves into the apostles of Christ" (v.13).

- His preaching, v.6. The words, "But though I be rude in speech" or "But if [I am] a simple person in speech" (JND), suggest that his detractors had made an accusation against him to this effect. Paul meets the charge 'head on': "But though I be rude in speech, yet not in knowledge; but we have been throughly made manifest among you in all things".

The accusation was that he was "rude in speech". The word "rude" *(idiotes)* means 'ignorant', and refers primarily to a private person in contrast to a State official, i.e., a person without professional knowledge: someone unskilled. It is translated "unlearned" in 1 Corinthians 14 verses 16, 23, 24, and "ignorant" in Acts 4 verse 13. Paul, however, deliberately eschewed oratory. See 1 Corinthians 2 verse 1, "And I, brethren, when I came to you, came not with excellency of speech, or of wisdom, declaring unto you the testimony of God". But "though I be rude in speech, yet not in knowledge" because it was the testimony - or mystery - of God that he declared!

Not only so, the Corinthians themselves knew the reality of Paul's spiritual knowledge and power, which he made manifest unto all men: "in everything we have made it manifest among all men to you ward" (RV) or "But in everything making [the truth] manifest in all things to you" (JND). "He humbly admits that his 'speech' is not that polished rhetoric so popular in Greek circles and perhaps not uncommon at Corinth, but when it came to what really counts, namely 'knowledge', he is ahead of any of his rivals. This claim could not be questioned amongst them for he had fully proved that it was true when he was with them. Ignorance, even though dressed in rhetorical garb, is no asset to anyone, nor can it profit the hearers. On the other hand, those who speak should strive to express what they know in the language suited to their hearers. 'Words easy to be understood' are seldom out of place" (A.McShane).

2) THE EXCLUSION OF THEIR SUPPORT, vv.7-12

We must notice here that *(a)* he refused support from Corinth (v.7); *(b)* he received support from others (vv.8-10); *(c)* he relates the reason for this apparent contradiction (vv.11-12).

a) He refused support from Corinth, v.7

"Have I committed an offence in abasing myself that ye might be exalted, because I have preached to you the gospel of God freely?". The sense of "exalted" is spiritually blessed: raised from the depths (perhaps referring to death) of sin.

The accusation here was that Paul had "preached...the gospel of God freely" at Corinth in his refusal of financial and material support, and therefore could not be an apostle of the highest order. He had a right, as an apostle, to receive remuneration. He had dealt with this in 1 Corinthians 9. He had every right to support: "thou shalt not muzzle the mouth of the ox that treadeth out the corn", and stated "Do ye not know that they which minister about holy things live of the things of the temple? and they which wait at the altar are partakers with the altar? Even so hath the Lord ordained that they which preach the gospel should live of the gospel. **But I have used none of these things**..." (1 Cor. 9: 9, 13-15). Compare Nehemiah 5 verse 15, "the former governors... were chargeable unto the people, and had taken of them bread and wine, beside forty shekels of silver... but so did not I, because of the fear of God".

In what sense then did he use the expression, "Or did I commit a sin in abasing myself that ye might be exalted, because I preached to you the gospel of God for nought?" (RV) It could be that reference was being made to the practice of "accredited rhetoricians and philosophers" (P.E.Hughes) to charge for their services, and therefore to live as a humble artisan (he was a tentmaker, Acts 18: 3) implied that Paul had broken the rules - inferring that he was worthless anyway. If this is the case, then Paul is, again, using irony. It seems more likely however that Paul was being charged with insulting the Corinthians by refusing their support, and demonstrating an arrogant independence.

Paul deliberately pursued this policy, not only at Corinth, but in Thessalonica: "Ye remember, brethren, our labour and travail: labouring night and day because we would not be chargeable unto any of you, we preached unto you the gospel of God" (1 Thess. 2: 9). Compare 2 Corinthians 3 verse 8. So too at Ephesus: "Ye yourselves know that these hands ministered unto my necessities" (Acts 20: 34). Paul's reason for this differed from place to place. At Corinth, it was "to cut off occasion from them which desire occasion" (v.12).

b) He received support from others, vv.8-10

"I robbed other churches (poor churches at that), taking wages of them, to do you service" (v.8). The word "wages" refers, strictly speaking, to soldier's pay: a soldier's "money for buying rations" (P.E.Hughes).

The words, "I robbed other churches" are explained: "And when I was present with you, and wanted, I was chargeable to no man: for that which was lacking to me the brethren which came from Macedonia supplied: and in all things I have kept myself from being burdensome unto you, and so will I keep myself" (v.9). He continues: "As the truth of Christ is in me (he expresses himself in the strongest terms), no man shall stop me of this boasting in the regions of Achaia". But why did Paul do this? This follows:

c) His reason for this, vv.11-12

"Wherefore? because I love you not? God knoweth" (v.11). It was evidently suggested that the reason for refusing financial support was lack of love towards them. He was cold of heart towards them. God knew otherwise: "God knoweth". (Sometimes we have to leave the matter there). See, for example 1 Thessalonians 2 verse 5.

"But what I do, that I will do, that I may *cut off occasion* ('the opportunity', JND) from them which desire occasion ('an opportunity', JND); that wherein they glory, they may be found even as we" (v.12). He was determined to act in this way to shew that they had no superiority over him at all: they accepted support for their so-called ministry: he did not. They could not claim that he was seeking his own interests.

The words, "That wherein they glory, they may be found even as we", are not without difficulty. The meaning appears to be this: *(i)* Paul's opponents were looking for "occasion" ('an opportunity', JND). What was it? *(ii)* It was evidently to induce him to take support, with this result *(iii)* that instead of being "cut off" from "occasion", and therefore disadvantaged, they would be on the same level as Paul himself. This explains 'the occasion' they desired: that in accepting financial support - and boasting in it - they would be precisely the same as Paul, because he did it too. As it was, they were disadvantaged - Paul did *not* do it!

3) THE EXPOSURE OF HIS OPPONENTS, vv.13-15

In this section, Paul denounces the false teachers in the plainest terms: he drops the irony, and goes straight to the point and describes *(a)* what they were (v.13); *(b)* who they served (v.14); *(c)* how they end (v.15).

a) What they were, v.13

"For such are false apostles, deceitful workers, transforming themselves into the apostles of Christ." We must notice that they were:

i)   *"False apostles".* Compare Revelation 2 verse 2, "thou hast tried them which say they are apostles..." There is a lot of falsehood in the Bible! False apostles...teachers...brethren, *et al.* See also Titus 1 verse 10, "vain talkers and deceivers, specially they of the circumcision"; Romans 16 verses 17-18, "mark them which cause divisions and offences contrary to the doctrine which ye have learned...by good words and fair speeches deceive the hearts of the simple ('unsuspecting', JND)".

ii) *"Transforming themselves".* They did this actively and deliberately. Not by the grace of God. Paul does not use the Greek word *metamorphoo,* where the emphasis is on *inward* change, but *metaschematizo,* where the emphasis is upon *outward* change. To change in fashion and appearance.

b) Who they served, v.14

"And no marvel; for **Satan** himself is transformed into an angel of light." The same word for "transformed" (*metaschematizo)* is used here. This reveals, very clearly, the power controlling the false teachers. Satan's presentation is totally incongruous. He is "a liar...the father of it" (John 8: 44). Darkness is his proper sphere. We cannot fail to notice the danger of this approach - there is no misunderstanding a "roaring lion" – but Satan's transformation "into an angel of light" is decidedly perilous. We have an early example , "And the serpent said unto the woman, Ye shall not surely die" (Gen. 3: 4).

c) How they end, v.15

"Therefore it is no great thing if his ministers also be transformed as the ministers of righteousness; whose *end* shall be according to their works." That is, it will be fitting: "whose end is destruction" (Phil. 3: 19); "whose judgment is just" (Rom. 3: 8 JND); "let him be Anathema" (1 Cor. 16: 22); "let him be accursed" (Gal. 1: 8-9). In summary:

How they appeared	What they were
"Apostles of Christ"	"False apostles"
"Angel of light"	"Satan himself"
"Ministers of righteousness"	"His ministers"

But how are they identified? They preach "another Jesus"; they have "another spirit"; they preach "another gospel" (v.4). They seduce from Christ.

4) THE EXPLANATION OF HIS FOLLY, vv.16-33

Paul now resumes his main theme. This commenced in verse 1: "Would to God ye could bear with me a little in my *folly*". So: "I say again, Let no man think me a fool; if otherwise, yet as a fool receive me, that I may boast myself a little" (v.16).

This section may be divided as follows: *(a)* he acts the role of a fool (vv.16-18); *(b)* he accuses them of accommodating fools (vv.19-20); *(c)* he admits the foolishness of his role (v.21); *(d)* he adopts the role of a fool (vv.22-33).

a) He acts the role of a fool, vv.16-18

"I say again, Let no man think of me as a fool; if otherwise, yet as a fool receive me, that I may boast myself a little" (v.16). So fools boast!

Paul makes it clear *(i)* that he should not be regarded as a fool, and *(ii)* but if they did regard him in this way, then he would act foolishly by glorying a little, even though it was foreign for him to do so. After all he does describe himself as "less than the least of all saints" (Eph. 3: 8), but as verses 17-18 demonstrate, he was simply taking the same ground of those who "glory after the flesh" (v.18). They 'gloried in the flesh', but he could beat them hands down there!

There was nothing spiritual in what he was about to do: "That which I speak, I speak it not after the Lord, but as it were foolishly, in this confidence of boasting" (v.17). In boasting of himself "a little", he did not speak "after the Lord". This is not a denial of inspiration: Paul is saying that he was not acting as the Lord Jesus who "humbled himself". *What* he did was not "after the Lord", but *why* he did it was!

There were two alternatives; *(i)* to speak "after the Lord" or *(ii)* to "glory after the flesh". He proceeds with the second alternative: "Seeing that many glory after the flesh, I will glory also". He was going to deliberately take the ground of his opponents. They gloried 'after the flesh'. Very well, although it was foolish for him to do so, he too would glory 'after the flesh'. He would meet their claims in full on their own ground!

b) He accuses them of accommodating fools, vv.19-20

Since "ye suffer fools gladly, seeing ye yourselves are wise" (v.19), then they could easily suffer him! Those fools gloried "after the flesh", the Corinthians could therefore accommodate him too!

But how did they 'suffer fools gladly?' "For ye suffer *(i)* if a man bring you into bondage; *(ii)* if a man devour you; *(iii)* if a man take of you; *(iv)* if a man exalt himself; *(v)* if a man smite you on the face" (v.20).

i) **"If a man bring you into bondage"**, meaning 'utter bondage' (*katadouloo*). Either bondage to the law (Gal. 4: 9; 5: 1) or bondage to themselves.

ii) **"If a man devour you",** meaning 'to consume by eating' or 'to swallow up'. They preyed on them - lived off them financially.

iii) **"If a man take of you",** meaning, to take captive. False teachers had ensnared believers at Corinth in the trap laid for them. Note the contrast with Chapter 12 verse 16.

iv) **"If a man exalt himself":** that is, they 'lorded it over the Corinthian flock': indulged in self-exultation.

v) **"If a man smite you on the face."** This could be figurative: "enduring gross affronts from the lips of these overbearing intruders" (P.E.Hughes). Although unlikely, it could be literal: see Acts 23 verse 2, where Ananias commanded Paul to be struck.

c) He admits the foolishness of his role, v.21

"I speak (regarding what he has just said) as concerning reproach, as though we had been weak". That is, if the things described in verse 20 are the marks of true authority - then he had been weak! This is, of course, ironical. But now he leaves that irony, and speaks boldly. So:

"Howbeit whereinsoever any is bold, (I speak foolishly), I am bold also." He now intends to assert himself - like the rest! So:

d) He adopts the role of a fool, vv.22-33

Paul does this in two ways: *(i)* in declaring his ancestry, verse 22 ("I speak foolishly", v.21); *(ii)* in describing his service, verses 23-33 ("I speak as a fool", v.23).

i)   In declaring his ancestry, v.22. "Are they Hebrews? so am I. Are they Israelites? so am I. Are they the seed of Abraham? so am I." Paul was equal to them nationally. In themselves, these things however count for nothing: see, for example, John 8 verse 39, Philippians 3 verse 3. It was "confidence in the flesh".

ii)   In describing his service, vv.23-33. Paul exceeded them in endurance. "Are they ministers of Christ? (I speak as a fool) I am more; in labours more abundant, in stripes above measure, in prisons more frequent, in deaths oft" (v.23). They might have called themselves "ministers of Christ", but they knew nothing of the sufferings of Christ.

He was equal to them in verse 22: now, utterly beyond them in experience. This was a sphere utterly unknown to his opponents. The catalogue exceeds the record in Acts, and fulfils Acts 9 verse 16, "I will shew him how many things he must suffer for my name's sake".

-   His service involved pain, vv.23-25. "In stripes above measure, in prisons more frequent, in deaths *oft.* Of the Jews *five* times received I forty stripes save one. Thrice was I beaten with rods, *once* I was stoned, *thrice* I suffered shipwreck, a night and a day I have been in the deep."

The statement, "Of the Jews five times received I forty stripes save one" refers to Deuteronomy 25 verse 3, "And it shall be, if the wicked man be worthy to be beaten...forty stripes he may give him, and not exceed". In practice, we are told, one less than the forty stripes was required to ensure that the maximum was not by miscalculation exceeded. "Thrice was I beaten by rods". These were Gentile beatings. See Acts 16 verse 22: "the magistrates...commanded to beat them with rods." (RV).

It has been suggested that verses 24-25 are a parenthesis, and illustrate "in deaths oft". In all the circumstances described, Paul could say, "We are killed all the day long" (Rom. 8: 36).

-   His service involved perils, v.26. Paul resumes the mainstream of his remarks: "In journeyings often, in *perils* of waters, in *perils* of robbers, in *perils* by my own countrymen, in *perils* by the heathen, in *perils* in the city, in *perils* in the wilderness, in *perils* in the sea, in *perils* among false brethren".

The last of these is the most feared. He faced what Corinth was experiencing: "false brethren".

- *His service involved privations, v.27.* "In weariness and painfulness ('in labours and toil', JND), in watchings often, in hunger and thirst, in fastings often, in cold and nakedness." Compare 1 Corinthians 4 verses 11-13: "Even unto this present hour we both hunger and thirst, and are naked, and are buffeted".

Note that the lowliness of his service is emphasised - not its greatness. Paul makes no reference to "bearing my name before kings" (Acts 9: 15).

- *His service involved pastoral concern, vv.28-29.* "Beside those things that are without, that which cometh upon me daily, the care of all the churches." Note: not now "oft...five times...thrice...once" (vv.24-25), but "daily". So his pastoral concern was more important to him than his privations. Observe the emphasis: "That which **presseth** upon me **daily"** (RV). "The care *(anxiety)* of all the churches" was a daily burden to Paul.

The false teachers wanted, not "the care of all the churches", but the control of all the churches. This explains Paul's attitude. He saw the danger facing the churches, and Corinth in particular. "The honour of Christ's name is a supreme concern. To see Christ's name dishonoured in the church above all places caused Paul the acutest grief" (P.E.Hughes). So:

"Who is weak, and I am not weak? who is offended, and I burn not?" Paul felt deeply the frailty of the churches. He identified with them in their weakness, and burned with indignation against the stumbling-blocks. This was a priestly attitude, reminding us that "we have not an high priest which cannot be touched with the feeling of our infirmities" (Heb. 4: 15).

- *His service involved personal infirmity, vv.30-33.* "If I must needs glory, I will glory of the things which concern mine infirmities" (v.30). The words, "If I must needs glory" are indicative of the distaste of this to Paul. His circumstances, that is, the self-commendation of the false apostles, made it necessary. Throughout the epistle, Paul has drawn attention to his own weakness (see, for example, 4: 7-11) to show that it has been the occasion of divine power in his life.

He calls upon the most solemn witnesses to attest what he has said. "The God and Father of our Lord Jesus Christ, which is blessed for evermore, knoweth that I lie not" (v.31). He had no desire to boast in his own achievements: he genuinely gloried in his own weakness, since, as noted above, it became the occasion of God's power. This will become clear in Chapter 12 verses 9-10. It was not a case of 'I'm ever so humble!'

Paul certainly left Damascus in anything but glory and honour. "In Damascus the governor under Aretas the king kept the city of the Damascenes with a garrison, desirous to apprehend me: and through a window in a basket was I let down by the wall, and escaped his hands" (vv.32-33). These verses are a example of his weakness, and occur immediately before a passage in which he speaks of his highest exaltation and privilege. He is about to speak of being "caught up". But here it is a case of being let down! It was hardly a distinguished and glorious exit from Damascus! It was most humbling, and indicated his great weakness. But the man who was shown to be so weak was given the highest conceivable privilege: "Caught up to the third heaven...caught up into paradise" (12: 2, 4). This illustrates the fact that "before honour is humility" (Prov. 15: 33; 18: 12), reminding us of Peter's injunction: "humble yourselves therefore under the mighty hand of God, that he may exalt you in due time" (1 Pet. 5: 6).

2 CORINTHIANS

"Caught up into paradise"

Read Chapter 12: 1-21

Chapters 10-12 are punctuated by boasting or glorying. But, to coin a phrase, there was 'a method in his madness'. Since the false teachers were given to boasting or glorying, Paul plays the same game, not willingly - he calls it 'folly' - but to secure the spiritual safety of the Corinthians: "I am become a fool in glorying (boasting); ye have compelled me" (12: 11). It was distasteful to him (11: 17).

Looking back, we should notice the following: *(i)* he boasted in his *authority* (10: 1-11): see verse 8: it was God-given; *(ii)* he boasted in his *ministry* (10: 12-18): see verses 13, 15-17: it was God-given; *(iii)* he boasted in his *policy*, that is, not to accept support (11: 1-15): see verse 10; *(iv)* he boasted in his *identity* (11: 16-32): see verse 18, "Seeing that many glory after the flesh, I will glory also": see verse 22, "Are they Hebrews? so am I..." *(v)* he boasted in his *adversity* (11: 23-33): see verse 30. Now, *(vi)* he boasted in his *revelations* (12: 1-13): see verses 1, 7.

2 Corinthians 12 may be divided as follows: *(1)* the third heaven (vv.1-5); *(2)* the thorn in the flesh (vv.6-10); *(3)* the true apostle (vv.11-13); *(4)* the third coming (vv.14-21).

1) THE THIRD HEAVEN, vv.1-5

"It is not expedient for me doubtless, to glory: I will come to visions (involving *sight*) and revelations (involving *hearing and dreams*) of the Lord" or "I must needs glory, though it is not expedient" (RV). He feels compelled to complete the 'boastful' course on which he had embarked, even though it was irksome for him to do so. What Paul is about to say, arises, not from his personal wishes, but because circumstances required it: see verse 11, "I am become a fool in glorying; ye have compelled me".

It has been suggested that "visions" relate to directions and service, whereas "revelations" relate to doctrine. For "visions and revelations", see Acts 10 verses 10, 17 ("he fell into a trance…doubted in himself what this vision which he had seen should mean"); Galatians 2 verse 2; Acts 16 verse 9; Acts 18 verse 9. Paul describes them as "visions and revelations *of the Lord*" We have to decide whether this is subjective, that is, revelations given *by* Him, or objective, that is, revelations given *of* Him. They are certainly "of the *Lord*", that is, of the *risen Christ*. "God hath made Him both Lord and Christ."

What follows is a further part of his strategy of taking his detractors on their own ground. Observe how he does this - not for one moment glorying in himself. We must notice *(a)* the person (v.2); *(b)* the period (v.2); *(c)* the place (vv.2-4); *(d)* the purpose (v.4).

a) The person, v.2

"I knew a man in Christ above fourteen years ago (whether in the body, I cannot tell, or whether out of the body, I cannot tell, God knoweth), such a one, caught up to the third heaven." We must notice the following:

i) Paul speaks of *"a man in Christ"*. Recognition that glory is due to Christ. He is accepted in Christ. He has no merit of his own. In the words of A.McShane: this is "a way of hiding his identity: the unimportant role he played in it".

ii) Paul speaks in the *third person.* There is no reference to "I". This he only uses again in verse 7 where, of course, it is made clear that he is fact speaking of himself. In this, he avoids speaking boastfully of his experience: it would have been a wonderful opportunity to say, 'I…I…I…I'!

b) The period, v.2

"Above fourteen years ago." He had kept it that long! No doubt others would have publicised the fact as soon as possible! Not so Paul! The matter was kept to himself. Compare David who killed a lion and a bear, but who evidently said nothing about it until required to prove his valour! (1 Sam. 17: 34-36).

A calculation will show that his experience must have been approximated to his call to service in Acts 13.

"Whether in the body, I cannot tell; or whether out of the body, I cannot tell, God knoweth." (See also v.3). Paul could not tell whether he was caught up **bodily**, or in a **disembodied** condition. Either were possible: *(i)* "in the body": see, for example, 1 Thessalonians 4 verse 17. In this connection, we think of Enoch and Elijah and, of course. the Lord Jesus Himself; *(ii)* "out of the body": see, for example, 2 Corinthians 5 verse 8, "absent from the body...present (at home) with the Lord".

c) The place, vv.2-4

"Such an one caught up to the **third heaven** (where it is)...he was caught up into **paradise** (what it is)." We should notice *(i)* the location: where it is; *(ii)* the description: what it is.

i)   The location: where it is

"Caught up to the **third heaven**" (v.2). The words "caught up", meaning snatched or caught away, are also found in 1 Thessalonians 4 verse 17. He was "let down" in Chapter 11 verse 33: now he is "caught up!"

The expression, "the third heaven" evidently describes the immediate presence of God, and His glorified Son. This is "**heaven itself**" (Heb. 9: 24), a term which is perfectly consistent with "made higher than the heavens" (Heb. 7: 26), and "ascended up far above all heavens" (Eph. 4: 10). The latter phrases emphasise His complete transcendence over every conceivable sphere, however elevated. See also Hebrews 4 verse 14, "Having therefore a great high priest who has passed through the heavens..." (JND). This must be the place where the saints are who are "with Christ" (Phil. 1: 23) and "present with the Lord" (2 Cor. 5: 8).

The "third heaven" is evidently "the heaven of heavens" (1 Kings 8: 27). Thus: the atmospheric heavens, the stellar heavens, **the third heaven.** The expression "heaven of heavens" is also found in Deuteronomy 10 verse 14 ("Behold the heavens and the heaven of heavens is the LORD's thy God") and Psalm 68 verse 33 ("him that rideth upon the heaven of heavens"). Perhaps, however, careful thought should be given to the fact that according to the Newberry Bible, both "*heaven*" and "the "*heaven* of heavens are in the dual number. This is also the case in Genesis 1 verse 1, but understandably so when we remember that God created the heavens by speaking from His uncreated dwelling-place.

The atmospheric heavens, the stellar heavens, *the third heaven*, have been likened to the tabernacle with its court, holy place, *and holy of holies*. The last is the ultimate: there dwelt the 'Shekinah Glory'.

ii) The description: what it is

"And I knew such a man (whether in the body, or out of the body, I cannot tell; God knoweth) how that he was caught up into paradise" (vv.3-4). We now have further information in connection with Paul's experience - his rapture. The repetition in verse 3 indicates, not a second experience, but the same experience: hence the one time given. In verse 2, it is "caught up to the third heaven", with the idea of *as far as* "the third heaven".

Now it is "*into*" Paradise. But what is "*paradise*"? According to Wm. Kelly, "paradise …not only heavenly, but the choicest part, as Adam's was of the earth". The word is probably of Persian origin, meaning an enclosure, and hence a pleasure-garden, or a park. The Greek translators of the Old Testament (the Septuagint, LXX) used *paradeisos* of the garden of Eden.

It occurs in Luke 23 verse 43, "Today thou shalt be with me in *paradise*": the penitent thief was assured of presence with Christ. That is, in a disembodied state. Not a *descent*: but an *ascent!* It occurs in Revelation 2 verse 7, "To him that overcometh will I give to eat of the tree of life, which is in the midst of the *paradise* of God".

In this connection we should notice the *correct* meaning of Hebrews 2 verses 14-15. Not deliverance from some mythical compartment in *hades,* but deliverance - like Israel - from bondage on earth. In this case, the bondage of sin! We should also consider the meaning of Ephesians 4 verse 8: "When he ascended up on high, he led captivity captive". This cites Psalm 68 verse 18, which in turn refers back to Judges 5 verse 12: "Lead thy captivity captive, thou son of Abinoam". We should notice that the words, "he led captivity captive", can be rendered 'a multitude of captives'. Judges 5 clarifies this: Barak led the captivity captive which had previously held Israel captive. The Lord Jesus has defeated the powers of darkness which held us in bondage. Now - in place of bondage - He has "*given gifts* unto men". He has bound the "strong man" and "divided the spoils".

"Paradise", therefore, is the present abode of the disembodied spirits of the redeemed, awaiting the day when they will be "clothed upon" with their "house which is from heaven" (2 Cor. 5: 2). It is, "absent from the body… present with the Lord". It is, "to be with Christ which is **far better**". See also 2 Corinthians 4 verse 17, "For our light affliction, which is but for a moment, worketh for us a far more exceeding and eternal weight of **glory**"; Romans 8 verse 18, "For I reckon, that the sufferings of this present time are not worthy to be compared with **the glory** which shall be revealed in us". How could Paul make such statements? The answer is evidently that **he had been there!** See our current passage.

"Paradise" is not "a shadowy waiting room, but a blissful abode within the very court of heaven itself...there they are beyond the reach of sin and suffering, without fear of being driven out, as happened in the first Paradise" (P.E.Hughes).

Just as Peter, James, and John - all of whom suffered for their faith - were given a vision of glory - so was Paul! But, so far as those three apostles were concerned, it was an **earthly** experience, and related to an **earthly kingdom.** But for Paul it was a **heavenly** experience, and related to a **heavenly home**.

d) The purpose, v.4

"And heard unspeakable words, which it is not lawful for a man to utter." If unable to say what he saw and heard, why take him up to heaven at all? It was for Paul **personally,** and in particular, with relation to his personal strengthening for his labour and adversity. If we assume that Paul was converted in AD37, called at Antioch in AD45, and martyred in AD67, he had over twenty years of intense suffering before him. See 2 Corinthians 11 and Luke's record (in Acts) of his sufferings. Hence the revelation was given to strengthen him for the future.

Paul refers here to **"unspeakable words"**. Not ecstatic language: rather that the revelation could not be translated into earthly or human terminology. The word "unspeakable" here differs from its usage elsewhere. In 2 Corinthians 9 verse 15, it means 'inexpressible' or 'cannot be related'; in 1 Peter 1 verse 8, 'cannot be told out'; here, literally, 'cannot be spoken'. "Unspeakable", possibly in the sense of 'too sacred to be uttered' (Moulton and Milligan cited by W.E.Vine).

"Of such an one will I glory (that is, of the "man in Christ"): yet of myself I will not glory, but in mine infirmities."

2) THE THORN IN THE FLESH, vv.6-10

In these verses, Paul describes how the Lord safeguarded him in two ways: *(a)* against the temptation to be *exalted* (vv.6-7); *(b)* against the temptation to be *depressed* (vv.8-10).

a) The temptation to be exalted, vv.6-7

We must notice here that *(i)* his testimony did not consist of a vision (v.6); *(ii)* that his humility was not endangered by the vision (v.7).

i)   His testimony did not consist of a vision, v.6

"For though I would desire to glory, I shall not be a fool; for I will say the truth: but now I forbear, lest any man should think of me above that which he seeth me to be, or that he heareth of me."

Paul again emphasises his desire to glory only in his weaknesses (v.5). He had every right to glory in what had happened fourteen years previously: what he had said was perfectly truthful: *so unlike his enemies.* But even so, he forebears to glory in it: "Lest any man should think of me above that which he seeth me to be, or that he heareth of me". He does not want to be regarded as some super-spiritual person, but simply as a frail mortal, sustained by divine strength. Nothing said for fourteen years! The important thing is not a vision, but that which "he *seeth* me to be, and that he *heareth* of me".

ii)   His humility was not endangered by the vision, v.7

Not only does he not wish *others* to think so, but "lest *I* should be exalted above measure through the abundance of the revelations, there was given to me a thorn in the flesh, the messenger of Satan to buffet me, lest *I* should be exalted above measure". We should notice:

-   *"there was given to me".* As a divine favour. Though apparently of Satan's malice, God intended it to be helpful: to counteract temptation to exaltation.

- **"a thorn in the flesh"**. While Paul's "thorn in the flesh" is completely unidentified - for very good reasons - it is the reason for its introduction that is important. Paul's "thorn in the flesh" was evidently most humiliating, and it seems quite clear that his enemies frequently alluded to it. See 2 Corinthians 10 verse 10, "his bodily presence is weak, and his speech contemptible". He now explains that, far from being a mark of weakness, it was the result of his highest exaltation.

The fact that it is unidentified is quite deliberate: every servant of Christ can point to his own weakness - physical, private, psychological - which keeps him in humble dependence upon God. Explanations are legion: perhaps Sir William Ramsay's suggestion of malarial fever being the best, but **the anonymity of the affliction is its greatest lesson**. We do not know exactly what it was, because, if we did, we would then reserve it for that situation alone.

We should notice the word, "**thorn**", meaning stake - a sharpened, wooden, shaft. We should notice the words, "**in the flesh**" or "**for** the flesh" (JND). Not necessarily physical: though probably so. See Galatians 4 verse 13: "Ye know how through infirmity of the flesh I preached the gospel unto you at first; and that which was a temptation to you in my flesh ye despised not, nor rejected, but ye received me as an angel of God, even as Christ Jesus".

- **"the messenger of Satan"**. Some understand this to be a person, for example, Alexander the coppersmith, but the sense seems to be that what happened was Satanic in origin. Better, it originated **with God**; Satan was the **instrument!** Satan only personally attacks key people: he is not omnipresent. So Job, so David, So Paul, and so, pre-eminently, the Lord Jesus.

- **"to buffet me"**. Literally, 'to strike with the fist'. Compare Matthew 26 verse 67.

We should notice how God overruled Satan. As a result of the "messenger of Satan", Paul was led **to pray** (v.8); Paul was led to **hear the Lord's voice** (v.9); Paul was led to **spiritual power** (v.9).

- **"lest I should be exalted above measure"**. Here is the purpose. Paul was to be constantly reminded of his weakness, though he was the recipient of "the abundance of the revelations".

b) The temptation to be depressed, vv.8-10

If his testimony did not consist of a vision (v.6), and his humility was not endangered by the vision (v.7), then his strength did not depend on the vision (vv.8-10).

"For this thing I besought the Lord *thrice,* that it might depart from me" (v.8). The word "thrice" probably refers to three occasions on which he was buffeted. The force of his buffeting turned him to utter dependence on the Lord for grace and strength. See above - God overruled Satan. As we have already noted, as a result of the "messenger of Satan", *(i)* Paul was led to pray (v.8); *(ii)* Paul was led to hear the Lord's voice (v.9) *(iii)* Paul was led to spiritual power (v.9). With this in mind, Paul *no longer* prayed that "it might depart from me"!

He prayed to One who in Gethsemane prayed three times, "O my Father, if it be possible, let this cup pass from me: nevertheless, not as I will, but as Thou wilt". The Lord Jesus was crowned with thorns and buffeted.

"I besought the *Lord."* The Lord Jesus. Compare Acts 7 verse 59, "Lord Jesus receive my spirit". Evidently he prays to the Lord Jesus here, who replied: "*My grace* is sufficient for thee: for *my strength* is made perfect in weakness". There are other instances in the Acts where the Lord Jesus is addressed directly. It has to be said, however, that these are private rather than public petitions.

"And He said unto me, My grace is sufficient for thee: for my strength is made perfect in weakness…" (v.9). The prayer of Paul was not unanswered: it was heard and heeded - but he was not promised deliverance *from* his affliction, but divine grace ("my grace…my strength") *for* the affliction. We should notice that *(i)* grace provides salvation in *the past* (Titus 1: 2); *(ii)* grace provides sufficiency for *the present* (2 Cor. 12: 9); *(iii)* grace provides satisfaction in *the future* (Eph. 2: 7). God had more use for Paul's weakness than He did for Paul's strength. Our strength is His rival: our weakness is His vehicle.

"Most gladly therefore will I rather glory in my infirmities that the power of Christ may rest upon me" (v.9). See also 2 Corinthians 11 verse 30, "If I must needs glory, I will glory of the things which concern mine infirmities"; 2 Corinthians 12 verse 5, "Of such a one will I glory, yet of myself I will not glory, but in mine infirmities".

He had spoken of "visions and revelations of the Lord": of them he had said, "It is not expedient for me, doubtless, to glory" (v.1). Now he says, "Most gladly therefore will I *rather* glory". Why the change? Because in his "infirmities" - 'weaknesses' - the "thorn in the flesh" - he can experience the strength of Christ. In his own words, "Most gladly therefore will I rather glory in my infirmities, that the power of Christ may rest upon me" or "spread a tabernacle over me" (RV margin).

"Therefore *I take pleasure* in infirmities, (then, expanding this) in reproaches (injuries), in necessities, in persecutions, in distresses, for Christ's sake: for when I am weak, then am I strong" (v.10). Compare Psalm 119 verse 71, "It is good for me that I have been afflicted; that I might learn thy statutes". Compare 2 Corinthians 4 verses 8-9, "We are *troubled* on every side, yet not *distressed*....*persecuted*, but not *forsaken*..." See also 2 Corinthians 4 verses 10-11, "Always bearing about in the body the dying of the Lord Jesus, that the life also of Jesus might be manifest in our body".

It was not that Paul found the experiences pleasurable, but he welcomed them nevertheless, since they brought divine strength for him to continue. It has been said that Peter was naturally strong, but weak, and Paul was naturally weak, but strong.

3) THE TRUE APOSTLE, vv.11-13

In these verses, we should notice *(a)* failure to support his apostleship at Corinth (v.11); *(b)* proof of his apostleship at Corinth (vv.12-13).

a) Failure to support his apostleship at Corinth.

Paul comments finally on all that he has said in this passage thus far: "I am become a fool: ye compelled me..." (v.11). It was the Corinthians themselves who had compelled Paul to take this line of argument. *They should have commended him.* It ought never to have been necessary for Paul to commend himself, taking a "foolish" position in so doing, though actually taking the same ground as ye have the false apostles who did commend themselves. The assembly at Corinth should have stood up for Paul against his opponents - after all, they were his letter of commendation (see 3: 1-3). They had witnessed his apostolic credentials: they had every reason to recognise him.

211

"The very chiefest apostles", is, again (see 11: 5), a reference to the 'super-apostles' as they are ironically described. Paul himself – "I be nothing" - could say, "But by the grace of God I am what I am" (1 Cor. 15: 10). It should be said, however, that some feel that the reference here could be to Peter, James and John since they had been with the Lord on earth, as opposed to Paul who had not.

b) Proof of his apostleship at Corinth, vv.12-13

Paul speaks of the "the signs of an apostle". These were, for example, in conversions resulting from his ministry: "If I be not an apostle unto others, yet doubtless I am to you: for the seal on mine apostleship are ye in the Lord" (1 Cor. 9: 2). As in other places, his ministry was attended by divine authentication: "signs, and wonders, and mighty deeds". See Mark 16 verse 20. For "signs…wonders…mighty deeds", see also Hebrews 2 verse 4, "God also bearing them witness, both with signs and wonders, and with divers miracles, and gifts of the Holy Ghost, according to His own will". The same three words are used in connection with the Lord Jesus in Acts 2 verse 22, "Jesus of Nazareth a man approved of God among you, by miracles, wonders, and signs…" The same three words are also used in connection with the "man of sin" in 2 Thessalonians 2 verse 9, "Even him whose coming is after the working of Satan, with all power and signs and lying wonders". Satan is the arch-counterfeiter.

"Signs" stresses the significance of what was done: "wonders" expresses the impact of what was done: "miracles" emphasises the divine origin of what was done. Notice that Paul does not say that *he wrought* "signs, and wonders, and mighty deeds". His humility is evident.

"For what is it wherein ye were inferior to other churches…" (v.13). They had been blessed as much as others through his ministry. But it had been evidently suggested, probably by the 'super-apostles', that he had really treated them badly, and that was why he had not accepted support.

The fact that Paul returns to the question of financial support shows just how much he had evidently been slandered and misrepresented. See Chapter 11 verses 7-12. Notice how he combats this:

4) THE THIRD COMING, vv.14-21

We should notice here *(a)* Paul's reason or motive for his coming (vv.14-18); *(b)* Paul's regret or apprehension at his coming (vv.19-21)

a) Paul's reason for his coming, vv.14-18

"I seek not *yours*, but *you*" (v.14). He had no desire for their goods or money - only a desire for their spiritual welfare. Compare 1 Thessalonians 2 verse 8. There were no "hidden things of shame (AV 'dishonesty')" with Paul (4: 2, RV). He did not "make a trade of (AV 'corrupt') the word of God" (2: 17, JND).

As their **spiritual parent** ("for the children ought not to lay up for the parents, but the parents for the children", v.14), he will do the spending: "And I will very gladly spend and be spent for you..." (v.15) or "Now I shall most gladly spend and be utterly spent for your souls" (RV & JND). For the first occurrence here of "spend" (*dapanao*), see Mark 5 verse 26, "She had suffered many things of many physicians, and had **spent** all that she had". The second occurrence of "spent" ('spend') means 'spend entirely' (*ekdapanao*). He was prepared to do this, not just out of a sense of duty, but "very gladly" or "most gladly" (RV). Less love on their part did not diminish his love for them: "Though the more abundantly I love you, the less I be loved" (v.15).

The verses that follow (vv.16-18) probably refute a charge that Paul has used "guile" in obtaining financial support, i.e. although not directly burdensome, he had, none the less, achieved financial advantage. Not so, as the Corinthians well knew. "But be it so, I did not burden you; nevertheless, being crafty, I caught you with guile. Did I make a gain of you by any of them whom I sent unto you? I desired Titus, and with him I sent a brother: Did Titus make a gain of you? Walked we not in the same spirit? Walked we not in the same spirit?" The importance of 2 Corinthians 8 verses 16-23 now becomes clear. Paul certainly used "guile", but in the best sense. He deliberately refused support evidently knowing that to do so would have given his detractors ammunition to be used against him.

b) Paul's regret (or apprehension) at his coming, vv.19-21

"Again, think ye that we excuse ourselves unto you?" (v.19) or "Ye have long been supposing that we excuse ourselves to you" (JND). It is thought that Paul commences on an interrogative note: 'Have you been thinking all this time that I have been defending myself before you?' But Paul **stood before the Lord** in all that he said: "we speak before God in Christ: but we do all things, dearly beloved, for your edifying" It was not **self-protection**, but **their edification** which he had in mind. "But all things, beloved, are for your edification" (ASV).

In all, Paul wished to avoid an unpleasant confrontation (v.20). He makes this clear in saying that if this were the case, then:

- "I shall not find you such as I would" or "I should find you not such as I would" (RV).

- "I shall be found unto you such as ye would not" or "I should…myself be found of you such as ye would not" (RV). Compare Chapter 10 verses 2, 11.

As to the first ("I should find you not such as I would"), Paul says "For I fear, lest, **when I come**" he would find "debates ('strifes', JND), envyings ('jealousies', JND), wraths, strifes ('contentions', JND), backbitings, whisperings, swellings ('puffings up', JND), tumults ('disturbances', JND)" (v.20).

As to the second ('I should…myself be found of you such as ye would not'), Paul says. "And lest, "when **I come again, my** God will humble me among you, and that I shall bewail many (grieve over many', JND) which have sinned already ('sinned before', JND), and have not repented of the uncleanness and fornication and lasciviousness which they have committed" (v.21).

Paul does not denounce what he has not seen, but expresses misgivings. He gives opportunity for them to deal with the situation before his arrival. Evidently, there was a continuance in some evils. P.E.Hughes puts it as follows: "The language of this verse suggests that numbers of those who in the past had been guilty of immoral conduct, characteristic of the viciousness of the surrounding unregenerate Corinthian society, did not repent of their past wickedness…even if they had outwardly abandoned it. This showed that their heart was not right with God, that the root of the matter was not in them, and that, instead of the fruit of the Spirit, their lives were still productive of the works of the flesh".

2 CORINTHIANS

"Examine yourselves"

Read Chapter 13: 1-14

In introducing this Epistle, we noted that its structure follows the order of its historical background. Paul had come from **Asia**, he was writing from **Macedonia,** and he was going to Corinth in **Achaia.** With this in mind the Epistle may therefore be divided as follows *(i)* what had happened in Asia (Chapters 1-7): that was past; *(ii)* what was happening in Macedonia (Chapters 8-9): that was present; *(iii)* what would happen in Corinth (Chapters.10-13): that was future or prospective. "This is the third time I am coming to you" (13: 1).

The third section of the Epistle (Chapters 10-13) deals with false apostles attempting to destroy Paul's authority, and Chapter 13 emphasises that he would not shrink from dealing summarily with his accusers: "I told you before, and foretell you, as if I were present, the second time; and being absent now I wrote to them which heretofore have sinned, and to all other, that, if I come again, I will not spare: since ye seek a proof of Christ speaking in me..." (vv.2-3).

The chapter may be divided as follows: *(1)* Paul exerts his authority (vv.1-4); *(2)* Paul exhorts his readers (vv.5-6); *(3)* Paul explains his motives (vv.7-10); *(4)* Paul expresses his greetings (vv.11-14).

1) PAUL EXERTS HIS AUTHORITY, vv.1-4

In this section, Paul deals with three aspects of his authority: *(a)* its probity (v.1); *(b)* its proof (vv.2-3); *(c)* its power (v.4).

a) Its probity, v.1

"This is the third time I am coming to you: in the mouth of two or three witnesses shall every word be established." Paul would assert his authority with integrity. He would not abuse his authority. We should notice, however, *(i)* the time of his visit as well as *(ii)* the testimony of witnesses.

i) The time of his visit

"This is the third time I am coming to you." While not all agree with the explanation, it does seem that Paul refers here to the third of three occasions on which he was "in *the process* of coming to Corinth" (J.Heading).

-    *The first visit* took place in Acts 18. "After these things, Paul departed from Athens, and came to Corinth" (vv.1-18).

-    *The second visit* had been planned and involved travelling directly to Corinth from Ephesus (2 Cor. 1: 15) and thence to Macedonia, but conditions in the assembly made it preferable for him to delay his arrival. He therefore altered his plan to travel to Corinth via Macedonia (1 Cor. 16: 5, JND).

-    *The third visit* was now imminent. "Behold, the third time I am ready to come to you…" (2 Cor. 12: 14): "This is the third time I am coming to you" (2 Cor. 13: 1).

In support of this, we should notice that Paul calls the forthcoming visit "the second time": "I told you before, and foretell you, as if I were present, the second time" (v.2). John Heading gives two possible explanations, of which the second is particularly appealing: that this refers "to his forthcoming visit, and he foretells them in writing what he will tell them verbally, and what he had already told them either in his epistles or else during his first visit".

ii) The testimony of witnesses

"In the mouth of two or three witnesses shall every word be established." This cites Deuteronomy 17 verse 6; Deuteronomy 19 verse 15, and emphasises the necessity to establish the accuracy of a charge, and to act at all times with absolute integrity. These passages are cited elsewhere in the New Testament:

- *Matthew 18: 15-16*, "And if thy brother sin against thee, go and tell him his fault between thee and him alone: if he shall hear thee, thou hast gained thy brother. But if he will not hear thee, then take with thee one or two more, that in the mouth of two or three witnesses every word may be established."

- *1 Timothy 5: 19*, "Against an elder receive not an accusation, but before two or three witnesses".

- **Hebrews 10: 28**, "He that despised Moses' law died without mercy under two or three witnesses". (It as been suggested that the "two or three witnesses" here were Korah, Dathan, and Abiram, but this is questionable).

The teaching is clear: while Paul would not hesitate to act against the guilty at Corinth, he would not do so without reference to the principles of justice laid down in the Mosaic law, and confirmed by the Lord Jesus. He would not act on hearsay, or on 'grape vine' rumours, but on attested facts. We cannot stress the lesson sufficiently. It is so important to verify the facts, particularly if charges are being levelled or character is being maligned. Rumour is capable of amazing embroidery! In the Old Testament the charge of idolatry could only be acted upon after thorough investigation: "If there be found among you...man or woman, that hath wrought wickedness in the sight of the Lord thy God...And it be told thee, and thou hast heard of it, and inquired diligently, and, behold, it be true, and the thing certain, that such abomination is wrought in Israel: then thou shalt bring forth that man or that woman...and shalt stone them with stones, till they die" (Deut. 17: 2-5).

b) Its proof, vv.2-3

"I told you before and foretell you as if I were present the second time, and being absent now I write to them which heretofore have sinned, and to all other, that if I come again, I will not spare; since ye seek a proof of Christ speaking in me, which to you-ward is not weak, but is mighty in you."

The words, "I told you *before*" (RV, "I have said beforehand") and "*foretell* you as if I were present with you the second time" translate the same word (*proereo*). The RV makes this clear: "I have *said beforehand* and I *do say beforehand*, as when I was present the second time".

The apparent repetition here ('I have *said beforehand* and I *do say beforehand*') emphasises Paul's consistency: "I have said" and "I do say" (RV). He had not changed his mind! But what were the two occasions on which he had warned them of apostolic censure?

i) **The first warning** ("I have said", RV) is in his *first letter*. "But I will come unto you shortly, if the Lord will, and will know, not the speech of them which are puffed up, but the power" (1 Cor. 4 verse 21). Compare 1 Corinthians 4 verse 21.

ii)   The second warning ("I do say", RV) is in **this epistle**: "as if I were present the second time and being absent now I write to them which heretofore have sinned, and to all other, that if I come again, I will not spare", or "as if I were present the second time, even though I am now absent" (RV margin), or "as present the second time, and now absent" (JND).

Paul relates his warning to "them which heretofore have sinned". That is, to those "puffed up as though I would not come to you" (1 Cor. 4: 18): those who were attacking his authority. But he adds, "and to all other" ('the rest', RV), which evidently refers to any who had subsequently swelled their ranks. We must not overlook the seriousness of undermining apostolic authority, either then or now. Paul tells the Corinthians, "I will not spare". Compare 2 Peter 2 verses 4-5. Bearing in mind that "If any man think himself to be a prophet, or spiritual, let him acknowledge that the things that I write unto you are the commandments of the **Lord**" (1 Cor. 14: 37), it is equally serious if **we** disregard apostolic teaching.

Paul's unsparing censure of his detractors in this way would be proof of his apostolic authority. "If I come again, I will not spare: **since ye seek a proof of Christ speaking in me,** which to you-ward is not weak, but is mighty in you". This is quite self-explanatory. Those who required evidence of his apostolic authority, "a proof of Christ speaking in me", would have it: "I will not spare". See also Chapter 10 verse 2. Compare Chapter 1 verse 23.

Paul's authority was not vested in his own personality or ability, but in Christ: "Christ speaking in me". This is expressed again in verse 10, "the power which the **Lord hath given** me to edification and not to destruction". Compare 1 Thessalonians 4 verse 2: "For ye know what **commandments** we gave you by the Lord Jesus".

If Paul's critics wanted evidence that Christ **had** spoken to them through Paul, they had only to remember their own salvation. "Which to you-ward **is** not weak but **is** mighty in you". Note: '**who** (JND/RV) to you-ward is not weak, but is mighty (*dunateo*) in you'. Their very salvation was a demonstration of Christ's power through Paul. See Chapter 3 verses 1-6, "Forasmuch as ye are manifestly declared to be the epistle of Christ ministered by us..."; See also Chapter 12 verse 12, "Truly the signs of an apostle were wrought among you in all patience, in signs and wonders and mighty deeds".

c) Its power, v.4

"For though he was crucified through weakness, yet he liveth by the power of God: for we also are weak in him, but we shall live with him by the power of God toward you."

Paul had evidently been accused of weakness (see 10: 10, "For his letters, say they, are weighty and powerful; but his bodily presence is weak, and his speech contemptible"), but there was no such weakness in his work at Corinth (v.3). In this he followed the pattern of the Lord Jesus: He had been "crucified through weakness, yet he liveth by the power of God".

In what sense was the Lord Jesus "crucified through weakness"? In no way was He weak: He was the master of every situation, including death. It was, on His part, a willing, voluntary submission to death. He **deliberately took the place of human weakness**: nothing demonstrates the weakness of man so much as death. They said, "He saved others, himself he cannot not save" (Matt. 27: 42). The words, "crucified through weakness", refer to the humiliation connected with it. In the eyes of men, it was an exhibition of human weakness. But "he liveth by the power of God". On the one hand, the death of the Lord Jesus was, apparently, a demonstration of weakness: on the other, His resurrection was a demonstration of divine power.

Following that pattern, Paul describes himself and his fellow-workers as "weak in him". That is, in sharing the place that He took: "always bearing about in the body the dying of the Lord Jesus ('the putting to death of Jesus', RV margin)" (2 Cor. 4: 10). But at the same time, participating in His risen power, "we shall live with him by the power of God **toward you**". That is, Paul would come, weak though he might seem, **in all the power and authority of the risen Christ.** They would prove that he was not weak: but powerful. He would act in all the authority and power of the risen Christ. As P.E.Hughes rightly observes, "It would be a misconception to understand Paul, when he says, "we shall live with him", to be speaking eschatologically of the future resurrection to everlasting glory at the end of the age. As the context shows, the reference is limited to his impending visit to Corinth and concerns the power of his authority which he will exercise there against any who are disobedient".

The Lord Jesus "humbled himself, and became obedient unto death, even the death of the cross. Wherefore God also hath highly exalted him…" (Phil.

219

2: 8-9). Bearing in mind the words, "Let this mind be in **you**, which was also in Christ Jesus" (Phil 2:5), we learn that humility must precede authority. This was demonstrated in Paul's life, and all who aspire to leadership amongst God's people must tread the same path. See 1 Peter 5 verses 5-6.

2) PAUL EXHORTS HIS READERS, vv.5-6

"Examine yourselves, whether ye be in the faith; prove your own selves. Know ye not your own selves, how that Jesus Christ is in you, except ye be reprobates. But I trust that ye shall know that we are not reprobates."

In verse 3, they had been examining Paul: now he says "examine yourselves". The overall direction of the passage is made particularly clear by inserting brackets: "Since ye seek a proof of Christ speaking in me, (who is not weak towards you, but is powerful among you, for if indeed he has been crucified in weakness, yet he lives by God's power; for indeed we are weak in him, but we shall live with him by God's power towards you) examine your own selves if ye be in the faith..." (vv.3-5, JND). In AV language, "Since ye seek a proof of Christ speaking in me, which to you-ward is not weak, but is mighty in you...examine yourselves".

That is, if the Corinthians had received the grace of God, then there was the proof they required! Compare 1 Corinthians 9 verses 1-2, "Are ye not my work in the Lord...the seal of mine apostleship are ye in the Lord". "The sole awful alternative to such certain knowledge is that they are reprobates – put to the poof and rejected as spurious" (P.E.Hughes).

The sequence of cognate terms gives structure to the passage. "Since you seek a **proof** (*dokimon,* v.3) of Christ speaking in me, you shall have it, for when I come again I will not spare...But it is your own selves, rather than me, you should **put to the proof** (*dokimazo,* v.5). Can it really be that ye do not know your own selves, that Christ Jesus is in you? - unless, and this is the sole alternative, yea are **without proof** (reprobate, not standing the test – *adokimoi,* v.5) – that is, Christ Jesus is not in you. But it is my hope that you will know that I am not **without proof** (*adokimoi,* meaning reprobate, v.6 – that is, of Christ speaking in me)" (P.E.Hughes). Hughes notes that this continues in verse 7. See below:

3) PAUL EXPLAINS HIS MOTIVES, vv7-10

We should notice three things in his connection: *(a)* he had no desire to be vindicated (vv.7-8); *(b)* he desired only their spiritual maturity (v.9); *(c)* he had no desire to censure them (v.10).

a) He had no desire to be vindicated, vv.7-8

"Now I pray to God that ye do no evil (this is what Paul wanted), *not* that we should appear approved (this is what Paul did not want), but that ye should do that which is honest, though we be as reprobates" (v.7).

P.E.Hughes (continuing his note on 'prove' and 'proof' above) proceeds by paraphrasing: "I pray God, however, that you may not do what is wrong, not that I may seem to have proof (*dokimoi* – that is, through coming to you with a rod); but that you may act honourably, and that I consequently may be like one without proof (*adokimoi* – that is, since it will then be unnecessary for me to give proof of my authority by the use of the rod)".

Paul had no desire to prove himself. He did not wish to come to Corinth in order to display his apostolic authority by 'not sparing!' He had no wish to "appear approved" or 'have proof' of his authority. Paul did not wish be justified or vindicated. That would be necessary if they did wrong, but it was *not* his desire at all. Hence he prayed that they would "do no evil" (RV), and therefore obviate the necessity for him to "appear approved".

This should be carefully noted. Paul had no desire to exercise discipline. He found no joy in wielding the rod. He would far rather see an enhancement of their spiritual welfare. In this, he displayed a divine characteristic: judgment is God's "strange work…his strange act" (Isaiah 28: 21). Hence, as noted above, he prayed "that ye should do that which is honest" (honourable: Greek *kalos*, meaning, good, fair, right), even though this meant that "we be as reprobates" (not 'we be reprobates' but "*as* reprobates", that is, 'without proof, *adokimoi*), that is, not able to prove, by exercising discipline, his apostolic authority.

He continues in this vein: "For we can do nothing against the truth, but for the truth" (v.8). The meaning of "we can do nothing against the truth" or 'we have no power against the truth', is that if, as Paul had prayed, the believers at Corinth did "no evil" and acted honourably, it would be totally inappropriate for him to come with a rod. That would be acting "against the truth".

b) He desired only their spiritual maturity, v.9

Moreover, this brought joy to Paul: "For we are glad (rejoice) when we are weak and ye are strong". He rejoiced when spiritual conditions rendered disciplinary measures unnecessary. The words, "when we are weak", doubtless refer to the language of his critics. But Paul found them a satisfying description, because they indicated that circumstances did not warrant the exercise of authority. To his critics, this was a sign of weakness, but Paul would far rather have strong Christians at Corinth, not needing discipline and the exercise of his authority, even though this gave his critics ammunition against him.

In it all, Paul put the welfare of the assembly before his own reputation. He makes this clear: "this also we wish (pray), even your perfection ('perfecting', RV)". This was his overmastering desire. The word "perfection" (*katartizo* not *teleioo*) means to render fit or complete. It is used of mending nets (Matt. 4: 21); restoration (Gal. 6: 1). It has a medical connotation: resetting what has been broken and dislocated. See 2 Timothy 3 verse 17 where "perfect" is often explained as 'all limbs present'. The relevance of this to Corinth is obvious.

c) He had no desire to censure them, v.10

"Therefore I write these things being absent (compare v.2), lest being present I should use sharpness, according to the power which the Lord has given me to edification and not to destruction." The word "sharpness" (*apotomos)* means 'abruptly, curtly, in a manner that cuts: hence, sharply, severely' (W.E.Vine). This concludes the section of the epistle beginning "who in presence am base among you, but being absent am bold toward you" (10: 1).

Paul did not renounce his authority by acting in this way: on the contrary he used it as primarily intended: "to edification, and not to destruction". This was wise pastoral care. He gave opportunity for matters to be rectified. We should notice, again, that his authority was not vested in his own personality or ability, but in Christ: "the power (*exousia*, meaning 'freedom of action, right to act', W.E.Vine) which the **Lord** hath given me".

4) PAUL EXPRESSES HIS GREETINGS, vv.11-14

The concluding verses of the epistle reflect an enlarging sphere: *(a)* locally (vv.11-12); *(b)* provincially (v.13); *(c)* heavenly, v.14.

a) Locally, v.11

"Finally, brethren, farewell. Be perfect, be of good comfort, be of one mind, live in peace and the God of love and peace shall be with you." The following should be noticed:

i) *"Farewell"*, meaning 'rejoice' (*chairo*). See Philippians 3 verse 1, "Finally, my brethren, rejoice in the Lord". As P.E.Hughes rightly observes, "Christian joy is one of the foremost fruit of the Spirit" (Gal. 5: 22) and it should be a foremost mark of every Christian community. He continues: "The rejoicing, it goes without saying, is not a mere high-spiritedness or the superficial affectation of a jovial attitude to life, but is the manifestation of a serene and heavenward-looking disposition, arising from a deep and exhaustless centre of origin, for, as is apparent from Philippians 3 verse 1 and Philippians 4 verse 4, it is rejoicing *in the Lord*". This rejoicing will be enriched by what follows:

ii) *"Be perfect"*. This is the same word as in verse 9. P.E.Hughes puts it as follows: "It implies the need… of a united, properly articulated, and therefore harmoniously functioning together of the members of Christ's body at Corinth".

iii) *"Be of good comfort"*. That is, 'be encouraged' (*parakaleo*). But here it evidently has the sense of admonition. It is elsewhere translated "heed my appeal" (RSV).

iv) *"Be of one mind"*. That is, agreement in the mind about truth. P.E.Hughes puts it nicely: This "does not mean that individual judgment and opinion should be set aside, but that as fellow-Christians, with all their diversities of ability and temperament, they should be united in what is essential, namely, in the love and doctrine of Christ". This leads to:

v) *"Live in peace"*. Yes, at Corinth, with all its factions and disorders! "Living in peace is, in fact, an outward consequence of the inward state of being of the same mind" (P.E.Hughes).

The result follows: "and the God of love and peace shall be with you". The order is significant: "the God of *love* and *peace*". By actively pursuing the things named above, the assembly at Corinth, and every other assembly, will know and experience His presence. As P.E.Hughes says, "The singleness of heart and purpose to which Paul has just exhorted the Corinthians may further be expressed or sealed by an external token of affection". To this we can add that where the presence of the God of love and peace is enjoyed, the mutual affection of His people will be deepened. Different kinds of kisses are mentioned in the Bible. See, for example, Luke 22 verses 47-48.

b) Provincially, v.13

"All the saints salute you." That is, the saints in Macedonia, from where Paul was writing. See Chapter 7 verse 5. These were the very believers who had been inspired by the "forwardness of…mind" displayed by the Corinthians. See Chapter 9 verses 2-3. The local unity at Corinth, and in every place, was part of a still greater unity. Every opportunity should be taken to express love and interest in fellow-believers, even though they may be personally unknown to each other.

c) Heavenly, v.14

"The grace of our Lord Jesus Christ, and the love of God, and the communion of the Holy Ghost, be with you all. Amen".

As J. Heading observes, "The unity of manifestation of the Godhead is a fitting thought to conclude an Epistle dealing with a background of disunity". A. McShane helpfully writes: "Paul closes all his epistles with some form of benediction and in doing so makes, without exception, some reference to 'grace', but the fullness of the blessing here is not equalled in any other of his writings. It begins with, 'The grace of our Lord Jesus Christ' and not with 'the love of God as we might expect. Perhaps the reason for this is twofold: first, the Corinthians, on account of their many failings, were in special need of 'grace'; and second, the order here is the order of experience, for faith in Christ is the beginning of life in the soul…The next phrase, 'the love of God', directs the thoughts to the fountain-head of all blessing". It is through the grace of God in Christ that we have experienced the love of God, and have been brought into the fellowship of the Holy Spirit. In connection with the 'communion of the Holy Ghost', A. McShane comments: "The 'communion of the Holy Spirit' is doubtless a reference to His operations, which enable us to enjoy what the grace of Christ and the love of God have brought to us".

The closing words, "be with you all. Amen", should not be overlooked. "The benediction is for 'all', and not just for the faithful few. The weakest saint needs 'grace', 'love', and 'fellowship', and most godly ones owe their all to these favours, favours which are found alone in the blessed Trinity" (A. McShane).